The Origins of Christian Morality

The Origins of
Christian Morality

❖ ❖ ❖ ❖ ❖ ❖ ❖ ❖ ❖ ❖

The First Two Centuries

Wayne A. Meeks

Yale University Press

New Haven and London

Published with the assistance of the Ronald
and Betty Miller Turner Publication Fund.

Designed by James J. Johnson. Set in
Aldus Roman by Keystone Typesetting, Inc.,
Orwigsburg, Pennsylvania.
Printed in the United States of America by
Vail-Ballou Press, Binghamton, New York.

*Library of Congress Cataloging-in-
Publication Data*

Meeks, Wayne A.
  The origins of Christian morality : the
first two centuries / Wayne A. Meeks.
    p.   cm.
  Includes bibliographical references and
indexes.
  ISBN 0-300-05640-0 (cloth)
       0-300-06513-2 (pbk.)

  1. Christian ethics—History—Early
church, ca. 30–600.   2. Ethics in the
Bible.   3. Bible. N.T.—Criticism,
interpretation, etc.   4. Sociology,
Biblical.   I. Title.
BJ1212.M43   1993
241'.09'015—dc20   93–10226
                                          CIP

A catalogue record for this book is available
from the British Library.

10 9 8 7 6 5 4 3 2

To Maurice and Paddy Wiles

Contents

❖ ❖ ❖ ❖ ❖ ❖ ❖ ❖ ❖ ❖

Preface

❖ ❖ ❖ ❖ ❖ ❖ ❖ ❖ ❖ ❖

This book sketches the beginnings of that process by which there eventually emerged the whole intricate fabric of sensibilities—perceptions, beliefs, and practices—that we call Christian morality. Superficially it may be mistaken for another in the large genre usually called "New Testament ethics" or "early Christian ethics," but this book is not one of those, for reasons to be explained in the first chapter. The reader will find here no answers to such piecemeal and historically naïve questions as, What do the early Christians teach us about abortion? or What is the New Testament's stand on homosexuality? or Ought Christians to be pacifists? Nor do I attempt to discover the central principles on which a system of early Christian ethics is based. If there was a system, it was an enormously complex one that defies reduction to basic rules or underlying principles. Rather, I have attempted in the following pages to lead the reader on a journey of exploration. The object of our quest is what Peter Brown has called, in a different context, "the ecology of moral notions."[1] The purpose of our journey is to attempt to construct a kind of ethnography of Christian beginnings.

The book began as a series of lectures, most immediately the Speaker's Lectures at Oxford University in 1990 and 1991. I am deeply indebted to the Faculty of Theology for having invited me to be the Speaker's Lecturer and for their warm hospitality during several delightful spring weeks in Oxford. To the staff of Christ Church and members of the Senior Common Room I am grateful for the comforts of college rooms, a splendid table and outstanding cellar, and many pleasant conversations. Many individuals made my stay memorable; I can single out only a few by name: Maurice and Paddy Wiles, to whom this book is dedicated as a small token of long friendship, Ernest Nicholson, Ed Sanders, Robert Morgan, Geza and Pam Vermes, Christopher Rowland, and Becky Gray.

Portions of the book, in rather different form, were given as the Rauschenbusch Lectures of 1986 at Colgate Rochester Divinity School and as the E. C. Westervelt Lectures of the same year at Austin Presbyterian Theological Seminary. I am grateful to both institutions for their invitations and for their kindness, and especially to Leonard I. Sweet, the Very Rev. William H. Petersen, Beverly Gaventa, Jack L. Stotts, E. Ellis Nelson, Ralph Person, and James Mahon.

The book retains the organization of the Speaker's Lectures, though it has been considerably expanded. I have somewhat altered the oral style, but the book like the lectures is intended for a general audience rather than specialists. Consequently I have kept references to scholarly literature to an absolute minimum; a regrettable side-effect is my inability to acknowledge in detail my debt to countless specialized works. Most of that debt will be obvious to colleagues; nonspecialists seeking to pursue questions raised here will find their way to a larger bibliography through the works I have cited. All translations of ancient texts are my own unless a translator or version (of the Bible) is named.

Maurice Wiles gave valuable advice about the shaping of a book out of the lectures he had heard. Elaine H. Pagels, Susan R. Garrett, and Martha F. Meeks each read the entire manuscript and made numerous and specific suggestions for its improvement, almost all of which I have gratefully accepted. Gene Outka read the first chapter and saved me from several blunders. The anonymous reader for Yale University Press was thorough and extraordinarily helpful. My deep thanks go to all of these kind and astute critics and to Charles Grench, Executive Editor, and all the staff of the Press. A grant from the A. Whitney Griswold Fund of Yale University funded the indexes, which were prepared by Craig Wansink.

CHAPTER 1

Morals and Community

❖ ❖ ❖ ❖ ❖ ❖ ❖ ❖ ❖ ❖

Even in an age that some describe as post-Christian, the beginnings of the strange movement that was to become Christianity in all its varieties continue to fascinate thoughtful people. Both the central story Christianity had to tell and all the histories we construct to explain its origin seem so improbable. Yet something more than mere curiosity about an ancient puzzle draws our attention to the first centuries of Christian history. Our interest in the question betrays our awareness that, whether or not we regard ourselves as Christians or in any way religious, we cannot altogether escape the tectonic shift of cultural values that was set in motion by those small and obscure beginnings. We sense that, between fifteen and twenty centuries ago, something changed. What was it that changed?

The insiders' stories—several kinds of stories, really—answer with more or less confidence: God's anointed one was shamefully crucified, but God overruled the shame by raising him from the dead and installing him as Lord of the universe. God became a human person, in order that humanity should become as God had always willed. A mysterious messenger arrived from the invisible world of pure light to awaken the drugged and forgetful bits of eternal Spirit who are capable of Knowing and thus escaping the world of matter and illusion and rejoining the primeval, motionless unity. And so on. Stories like these we often call "myths," and much of the modern effort to understand Christian beginnings has focused on them. Yet our difficulties in saying just what it was that Christianity brought into the world do not lie simply in the fact that the new movement spoke the language of myth. It is not the case, as the famous demythologizer Rudolf Bultmann believed, that modern people cannot think in mythic terms; our common problem is rather that we believe too many myths, and most of them too cheap and sordid—but myths of the Christian kind do give us trouble when we try to connect them with what passes for the reality of everyday. It remains problematic how the insiders' stories can be made to cohere with mundane explanations of the way things happen. Nevertheless, that problem is not the only or the primary obstacle to historical understanding of this phenomenon.

There is a different way of answering the question, What changed as Christianity gathered itself out of the other sects and movements of Judaism and the welter of religious cults and practices of the Roman Empire to become a dominant cultural force? Looked at from the perspective of cultural history, what changed was a broad range of sensibilities. There emerged altered convictions about the kinds of behavior that are fitting, right, and salutary for human flourishing. A new vocabulary appeared in talk about what one ought to do and why, new senses of the end toward which a virtuous human life would strive, new hopes and new fears. New institutions and sanctions came into being, which undertook to direct the formation of character and to offer to or impose upon the most diverse levels and groups of the population that "guidance of souls" that used to be the domain of the elite's philosophy. In short, by the time Christianity became a political and cultural force in the Roman Empire in the fourth and fifth centuries of the common era, it had become an institution and an idiom of morality. What had changed was morality.

To be sure, it is curiously difficult to say exactly what was new about Christian morality, or to draw firm boundaries around it. The language of virtue that Christians spoke was adapted from older traditions of moral discourse, rather than being invented from scratch. The daily practice of most church members was doubtless indistinguishable in most respects from that of their unconverted neighbors. Differences in moral judgment and practice between one Christian, or group of Christians, and another often seem as great as or greater than differences between the Christians and the "pagans." Attempts to discover overt changes in those areas of public discourse, practice, or legislation that we would identify as morally sensitive—the use of deadly force by authorities, the treatment of slaves, relations between the sexes, the distribution of power and goods, and a host of similar issues—turn up embarrassingly few examples of a clear difference that could be ascribed to Christian influence. Worse, what trends can be confirmed are, often as not, in the opposite direction from what most Christians today would think the morally desirable one.[1]

Nevertheless, it is clearly not meaningless to speak of "Christian morality," however many qualifications may be necessary as one attempts to delineate it. Within all the diversity that must be acknowledged in Christian moral practice and moral discourse, there is to be discovered a family resemblance of moral traits. Moreover, it can hardly be doubted that the Christian family of moral sensibilities has profoundly affected the history of morality, most clearly in European culture and its diasporas, but also to some extent in every part of the modern world. The task of this book is not to *define* Christian morality but to describe its rough contours in its formative years, from the crucifixion of Jesus of Nazareth to the end of the second century of the common era.

Ethics and Morality

In modern English, the word *ethics* has come to have a more stately resonance than the word *morality*. The reader may therefore wonder why I have chosen to talk about early Christian *morality*—especially as the project of this book seems superficially to resemble that of a vast array of books on the topic "New Testament ethics." To begin with the larger phrase, there are several reasons why "New Testament ethics" or, for that matter, "New Testament morality" would be a misleading label for the kind of historical description I have in mind. First, while much, perhaps most, of the evidence I will explore will be found in the New Testament, it will not do to limit our purview to its documents alone if we are interested in tracing the whole picture of Christian moral development in the first two centuries. We will also want to look at documents that are later than any in the New Testament; at others that were contemporary and, in those centuries, often accorded equal status with the New Testament, only later being excluded from the normative canon; and at still others that expressed the beliefs and practices of Christian movements that were stigmatized and eventually suppressed by the emerging dominant institutions and tradition.

Second, "New Testament ethics" is misleading as a historical category because, by the end of the period I am interested in, the New Testament as we know it had not yet fully taken shape. The first Christians, the Christians who began to invent Christian morality, did not have a New Testament. This obvious fact is often forgotten. If there were a modern group of Christians who claimed that their ethical standards were derived entirely from the New Testament, then it would be appropriate for them to designate *their* ethics "New Testament ethics"—but that would be a normative category, not a historical or descriptive one. For traditional Christians of even the most biblicist persuasion, however, such a claim would itself be odd, for the New Testament is always read normatively as part of a larger canon including at least the Old Testament as well as the New. To speak of "biblical ethics" would therefore be preferable to "New Testament ethics" if we were talking about the normative use of scripture by modern Christians. Now this is not the question addressed here; I mention this different question in order to underline the distinction between the normative use of texts in moral discourse and the historical use of texts as witnesses to norms and practices of the past. Further, I hope this digression will remind us that when we speak of morality or ethics we are talking about people. Texts do not have an ethic; people do.

Still, why not early Christian ethics rather than morality? "Ethics" and "morality" are often used synonymously—the one word comes from the Greek, the other from the Latin word that Cicero coined to translate the Greek—but in common speech there is often a nuance of difference on which I want to capitalize in order to make a particular point. Some moral philosophers also distinguish the two, but not always in the same way, nor usually for the purpose I have in view. I take "ethics" in the sense of a reflective, second-order activity: it is morality rendered self-conscious; it asks about the logic of moral discourse and action, about the grounds for judgment, about the anatomy of duty or the roots and structure of virtue. It is thus, as the *Oxford English Dictionary* has it, "the science of morality." "Morality," on the other hand, names a dimension of life, a pervasive and, often, only partly conscious set of value-laden dispositions, inclinations, attitudes, and habits.

The moral admonition I heard most often in my childhood was the simple command, "Behave yourself!" The phrase seems on its face semantically empty—it would certainly not be easy to translate into another language—yet parents in my neighborhood never doubted its power to communicate. Such a command presupposes that the child has learned what behavior is required: some stage of morality has been internalized. If the parent finds it necessary to tell the child exactly what must be done ("Stop throwing mud at your sister!"), and if the child asks, "Why?" then the stage might be set for a rudimentary level of *ethical* discourse. Not necessarily, however, for the parent may respond, "Because I say so" or "Because it's wrong" or "We don't do that to other people" or "How would you feel if someone did that to you?" Thus, by appeal to authority, or to a more general moral sense, or to a sense of family standards, or to an assumed capacity for empathy, the parent undertakes to advance the process of internalization of moral values or rules. If the parent were in fact to engage in a more rational explanation, then the two would be "doing ethics" in the special sense I am adopting here. To avoid misunderstanding, however, note that if the parent did engage the child in *ethical* reflection, the immediate aim in view would be the same: to help the child to become a dependably *moral* agent. The reflective activity of "ethics" is thus not unimportant for "morality"; I am using the latter term not to drive a wedge between "the science of morality" and "morality" itself, but only to focus attention on the broader dimensions of the latter.

Moral Heroes and Moral Communities

Almost without exception, the documents that eventually became the New Testament and most of the other surviving documents from the same period of Christianity's beginnings are concerned with the way converts to the movement ought to behave. These documents are addressed not to individuals but to communities, and they have among their primary aims the maintenance and growth of those communities. In these documents we can see, though not always very clearly, the very formation of a Christian moral order, of a set of Christian moral practices. My thesis is that we cannot begin to understand that process of moral formation until we see that it is inextricable from the process by which distinctive communities were taking shape. Making morals means making community.

In one way, this claim runs counter to some cherished views of morality in our present culture: aren't morals essentially an individual matter? Our moral heroes are the great-souled individuals who stood up against the community's standards and the prevailing ethos. Martin Luther, with his "conscience held captive by the word of God," crying out against the whole institutional power of the church, "Hier stehe ich; ich kann nichts anders. Gott hilfe mich!" Or his namesake Martin Luther King, standing against mobs and police and unjust laws. Or Ann Hutchinson, resisting the complacent power of the New England religious establishment. Or Ghandi's lone and seemingly fragile nonviolent stubbornness against an empire's might and self-righteousness. The second-century martyr Perpetua commanding Roman jailers, confuting a Roman governor and her own father, going fearlessly to the arena to die. Or the apostles before the Sanhedrin in Acts, declaring (in an echo of the famous words of Socrates), "One must obey God rather than human beings."

We must pause a moment with this allusion to Socrates to observe a debate in modern ethics that may be pertinent to our project. Some moral philosophers are now suggesting that it was Socrates—Plato's Socrates, especially as read by the Enlightenment and by Kant—who put us on the road to confusion. Plato's Socrates, by his incessant questioning, argues people into being rational, needles them into thinking back and back and back to the highest levels of abstraction, from which the essential categories can be deduced: What is Justice? What is Liberty? What is the Good? the Beautiful? This was possible in the Platonic myth because the rational soul was transcendent; it came from elsewhere. Its reflection was a remembering of what it had known in that other realm before it descended into our cave of relationships and becoming. The portrait of Socrates who thus emerges as the ideal moral agent—provided we ignore the real political and social world of fifth-century Athens—is itself bloodless and abstract. We are tempted too often to think of the moral agent as a solitary mind and (since Augustine) will that think themselves free from all the accidental connections of history and society and community to decide what is good and true for everyone in all times.

The author of Acts did not mean to put his readers on that road when he cleverly made Peter allude to Socrates' defense. "Luke" knew that the God Peter was obeying was not the inner *daimōn* of Socrates. Peter did not learn God's will by Socratic questioning and rational reflection, but as the member of a group who had been with Jesus "from the beginning in Galilee," and all who joined that group "were adhering diligently to the teaching and community of the apostles, to the breaking of bread and the prayers" (Acts 2:42). The matron Perpetua and the slave Felicitas did not stand as lonely philosophers against the power of Rome, but as part of a larger group of catechumens who had recently been converted to the Christian community, a community which they now represented in the struggle and which stood with and behind them. Ann Hutchinson would not have been who she was without the circle of strong believers around John Cotton, nor without the radical stream in Puritanism within which her prophetic consciousness was formed and out of which, after her, would emerge the American Quakers. Martin Luther King would not have been who he was without the Black church and without the liberal theological tradition he learned at Boston University. Martin Luther's revolutionary interpretation of scripture and his leadership of the Reformation would not have been possible without the Augustinian tradition and Erasmian humanism and the beginnings of a German national consciousness. And we ourselves, when faced with moral dilemmas—when we try to get agreement between people who hold radically different opinions about, say, abortion or capital punishment—we often find that reasoning does not bring them closer together, because they reason from different starting points. Their visions of what is moral are different, and the differences seem to be connected with their differing personal histories, the different traditions in which they stand, the different circumstances that shape their lives.

Lessons from Aristotle

A number of philosophers and theologians have recently suggested that we ought to look back not to Plato and the Socrates he defined for us, but to Aristotle, who had started out in Plato's school, but then went quite a different way.[2] Aristotle said that a human being is a *politikon zōon*—an animal designed by nature to live in an ordered community, a *polis* or city-state. It would be strange, he said, to represent a recluse as really happy (*makarios, EN* 9.9.3). When Aristotle came to write his *Nicomachean Ethics*, it did not take the form of exhortations to behave properly, nor of the kind of dialogues Plato wrote, seeking to reason one's way to the fundamental ideas on which ethics were based. Rather, he addressed his essay to people who were already virtuous, intending to help them to reflect on the common moral experience they shared with their peers "to develop a self-conscious and coherent ethical outlook: to reinforce reflectively the lives they [were] already inclined to lead."[3] Hence when we read the *Ethics* we are struck by how often Aristotle quotes proverbs and how often he uses the verb *dokei*, which means here "the common opinion is . . . ." Aristotle did not think one could persuade people to be good by rational argument; a person becomes virtuous by training, by forming good habits. "Habit [*ethos*] makes character [*ēthos*]" became a cliché in Greek moral philosophy. Aristotle was among the first to analyze the educative function of communal practice in the formation of virtue. To develop a character that was virtuous, then, a child had to grow up within a moral and educative community. Aristotle, accordingly, focuses his attention in the *Nicomachean Ethics* on the kinds of relationships that are common both to the household and to the city-state as a whole. The various shapes that friendship could take occupy a large part of the discussion. The unequal relationships of power and responsibility for rulers and ruled, husbands and wives, masters and slaves, parents and children are discussed. So are the kinds of exchanges by which they function—exchanges of goods, of honor and esteem, of command and obedience, of support and protection, and so on.

Now the point here is obviously not to discuss Aristotle's ethics in detail, but to learn from him one central insight into the genealogy of morals, which we moderns too often have forgotten: individuals do not become moral agents except in the relationships, the transactions, the habits and reinforcements, the special uses of language and gesture that together constitute life in community. Our moral intuitions are those unreflective convictions about what is right or wrong, fair or unfair, noble or despicable, with which all the more complicated moral decisions must begin and which they must take into account.[4] These intuitions are not given by nature, but are shaped in the same communities and by the same kinds of interpersonal processes by which we become conscious and competent selves. This is the process which is often called "socialization," though the word is ugly and may seem to imply a one-sided and mechanical process rather than the personal and dynamic interactions that are really involved. Still, "socialization" and "resocialization" are convenient labels for processes central to the development and change of moral sensibilities.

An Ethnography of Morals

We need then a procedure that will enable us to see into the process of socialization and resocialization that produced the early forms of Christian morality. We find a further clue to an effective approach in the writings of another ancient author rather less well known than Aristotle and somewhat more off-putting in his style. In the time of the emperor Hadrian or shortly thereafter, an Athenian Christian, Aristides, wrote a defense of his faith that made some extraordinary claims for Christian morality. The Christians, he said,

> are the ones, beyond all the [other] nations of earth, who have found the truth. For they know the God who is creator and maker of everything, and they worship no other God but him. . . . They do not commit adultery, they do not engage in illicit sex, they do not give false testimony, they do not covet other people's goods, they honor father and mother and love their neighbors, they give just decisions. Whatever

they do not want to happen to them, they do not do to another. They appeal to those who treat them unjustly and try to make them their friends; they do good to their enemies. Their women are chaste and are virgins and do not engage in prostitution. Their men abstain from all unlawful intercourse and impurity, and all the more the women likewise abstain, for they look forward to a great hope that is to come. Moreover, if they have male or female slaves or children, they urge them to become Christians so that they can hold them in affection, and when they do become such, they call them brothers without distinction. They do not honor strange gods. They are humble and gentle and modest and honest, and they love one another. They do not overlook widows, and they save orphans; a Christian with possessions shares generously with anyone without. If they see a stranger, they bring him into their own homes and greet him like a real brother—for they call one another "brothers" not by physical connection but by the soul.[5]

Some readers may envy the moral confidence of Aristides. Others may merely be embarrassed by what is likely to appear uncomfortably like Mr. Thwackam's contented belief in the superiority of his own religion in Fielding's *Tom Jones*. Whatever one's response, there is one peculiarity of Aristides' apology that will repay our close attention. Aristides describes the Christians as a people or nation, an *ethnos*. He contrasts their knowledge and their behavior with Babylonians, Greeks, and Egyptians, and then with the Jews. The traits upon which he focuses to distinguish among these different peoples are theological and moral—beliefs about the divine and human worlds and consequent practices. Each people has its own picture of reality and, following therefrom, its own code of behavior. The Jews, in Aristides' view, are better in both respects than Greeks and barbarians, and the Christians better still. Thus Aristides has written an apology in the form of comparative ethnography—capitalizing on the fad for comparing customs and religions that was prominent in the age of Hadrian[6]—and he has made morality the centerpiece of his idealized description.

There is something odd about Aristides' starting point: the Christians are obviously *not* a natural *ethnos* like the Babylonians, Egyptians, or Jews. Yet Aristides assumes without argument that observers will consider them in such a way. As a matter of fact, opponents of the new movement early on began to ridicule it as a "third race"—that is, neither Greek nor barbarian but something outside the usual categories. Christian apologists took up the taunt and gave it a positive sense: outside the usual divisions and therefore something special.[7] There is something about the way early Christians understand themselves that can be expressed, at least sometimes in defensive situations, in terms of their being a distinctive community, separate from all others. We will see soon enough that, in other contexts, they made just the opposite claim. As the *Letter to Diognetus* says, "Christians are distinguished from other people in neither land nor speech nor customs" (5:1)—though this text, too, goes on to describe the relation of Christians to Greeks and barbarians as highly paradoxical. Tension between the sense of sharing the culture around them and the sense of standing opposed to it runs strongly through the history of early Christianity, and we will meet it in many forms in this investigation. For the moment, however, we will follow Aristides in focusing only on the sense of uniqueness. To see the Christians as a new *ethnos*, as they and their opponents sometimes saw themselves, suggests a model for exploring their moral sensibilities.

Like Aristides, I shall attempt to sketch an ethnography of early Christian morality—though our notion of ethnography is obviously rather different from his. An ethnographic approach treats the texts that are our primary sources for the history of Christian beginnings as an anthropologist today might treat information gleaned from natives in a tribe among whom the anthropologist is living for a time. I speak analogically, of course, for in any literal sense an ethnography of people long dead is impossible. In the absence of a time machine, we cannot do field work among them. Nevertheless, the perspectives of anthropologists, if not their specific methods, can help the historian of morals and of religion to develop a fuller picture of the past.

These perspectives enable us to see things overlooked by both the purely cognitivist and the existentialist modes of interpretation, which between them have dominated most recent studies of early Christian ethics. Rather than a system of ideas or individual, subjective decision making, the object of an ethnographic approach is *culture*. Morality is an integral part of a community's culture. More precisely, our task is to describe the moral dimensions of the subcultures of several varieties of the early Christian movement, seen within the larger complex culture of the Roman Empire.

Second, I agree with such anthropologists as James Peacock that an adequate understanding of culture may be hoped for only if we take a *holistic* approach.[8] That is, we must be aware that the culture of any particular society or group, however complex, is so internally interconnected that if we pull out any one of its components—its ideas, its myths, its rules, its logical

structures, its material supports—and disregard that element's embedded-
ness in the whole, we will fail to understand it. For that reason the logic of
the succeeding chapters has to be circular—or, more optimistically, a spiral.
The ten or a dozen bites out of early Christian moral culture represented by
these chapters must somehow be chewed together before we can claim to
have caught any of the flavor of the whole. But the division into bites is
necessary, because every attempt to understand the whole must be firmly
anchored to a particular instance, must look from some particular angle.

Finally, the kind of ethnography that seems to me most promising as an
analogy for the historian of morals is an *interpretive* ethnography. That is, I
agree with Clifford Geertz, the doyen of interpretive anthropologists, who
says: "Believing, with Max Weber, that man is an animal suspended in webs
of significance he himself has spun, I take culture to be those webs, and the
analysis of it to be therefore not an experimental science in search of law but
an interpretive one in search of meaning."[9]

My perception of the way in which the subculture of a religious community provides the context, grounding, and meaning of that community's
moral life is also close to the view that Geertz articulated in his classic essay
of 1957, "Ethos, World View, and the Analysis of Sacred Symbols": "Religion supports proper conduct by picturing a world in which such conduct is
only common sense."[10] It is thus not the great ethical principles of the early
Christians that I am trying to deduce, but the ways in which they developed
something like a moral common sense, a set of moral intuitions.

Mapping Early Christian Morality

If I am right about the way moral dispositions are shaped and the way
they work in a community, then a description of early Christian morality
cannot be limited to an account of the Christians' theological ideas that bear
on ethics, or of their moral rules, or of the structures of their moral
arguments—though these all have a place in the description. Rather we
approach them as if we were ethnographers of the past, inquiring about the
forms of culture within which the ethical sensibilities of the early Christians
have meaning. Practically, it is necessary to look at the texts, our only means
of access to the communities we want to study, from a series of different
perspectives, one after the other. At each look, we will be asking about a
different facet of the social practices and the cultural webs of meaning that
together constitute "early Christianity."

Moral Consequences of "Conversion"

In the next chapter, we shall return once again to the puzzle of the "ethnic" self-consciousness of early Christians that Aristides of Athens took for granted. When Aristides compared Christianity with *ethnē* like the Greeks, Babylonians, Egyptians, and Jews, he implied that becoming a Christian meant something like the experience of an immigrant who leaves his or her native land and then assimilates to the culture of a new, adopted homeland. Such a transfer of allegiances and transformation of mores requires a re-socialization. That is, something like the primary socialization that occurs normally in the interactions between child and family, the process in which the self receives those components of its structure and those basic values that are contributed by its environment, is reenacted in a new context.[11] The language the early Christians use implies that this supersession was, at least ideally, quite radical. For example, kinship language—calling one another "brother," "sister," "parent," "child," a practice to which Aristides alludes— pictures the displacement of the natural family by new relationships and obligations.

In describing the evolution of a distinct moral ethos among the early Christians, we must take seriously the fact that they depict themselves as a movement of converts. At the earliest stage of the movement they created a rite of passage to dramatize the separation from one life and one society and the joining of another, leaving the family of birth and the culture of residence and becoming a sister or brother of those who are God's children. Reminders of the boundaries between the old world and the new are a constant element in early Christian moral exhortation. We will need to explore the antecedents of such conversion and to ask to what extent the radicality of conversion language corresponds to realities of social experience.

City, Household, People of God

The radical notion of "conversion" that some early Christians developed could lead to a certain ambivalence about the towns, cities, and neighborhoods in which they actually lived. The second set of questions we must ask has to do with that ambivalence. The importance of these questions is suggested by recalling again the structure of Aristotle's ethical discourse, for his starting point was the way citizens of Athens in his time lived their lives and talked about their moral obligations. Ethical life for him was life in a polis, the unique Athenian city-state, and in this respect Aristotle set the pattern for the subsequent discussion of ethics by the philosophical and rhetorical moralists who stood in the Greek tradition.

Life in the Mediterranean cities in which Christianity took root was very different from life in the golden age of Athens. The superimposition of Roman power on the towns of Italy and the East, the linkages of local aristocracies with the Roman leaders, the migration of peoples in the age of freer and safer travel and commerce—all these factors and more changed the face of urban culture. Nevertheless, for the elites who articulated the language of moral obligation, the city remained the primary framework of reference. This was true even of those communities of immigrants that established themselves in every city in the Roman era, and even of that unique case among such communities, the diaspora Jews. The Jews' distinctive religious scruples made the issue of assimilation and identity, which every immigrant group faced, peculiarly uncomfortable and potentially dangerous. Nevertheless, the classical tradition of the polis still provided them with the essential language for discussing both their belonging and their distinctiveness, as we can see, for example, throughout the writings of both Philo and Josephus. But what did the polis mean for the Christians, those "converts" who would come to accept their stigmatization as a "third race," neither Greek nor Jew, who could sometimes say that their *politeuma* (a revealing term, often used of an organized body of immigrants, resident aliens, for example the Jews in a Greek city) was in heaven, not on earth (Phil. 3:20)? It was nevertheless the earthly cities of Rome and its provinces where the Christian movement found the fertile soil for its earliest and most rapid expansion. It was in the neighborhoods and streets and households of those cities where the colonists of heaven had to rub elbows and do business with citizens and fellow residents of Ephesus and Alexandria and Corinth. Was the classical polis still their chief model for the language of morality? If not, what took its place?

Loving and Hating the World

Whatever we may decide about the Christians' attitudes toward the urban culture in which their institutions took shape, we shall see that the city was not the whole world for them. Indeed, one of the things that strikes us as we read the hortatory literature of the early Christians is how frequently they talk about "the world," *ho kosmos.* Here we see a paradox that has often been repeated in the history of religions: a cult that is, in the world's eyes, infinitesimal believes that the actions of its members take their meaning from a cosmic process. The One who called them into existence by rescuing them from the present evil age is none other than the creator of the universe—its "founder and craftsman," as Aristides put it. That world's creation, its present corruption, and its ultimate destiny in God's salvation form the plot of a vast drama in which each Christian actor must play her or his part.

The Christians were not all of one mind about the world's nature or its destiny. Paul could speak of "the god of this world," meaning Satan. Yet he could elsewhere depict the creation "groaning in travail" for its liberation to share in "the glory of the children of God." The Fourth Gospel identifies Jesus Christ with the very Logos through which all things came to be, but it tells the story of the utter rejection by "this world" of this one who came to save it. In the apocalyptic visions of John of Patmos, not merely the Great City, but this world itself dissolves in cycles of violent destruction; only a new heaven and a new earth can provide safe refuge for those who hold fast to the commandments of Jesus. By the time Aristides wrote his paean to absolute monotheism, Marcion was already puzzling out his solution to the ambivalence expressed by Paul. This world, Marcion thought, could not have been made by the same loving God who came in the Christ. The world must perish with its creator. The Gnostic sect taught Valentinus to read the creation stories upside down and to transform the Christian gospel into a message of the rare enlightened soul's escape from the cosmic prison. Ascetic Christians of varied theological persuasions saw the world as enemy; to be baptized was to enlist in God's war against it. The formative centuries of Christian morality are thus marked by oscillation between extreme visions: is it the Christian's moral task to do battle against the world, to flee from it, or to participate in its transformation?

The Language of Obligation

So far I have sketched out some broad outlines of the symbolic world within which the early Christians made sense of the moral life they understood to be required of them. We must also look at the language they use to provide explicit action guides for one another. Early in the second century, the Roman governor general of Bithynia and Pontus wrote to the emperor Trajan that he had been interrogating Christians to learn what he could of their superstition. One of the things he learned, from former Christians who had recanted, was that one Christian practice was "to bind themselves by oath . . . to abstain from theft, robbery, and adultery, to commit no breach of trust and not to deny a deposit when called upon to restore it."[12] A commonplace list of vices; it resembles the list of things Christians do not do according to the longer recension of Aristides' apology. Lists of vices and virtues are found scattered through all the earliest literature of the Christians, and for the most part they differ little from those we could glean from any of the moralizing philosophers and rhetoricians of the same era. Much of the language of Christian morality is language shared with the culture around them.

Other language is more peculiar. For example, the most shocking and central claim of the early Christian proclamation was that the Lord and Son of God was none other than the Jesus who died by Rome's most shaming form of execution, but whom God then raised from the dead and exalted to heaven. That claim early became a metaphor patient of manifold transformation. It thus became a pattern by which a way of life, a claim of authority, an assertion of value could be measured. The concept of "humility," for example, was transformed by juxtaposition with this metaphoric pattern. The pervasive notions of honor and shame, so determinative to the ancients' understanding of a well-lived life, are jarred and occasionally inverted by the force of this new paradox.

The Grammar of Christian Practice

If we are to be historical ethnographers of early Christians' morality, it will be important to set their moral talk within the context of social forms. The uses of ritual to reify the symbolic moral universe are one example. The regular practice of admonition, which set the churches apart from other cultic groups of antiquity, is another. We must accordingly explore the question whether we are justified in speaking of a peculiar social practice, or set of social practices, that characterized the early Christian movement.

Knowing Evil

Every map of a moral world depends heavily for its delineation upon the dark colors that are used to sketch in the enemies of virtue. What are the things that stand against our being good? Why is it so hard both to know and to do what we ought? The ways in which evil appeared to the early Christians and how they named it, what things to them were moral abominations and why—these are questions we will have to pursue.

The Body as Sign and Problem

The extraordinary book by Peter Brown, *The Body and Society,* has illuminated a vast and complex array of social realities and metaphors to which we shall have to pay special attention.[13] That the body could be a metaphor for society was a commonplace in antiquity. That the body and its relationships were the arena in which the moral contest of life must take place was also nothing new. Yet, for Christians, ascetic and nonascetic, both commonplaces became peculiarly intricate topics of elaboration and controversy.

A Life Worthy of God

Belatedly we shall come to the topic with which our apologist Aristides began: the claim that the things one believes about God affect the way one behaves. We may think Aristides naïve in his apparent claim that proper monotheistic belief will assure that the believers will behave properly in their marriages and economic relationships. Nevertheless, it is clear that the intersection of theology and ethics in early Christian texts is different in notable ways from the connections made by pagan moralists of the same era. It will be important for us to try to sort out various ways in which Christian talk about God interacts with talk about behavior.

Senses of an Ending

Biblical theology in this century has been preoccupied—some would say "obsessed"—with the question of eschatology. Albert Schweitzer popularized the alarm that continental theologians began to feel, around the turn of the century, about the rediscovery of apocalypticism as the historical context of the Jesus movement. If the urgency of early Christianity's claims was posited on the expectation that the world was about to end, an event which did not occur, then the basis of Christian ethics seemed to be undermined. Without promising to solve that particular dilemma, I do think it essential for us to consider the ways in which various senses of an ending set the terms for early Christian moral discourse. The Christian life is always life lived toward a final act, a summing up and judgment, that lies entirely in God's hands and in God's time.

The Moral Story

The Ending, moreover, presupposes a Beginning and a very distinctive and complex Middle. The moral life has a plot, and it is a plot that implicates not merely each individual, but humankind and the cosmos. It may be that what most clearly sets Christian ethics apart from all the other ethical discourse of late antiquity, with which it otherwise shares so much, is just the creation of this peculiar story in which each of us is called on to be a character, and from which character itself and virtue take their meaning. The discovery of this story's roots, its plot, and its functioning will be the final step in which I invite readers to join with me in our ethnographic pursuit of that strange tribe that some of us strangely claim as our ancestors, the early Christians.

The Parts and the Whole

The investigation I have just outlined is not very systematic. It is intended to emulate the negotiations, the trials and errors, of the ethnographer just coming to know the natives in their own place and trying to learn what each of them has to know in order to be a morally competent member of that community. We have a great deal to learn, and most of these natives we want to know about are silent and invisible behind the impenetrable curtain of past time. Even so, this one sojourn among them cannot digest all the pertinent facts we could glean from what they have left us. Every informed reader will think of other texts I might have analyzed in each chapter, other avenues I could well have explored. What follows, then, is more in the way of a series of case studies, some preliminary trenches in the archaeology of the past, not a complete excavation. Each case, the finds of each trench, must be set alongside the ones before, and in the end, if we are lucky, we may see something of the patterns implicit in the whole.

CHAPTER 2

Turning: Moral Consequences of Conversion

❖ ❖ ❖ ❖ ❖ ❖ ❖ ❖ ❖ ❖

Early Christianity was a movement of converts. That is, the Christians thought of themselves as people who had turned their lives around, from one state to another profoundly better. Turning around (Greek *epistrophē*, Latin *conversio*) is a metaphor that could have broad and multiple consequences for the way the early Christians perceived their moral possibilities and obligations. Its generative potential is visible already in the earliest Christian document we have, the Apostle Paul's First Letter to the Thessalonians. First Thessalonians is a letter of moral advice. It aims to reinforce a variety of things that Paul has taught the new Christians of Thessalonica about the behavior and the dispositions appropriate to people who have been "chosen" and "called" by God. At the beginning of the letter, he reminds them of and congratulates them for the way they first received the gospel and its messengers. Everywhere Paul has been, he says, other Christians are talking about them. They recount "how you turned to God from idols" (1 Thess. 1:9). It is this "turning," then, that they are to keep firmly in mind as the letter goes on, encouraging them to persist in the new way they have taken. The letter continues the paternal admonitions that Paul and Silvanus and Timothy gave them at the time of their conversion, "that you should walk in a way worthy of the God who calls you into his own kingdom and glory" (2:12). Thus our earliest extant Christian writing wants to root the moral sensibilities of its readers in their consciousness of having turned around.[1]

Behind the Metaphor

In order to understand the converts' consciousness, we would like most of all to hear their own descriptions, first-hand. The texts disappoint us in that regard. Before Augustine's masterpiece of introspection—and retro-spection—we have no Christian autobiography, nothing to compare with the "testimonial" so beloved of modern conversionist sects. In the period we are concentrating on, only two converts tell us more or less directly what the event meant to them, and they do not tell us very much. Those two are Paul and Justin Martyr.

Paul was destined to become the prototypical convert in the imagination of western Christianity, but his own comments about the radical change in his life are few, and each is embedded in a highly rhetorical passage.[2] There are only two such passages that offer anything to our immediate purpose: Gal. 1:13–17 and Phil. 3:4–11.[3] Both are parts of arguments that seek to dissuade non-Jewish Christians from accepting the premise that in order to be fully a part of God's people they must take up some level of Jewish practice. In Galatia the demand that they do so is present and urgent; the primary aim of Paul's letter is to counter it. In the Letter to the Philippians, there is no indication that the matter has already become an issue in the colony (though some commentators think otherwise). Rather, Paul writes to inoculate his friends against the potential threat, alluding to his experience recently in another Roman colony, Corinth (compare 2 Cor. 10–13).

In both passages Paul depicts himself, prior to what we call his conver-sion, as the very model of an observant Jew. The rhetorical point of that depiction, of course, is to say that he then embodied what his opponents are advocating for proselytized gentiles, but to a degree of perfection beyond their reach, only to set all that behind him, even to regard it as "garbage, in order to acquire Christ and to be found in him" (Phil. 3:8–9). The personal example—of one kind of "convert" for quite a different kind—is intended to reduce the rival point of view to absurdity.

The controversy itself need not detain us here. Our question is whether Paul's transformation from "a zealot for my ancestral traditions . . . per-secuting the congregation of God and trying to destroy it" (Gal. 1:13–14) to an equally zealous promoter of that congregation (that is, the Jesus sect) among uncircumcised gentiles, entailed a change of *moral* outlook or prac-tice. It is not an easy question to answer, and the reasons for the difficulty are rooted in the problem alluded to in the previous chapter, of defining in advance what morality meant for the people we are investigating. On the one hand, Paul's behavior now is quite different from what it was when, as Pharisee and zealot, he was undertaking to stamp out the new Jewish sect. Obviously, too, his reckoning of value has changed radically, if things previously central to his sense of "right" and "profit" he now regards as "loss" and "garbage." On the other hand, there is no hint really—despite a powerful tradition of reading these texts that begins with Augustine and is elevated by Luther into a defining component of Christian self-understanding—that those things Paul valued before are no longer, in his eyes, good in themselves. The moral goods taught in the Torah have not become evil—as "works-righteousness." The shape of Paul's rhetoric is rather one of contrast: even the relatively good has been eclipsed by what is far superior (*to hyperechon*, Phil. 3:8). The moral admonitions that Paul teaches to his gentile converts could be heard in any synagogue (and, with few exceptions, from any moral philosopher of the Greek world: another issue). When Paul draws boundaries in terms of moral behavior, it is not between "Christians" (a word not yet available to Paul) and Jews, but between the groups he addresses and "the gentiles"—as, for example, in 1 Thess. 4:5: "not as the gentiles who do not know God." Later Christians, including one writing in Paul's own name not more than a generation later, could make the pre-Christian Paul into "the first of sinners" and his turning-about thus the paradigm of conversion as moral rescue (1 Tim. 1:15–16). That, however, is not the way Paul himself describes the change. He is not, in his self-description, a despairing Jewish sinner who has been "saved" by becoming a Christian, but a confident and zealous Jew whose zeal has been turned in a radically new—but still "Jewish"—direction by the God he has always sought to obey.

Justin, writing in the middle of the second century, draws quite a different picture. In his *Dialogue with Trypho* he presents himself, following a common literary convention and perhaps an experience familiar among some of his contemporaries, as a philosopher who once tried each of the schools of philosophy before being led to the true philosophy, Christianity, by a mysterious old man.[4] In his *Apology*, however, it is the moral qualities of the Christians that he singles out as the impetus for his conversion. Previously, while devoted to Plato's doctrines, he had heard the Christians slandered, but when he saw their fearlessness in the face of death and other threats, he recognized that the slanders must be false. For no "pleasure lover or dissolute person or cannibal" ever showed such indifference to death (2 *Apol.* 12.1). Still, Justin does not here suggest that his conversion entailed a reversal of his moral values. Rather, he wants to be seen as a person who was engaged in an intellectual and religious quest until he found what he was looking for. Indeed, as we shall see later, he will argue that the conversion to

Christianity makes better members of the society, better citizens of the Empire.

Now we should bear in mind that neither Paul nor Justin has given us an unretouched account of his experience. All these reports are retrospective, written many years after the event, and all are shaped by conventions both of the larger culture and of the movement the writers have joined, as well as by the rhetorical strategies that led each author to recall his conversion. Thus, while we do not obtain from them a clear picture of the experience of Paul and Justin, we are able to discover in their use of the conversion reports moments in the process of the institutionalization of conversion.[5]

Sociologists studying modern conversionist sects report a similar phenomenon. Converts create retrospective stories of their own conversions that serve several functions in the process by which they come to be at home in the new group or movement. Their own understandings of their identity and their relation to their new reference group and to former reference groups and individuals are transformed by the making of the story, which follows the model of a typical "conversion career" that is believed in by the group. In turn, each new convert's story reinforces and may enlarge or modify that model.[6] While we may be disappointed that we do not have more autobiographical facts about our subjects, the uses of the conversion stories that we see in the early texts are themselves important clues to the process of resocializing moral intuitions that is the real object of our inquiry.

Reform or Transformation?

Modern stories of conversion are of at least two kinds. One kind, most often told by the converts themselves or by others inside conversionist groups, describes someone who was leading a dissolute, barren, or otherwise deplorable life, who turns about, shapes up, and henceforth exhibits deportment approved by all. The drug addict, the prostitute, the juvenile delinquent becomes a model citizen. The deviant has been won over to the norms that society at large upholds.

In the other kind of story, most often told by outsiders about the converts or about their converters, the change is not from deviance to moral conformity, but may be quite the opposite: from ordinary citizen to fanatical member of a group that itself deviates from the norms of the larger society. Thus middle-class American parents in the 1960s and '70s feared the "capture" or "brainwashing" of their children by "cults." A mild and lonely adolescent might overnight become a "world-saver," with wild eyes or shaved head, aggressively soliciting in airports or handing out tracts on street corners. Usually told by opponents, such stories can of course also be told by members of what Bryan Wilson calls a "conversionist sect," whose "response to the world" stigmatizes the culture from which they have "turned" as itself depraved and wicked.[7] Turning to the sect or cult is therefore turning from the world. Both kinds of stories were told by and about the early Christians.

The former kind of story—rescue and restoration of the deviant—was very familiar in the culture into which Christianity was born. One of the most famous concerned the Athenian Polemo, head of the (Platonic) Academy from 314 to ca. 276 B.C.E., but formerly, we are told in one account, "so profligate and dissipated that he actually carried about with him money to procure the immediate gratification of his desires, and would even keep sums concealed in lanes and alleys."[8] Among the many versions of his transformation that circulated in antiquity was the comic satire by Lucian, "The Double Indictment," in which the courtesan named Carousing *(Methē)* accuses the proper maid Academy of having stolen her lover. Academy replies, "I converted *(hypestrepsa)* him and sobered him and made him from a slave into a well-behaved, temperate man, very valuable to the Greeks."[9]

Although Lucian knew how to joke about conversion, as about most other topics, he could also be serious, as in his dialogue describing a conversion, perhaps his own, by the philosopher Nigrinus. "Once a slave," says Lucian's spokesman, "I am now free! 'once poor, now rich indeed'; once witless and befogged, now saner."[10] Such metaphorical contrasts are typical of converts' stories, and we encounter similar contrasted pairs frequently in early Christian literature: slave, free; asleep, wakened; drunk, sobered; blind, seeing; stupid, understanding; captive, released. Often, too, the "turning" of the convert is said to be a "turning to oneself," a return to one's natural state.[11] This is the kind of conversion we see in Jesus' parable of the Prodigal Son, who "came to himself" among the pigs and went home to submit to his father (Luke 15:17). Or the Legion-possessed demoniac, whom Jesus exorcized and thus rescued from his naked and isolated life in the graveyard. Jesus sent him, "clothed and sensible," home to his people (Mark 5:1–20 and parallels). This kind of conversion is the restoration of an individual. Its stories confirm the mores that are commonly approved, at least in theory, by those who articulate the moral consensus of the society, though, to be sure, the stories often contain an implicit or explicit criticism of the way the majority of the society in fact live. If that criticism goes so far that the convert in the story undergoes not reintegration into the society but separation from it, then we have moved into the other type of story. More on that later.

Conversion by Philosophy

In antiquity, conversion as moral transformation of the individual is the business of philosophy rather than of religion. The chief instrument for bringing it about, in the stories told by the philosophers themselves or their admirers, was the protreptic speech of the philosopher. In the word *protreptic* itself, we see again the metaphor of "turning." The purpose of protreptic is to persuade those capable of hearing the message to adopt the philosopher's point of view and form of life. It is such a speech that Lucian describes, in his dialogue *The Wisdom of Nigrinus,* as like a well-shot arrow that, penetrating the soul with exactly the right force, pervades it with the drug of philosophy (35–37). It is precisely a change of life at which the philosopher aims with his rhetoric, says Epictetus. The hearer who is rightly moved will not merely compliment the philosopher on his style. Rather he ought to say, "The philosopher touched me nobly; I must no longer act this way."[12] This confidence in the power of the spoken word to alter lives echoes often in early Christian writings, too. Thus the response of the Thessalonian converts mentioned at the beginning of this chapter was to "the gospel" *(to euangelion),* "the word [of the Lord]" *(logos tou kyriou)* (1 Thess. 1:5,6,8).

Conversion stories always idealize. The turn-about is instantaneous, for so the economy of the narrative requires. The ancients knew as well as we, however, that in reality lives do not change so easily or so suddenly. One of the more popular versions of the conversion by philosophy to the life of virtue was in an odd little tract called the *Tablet of Cebes.* This pamphlet, written perhaps in the first century c.e., has often been called "the Greek *Pilgrim's Progress.*"[13] It purports to be a kind of tour guide's lecture explaining a peculiar painting found in a temple in Athens. The painting shows crowds of people on a road called "Life" that leads, by devious paths with certain byways, through various gates and past walls, towers, distractions, and culs-de-sac, to an enthroned and gracious lady called *Eudaimonia:* "Happiness." The old man who explains the allegorical meaning of the picture points out that very few reach the goal—and they only by the intervention of a lady known as "Repentance" or "Transformation of Mind" (*Metanoia* or *Metameleia*—again we could perhaps translate "Conversion").

The *Tablet of Cebes* illustrates three characteristics of the moral conversion promised by ancient schools of philosophy that are significant for our comparisons with the early Christian notions. First, popular philosophy stresses how hard it is to be good. The life of virtue is an *agōn*, a struggle, a contest, a race to be run. Second, the choice between the easy life of vice and the difficult life of virtue is an exceedingly lonely one. Third, indispensable to the proper choice is the right kind of education *(paideia)*. It follows that philosophical conversion and the virtuous life to which it leads are attainable only by an elite. An elite of intellect and self-discipline, all the schools of philosophy would agree, but those who win through in "Cebes'" allegory are also an elite, in a sense rarely acknowledged by the philosophers—an elite of luck. Education cost money and demanded leisure.[14]

Yet there is in the *Tablet* itself a suggestion that what commonly passes for a good education is not truly so, but only a *pseudopaideia* (11.1). To attain "true education" requires "repentance" (or "conversion") and the assistance of the ascetic sisters Self-control *(Enkrateia)* and Perseverance *(Karteria)* (16.2). These words denote virtues in all kinds of Greek moral discourse, but when "Cebes" depicts them as leading the candidate for the good life *away* from the kind of *paideia* taught in the schools, the implication is that what even the elites of the culture teach as morally good is not truly so. Fitzgerald and White observe, in a note on this passage, that the language here resembles that used often by Cynics.[15] It is among the Cynics, and among those Stoic philosophers influenced by the Cynics, that we most often hear of conversion as rejection of or rescue from the perverted values of the dominant culture. For example, a Cynic letter, written probably in the second century of our era and pretending to be from the founder Diogenes, tells this story of a conversion:

> Once when I went to the house of a lad, the son of extremely prosperous parents, I reclined in a banquet hall adorned all about with inscriptions and gold, so that there was no place where you could spit. Therefore, when something lodged in my throat, I coughed and glanced around me. Since I had no place to spit, I spit at the lad himself. When he rebuked me for this, I retorted, "Well then, So-and-so (speaking to him by name), do you blame me for what happened and not yourself? It was you who decorated the walls and pavement of the banquet hall, leaving only yourself unadorned, as a place fit to spit onto!"

He answered, "You appear to be criticizing my lack of education, but you won't be able to say this anymore. I don't intend to fall one step behind you."

From the next day, after he distributed his property to his relatives, he took up the wallet, doubled his coarse cloak [these two items, with a staff, constituted the identifying kit of the Cynic], and followed me. (Pseudo-Diogenes, Epistle 38)[16]

This is obviously an example of a conversion story of the second type identified above, here used to approve the radical change. Conversion means leaving the conventional forms of life. The Cynic's freedom from moral contingency is purchased by a conspicuously ascetic way of life, which stands at the same time as a radical critique of popular conventions and values. The many anecdotes about the "shamelessness" of Diogenes make the same point.[17] To be converted by a Cynic was to abandon convention as a guide to life. But *to what* were such people converted?

Conversion to Cynicism was conversion to a radical individualism. Abraham Malherbe has shown that Cynics in the period of the Roman principate divided themselves into two types. The one was concerned only with the Cynic's own attainment of happiness by the rigorous self-discipline of the "Diogenean short-cut." Cynics of this type despised the masses and sought to distinguish themselves from all who followed conventional mores. The other Cynics were milder in their condemnation of those around them and even saw themselves as engaged in improving society. In neither case, however, could one speak of a Cynic community. Conversion was to an austere self-sufficiency *(autarkeia)*.[18]

The case is not much different with a Stoic like Epictetus (who admired much about the Cynics). He warned his pupils against continuing to associate with nonphilosophers, who might reinforce old habits. "It is for this reason that the philosophers advise us to leave even our own countries, because old habits *(ta palaia ethē)* distract us and do not allow a beginning to be made of another custom *(ethismos)*" (*Diss.* 3.16.11). Hence Epictetus's advice is: "Flee your former habits; flee the uninitiated *[idiōtai]*, if you want ever to be anyone" (3.16.16). Epictetus was well aware that those who followed this advice would feel isolated and uprooted, but that was simply the cost of becoming a philosopher and had to be borne.[19] The interaction among the students in his lectures may have provided temporary respite from influences of the larger world, but the school pretended to be no lasting community.

Many philosophers did acknowledge the need for a common life and discipline in order to acquire the moral habits of the philosophical life. For example, Seneca—tutor and counselor of the emperor Nero, hardly a countercultural figure—devotes much of his Epistle 6 to this theme. He is sending books, with marked passages, to Lucilius:

> Of course, however, the living voice and the intimacy of a common life [*viva vox et convictus*] will help you more than the written word. . . . Cleanthes could not have been the express image of Zeno, if he had merely heard his lectures; he shared his life [*vitae eius interfuit*], saw into his hidden purposes, and watched him to see whether he lived according to his own rules. Plato, Aristotle, and the whole throng of sages who were destined to go each his different way, derived more benefit from the character than from the words [*plus ex moribus quam ex verbis*] of Socrates. It was not the class-room of Epicurus, but living together under the same roof [*non schola Epicuri sed contubernium*], that made great men of Metrodorus, Hermarchus, and Polyaenus.[20]

Seneca's final example is a significant exception to the general rule of Hellenistic philosophy's individualism, although Seneca's own point is simply a variation on the familiar theme of the importance of personal example. The formative relationship is between teacher and disciples, not among the disciples. For Seneca the philosophical life is aided by friendship, but it establishes no alternative community. The transformation of the mind (*animus eius transfiguratus est*) necessary for any progress toward true wisdom (*Ep.* 94.48) remained for him, a Stoic, essentially a lonely task. In point of fact, however, the Epicureans do seem to have formed intentional and highly structured communities, and it is in them that we find the closest social analogy, at least among the philosophical schools, to early Christianity. In the Epicurean "Garden," if not in other philosophical schools, we find that dimension which, I will argue, is essential to early Christian conversion: the change of primary reference groups, the resocialization into an alternative community.[21]

Religious Conversion

In one obvious respect, however, a conversion to Epicureanism seems at the opposite pole from a conversion to Christianity. While the "atheism" of which both were accused in antiquity was clearly as mistaken in the one case as in the other—if we understand atheism to mean, as in our usage, the belief that no god exists—still the theology of Christians was profoundly different from that of the Epicureans. For Epicurus the one thing to be kept firmly in mind about the gods was that they could not possibly be concerned about human affairs; they needed no human worship and people had no need to fear them. Frischer may very well be right that the Epicurean sage attracts new recruits by his resemblance to the gods, but that resemblance is precisely detachment, impassiveness, insulation from contact with anything or anyone worldly.[22] That is hardly to be compared with Paul's "how you turned to God from idols, to serve the living and genuine God." Was there in the religious world in which Christianity began some familiar model that would have resonated in Paul's audience with this talk about a transformation of one's self and one's behavior by the act of turning to a different god?

Sixty years ago A. D. Nock, in his classic book on conversion in antiquity, drew a sharp distinction between *conversion*, understood in a Christian sense, and *adhesion*, a less thoroughgoing change of religious allegiance. An initiate into one of the older or newer mysteries became only an adherent to that cult, not a convert. Nock sums up, "Our survey of paganism has given us little reason to expect that the adhesion of any individual to a cult would involve any marked spiritual reorientation, any recoil from his moral and religious past, any idea of starting a new life." Nevertheless, Nock makes one exception. He devotes a chapter of his book to "the conversion of Lucius," the story told in the eleventh book of Apuleius's novel *Metamorphoses*. Taking the story to have "more than a touch of autobiography," Nock compares it with a modern conversion to Roman Catholicism.[23]

The old story that Apuleius used as the armature of his novel tells how a young man's experiments with magic leave him transformed into a donkey. After many adventures he receives the antidote that returns him to his normal shape. In Apuleius's retelling, the hero's salvation comes by the mediation of the goddess Isis, and his initiation into her cult leads him into lifelong devotion to her. The centerpiece of the narrative is the nearest thing we have from antiquity to a first-hand account of initiation by an initiate. But is it a conversion?

Certainly the central plot of the story turns on transformation, and a number of elements in Apuleius's language reinforce this transformation's deeper implications. Witnesses to Lucius's restoration marvel that he is "as it were born again" *(renatus quodam modo)* and remark that he "has at once pledged himself to service in the sacred rites" (11.16 [Helm 278.9]). His devotion is further described at §19 (281.6–9), as Lucius delays his initiation out of "religious fear."[24] The reasons for his fear sound rather like the anxieties of a young Augustine, at least in the standard translation: "For I had taken care to ascertain how arduous was the service of the faith, how extremely hard were the rules of chastity and abstinence" (11.19 [281.7]). This translation, however, is a bit tendentious. "Submission to the required rites" would better represent *religionis obsequium* than "service of the faith." As for the "rules of chastity and abstinence," it is evident in what follows that they refer to preparation for the initiation, not a lifelong discipline entailed by devotion to the goddess. See, for example, §23 (284.24–25): "For the ten following days I should curb my desire for food, abstaining from all animal flesh and from wine" (Griffiths 1975, 99). Just before this Griffiths has again introduced too "Christian" an interpretation when he translates *praefatus deum veniam* as "Then he prayed for the forgiveness of the gods," when "asked permission" or "sought indulgence of the gods" would fit the context better. Lucian is represented as entering on a lifelong devotion to Isis and eventually also Osiris, including his joining the *collegium pastophorum* of the latter (§30 [291.12–14]). Moreover, this dedication can be expressed (in §15) by the metaphor of enlistment in military service.[25] This devotion and its regimens, however, do not interfere with the fictional Lucian's developing a lucrative practice of legal rhetoric in Rome (§§28–30, especially 290.1–4; 291.3–11). Apuleius himself, if we are to believe with most commentators that the report has some autobiographical element, very likely felt a comparable devotion to Isis—but it was by no means exclusive, as he makes clear in his *Apologia* 55: "I have taken part in a number of initiation ceremonies in Greece."[26] There is after all rather little in Apuleius's tale to support a view of initiation as a moral transformation, and nothing at all to suggest induction into the kind of community we see among the Epicureans and the Christians.[27] Being or becoming religious in the Greco-Roman world did not entail either moral transformation or sectarian resocialization.

Yet there is one religious community to be found in each of the cities where Christianity took its lasting shape that did receive converts in the full moral and social sense. That community, of course, was the association of Jewish residents. Conversion to Judaism in antiquity is often discussed in modern scholarly literature, but there remains no fully satisfactory treatment of the topic, and certainly none can be attempted here.[28] Shaye J. D. Cohen has warned of the danger of imposing a single pattern on the great variety of ways in which non-Jews might express a positive interest in Judaism in different parts of the Roman Empire. These ranged from "admiring some aspect of Judaism" to "converting to Judaism and 'becoming a Jew' "; moreover, each of these kinds of behavior and the others in between might be understood differently by various groups of Jews at different times and places.[29] Certainly no one would call Philo of Alexandria typical of Jews in the first century, but nevertheless several passages in his works provide a useful point of comparison with our early Christian texts. These passages at least offer a construal of what it meant to become a full proselyte that would have been plausible to Philo's audience, an urban, Greek-speaking community of the Diaspora contemporary with the beginning of Christianity.

Philo treats the speeches of Moses in the latter part of Deuteronomy as a philosophical discourse "on the virtues." In his treatise by that title, Philo notes that Moses paid special attention to the needs of proselytes (in the original, these provisions were for resident aliens in the territory of Israel, but the Septuagint had already translated *ger* by *prosēlytos*):

> Having laid down laws for members of the same nation *[homoethnoi]*, he holds that the incomers *[epēlytoi,* a synonym for *prosēlytoi]* too should be accorded every favour and consideration as their due, because abandoning their kinsfolk by blood, their country, their customs and the temples and images of their gods, and the tributes and honours paid to them, they have taken the journey to a better home, from idle fables to the clear vision of truth and the worship of the one and truly existing God. He commands all members of the nation to love the incomers, not only as friends and kinsfolk but as themselves both in body and soul. (*Virt.* 102–03)[30]

Here we see clearly that our notion of *religious* change, determined by our society's segmentation of "religion" from the rest of social life, cannot encompass the sort of conversion that Philo, and presumably his audience, had in mind. The change is a "journey to a better home"; that is, it is as much social, moral, and political as religious. It entails "abandoning their kinsfolk by blood, their country, their customs and the temples and images of their gods," and becoming members of the Jewish community.

Further on in the same treatise, Philo imagines Moses delivering a protreptic address in which he "exhorts *[protrepei]* everyone everywhere to pursue piety and justice, and offers to the repentant in honour of their victory the high rewards of membership in the best of commonwealths [politeia]" (Virt. 175, trans. Colson). Here again the word Philo chooses to name the virtue described in this part of the treatise, metanoia, "transformation of mind," could as well be translated "conversion" as "repentance." The contrastive language we heard earlier in gentile philosophical descriptions of conversion echoes liberally through this address, as at the end of §179: "as if, though blind at the first they had recovered their sight and had come from the deepest darkness to behold the most radiant light." Perhaps at one level Philo intends the metaphors to represent that philosophical change in the individual progressing toward wisdom that he so often reads into biblical accounts of journeys, changes of name, and the like. The primary focus in this passage, nevertheless, is the case of the proselyte. The "first and most necessary step to conversion" (§180, my trans.) is taken by those who "did not at the first acknowledge their duty to reverence the Founder and Father of all, yet afterwards embraced the creed of one instead of a multiplicity of sovereigns" (§179, trans. Colson).

Furthermore, Philo sees the political and social conversion as entailing a moral transformation:

> For it is excellent and profitable to desert without a backward glance to the ranks of virtue and abandon vice that malignant mistress; and where honour is rendered to the God who IS, the whole company of the other virtues must follow in its train as surely as in the sunshine the shadow follows the body. The proselytes become at once temperate, continent, modest, gentle, kind, humane, serious, just, high-minded, truth-lovers, superior to the desire for money and pleasure, just as conversely the rebels from the holy laws are seen to be incontinent, shameless, unjust, frivolous, petty-minded, quarrelsome, friends of falsehood and perjury . . . . (Virt. 181–82, trans. Colson)[31]

I have devoted this much space to Philo's evidence—still far less than the complexity of his situation and the importance of his testimony deserve—because several dimensions of the picture we see here offer such close analogies to things we see in the early Christian documents. Here conversion is described as the transformation both of a way of thinking and of a form of life, as a change of allegiance from many false gods to the one true God, as a radical resocialization, abandoning one's closest and most familiar ties and finding new ones, and as a fundamental reformation of morals. Here, too, one is struck by the deep ambivalence of the religious community toward the surrounding society and its culture. On the one hand, the society whose religion is polytheistic appears incorrigibly benighted, irrational, and wicked: virtue can be attained only by a change of citizenship, transferring to the people of the one God. On the other, the virtues the community seeks and its way of reasoning about them are described in the language of that same society's high culture. In this tension we see the ambivalence of people whose identity, expressed as loyalty to their one God through the ethos laid down in his covenant, condemns them to the status of resident aliens in the cities where they reside. When we sense often in the Christian texts a similar ambivalence, we have to ask whether it is rooted in some set of social relationships analogous to the alien status of the Jewish communities, or whether the moral vision of the world inherited from communities like Philo's leads to social alienation.

Christian Conversion as a Social Act

It is obvious in Paul's letter to the Thessalonian Christians that their "turning from idols" to the "living and genuine God" was simultaneously a transfer of loyalty and sense of belonging from one set of social relations to another, quite different set. The social relocation and the theological transformation are mutually dependent; each implies the other, and each reinforces the other. There are several ways in which Paul's letter emphasizes—and perhaps exaggerates—the social and theological "turn," ways that have direct implications for the moral reformation of these converts that he and his coworkers were trying to bring about. For one thing, he repeatedly stresses the "pressure" (thlipsis) that the converts have experienced from their neighbors,[32] and seeks to integrate this experience into a theological picture of reality: it is the kind of thing he warned them to expect when he first preached to them (3:4); it is a replication (mimēsis) of the foundational story of Christ crucified and of the life of the apostle (1:6) and of the experience of other Christian groups, including those in Judaea (2:14). Second, the letter stresses in several ways the strong ties that the converts now have with the apostle and with each other and with other Christians elsewhere. Virtues are redefined relative to the community: "familial affection" (philadelphia), for example, becomes love for the "brothers and sisters" of the Christian community (4:9). Third, Paul explicitly draws the line between insiders and outsiders in moral terms. The converts' behavior must be "worthy of the God who calls you"—that one, "living God" radically distinguished from the "idols" (2:12; 4:1). Sexual relations, a paradigm of distinctive behavior here as so often in early Christian moralizing and apologetics, must be "not in the passion of lust, like the gentiles who do not know God" (4:5).

As I said, Paul exaggerates the difference he urges. Pagan moral philosophers of Paul's era commonly advocated monogamous marriage. Paul's phrase "passion of lust" could be found describing the root of vice in the lectures of just about any of those philosophers, and in fact this whole letter is shot through with phrases and topics that were discussed regularly by pagan moralists.[33] Yet the fact of the exaggeration is itself important. The moral sphere within which the new Christians are urged to think about their own behavior is a strongly bounded space. Its symbolic shape and texture are formed by Jewish conceptions and stories about the one God and by the peculiar Christian story about God's crucified and resurrected Son. Its social boundaries are determined by the "turning" of those who have received these stories as their own and by the separation from "the gentiles"—who include those formerly their families and associates.[34]

Ritualizing Conversion

From the earliest years of the Christian movement, conversion, this movement from the common social sphere to a special one, was ritualized in the actions of baptism. From the second-century church we have several fragmentary glimpses of the way conversion was being institutionalized. From the beginning of the third century we have a document, the *Apostolic Tradition* attributed to Hippolytus, that depicts, in rules that may describe the ideal more closely than common practice, the elaborate procedures that had evolved in Rome in the second century for the reception of converts.[35] Reading those procedures, we are struck by the multiple ways they symbolically protect the purity of the community that the catechumens were joining and by the definition of that purity in a mixture of theological and moral terms.

Purifications of various kinds were often preliminary to initiations in antiquity. By making the act of washing the central act of the initiation itself, Christianity had from the beginning implied a boundary between an impure society and a pure community.[36] What we see in the Roman rite of Hippolytus is a dramatic emphasis on that boundary. Now candidates are screened before they are even permitted to take instruction, and people with morally suspect occupations—such as male and female prostitutes, school teachers, and sculptors—are excluded or required to change their jobs. Further screenings take place during the period of instruction, normally three years, and finally before admission to the water. Moreover, repeated exorcisms of the candidates dramatize a picture of the world outside the church as a realm under the devil's power.[37]

When we focus our attention on these boundary-drawing elements in Christian forms of initiation, early Christian conversion looks much less like the first type of conversion we considered—moral reformation of individuals according to socially approved norms—and much more like the second—detachment from the larger society's norms and joining what modern sociologists would call a "cult." The steps laid out in the *Apostolic Tradition*—scrutiny, instruction, exorcism, extended time of catechumenate, renunciation, washing—all serve to stigmatize "the world" being left and to distinguish the sacred space being entered.

Comparison between the Christian ritual and initiations like that of "Lucian" into the Isis cult discussed above will make the point plainer. In both cases, washing, sprinkling, or other acts of purification play a large role. In the initiations of the mysteries, however, what is protected as "pure" is the sacred space or the sacred rites themselves. Hence, for example, washing *precedes* initiation. In Christian initiation, what is to be kept pure is the *community.* Moreover, that purity is defined in moral as well as theological—that is, monotheistic—terms. Moral scrutiny of candidates is for the Christians not merely a temporary measure to assure purity at the moment of entering the sanctuary, as is often the case with the sacral rules found in inscriptions from ancient cult places.[38] Rather, the initiation is understood by Christian writers as the anchor and beginning point for a process of moral re-education that is conducted by and within the community of converts.

Remembering Conversion

Reminders of conversion and stories about conversion could serve important functions in that process of moral formation itself, as we have already seen in Paul's letter to the Thessalonians. By reminding them of their conversion and by stressing their relationship both to himself and to the larger Christian movement, Paul places the moral exhortations of the letter into a specific social and symbolic context. At the same time, he associates these directives with all the other moral exhortations that the converts heard at the time of their conversion and all the admonitions that they are to heed from their local leaders and which they are urged to make to one another. The letter depicts the "converted" life as having a certain shape and texture. The specific admonitions given in the letter are far from being a comprehensive picture of that life; they are only samples of and pointers to its shape and texture. The foundation doctrines and stories and the personal relationships engendered in the process and rituals of conversion imply much more.

Such reminders of conversion, with similar implied functions, occur elsewhere in the Pauline letters as well, for example in 1 Cor. 6:9–11: "Do you not know that unjust people will not inherit the kingdom of God? Do not be deceived: neither fornicators nor idolaters nor adulterers nor the morally flabby nor sodomites nor thieves nor greedy folk nor drunkards nor slanderers nor robbers will inherit the kingdom of God. And some of you were these things—but you were washed, you were made holy, you were justified in the name of the Lord Jesus Christ and in the spirit of our God."

This mode of exhortation was one well learned in the Pauline school and elsewhere, for it dominates the letters to Colossians and Ephesians, which are probably the work of disciples of Paul, as well as the rather similar letter called 1 Peter. All these letters are filled with language that recalls the ritual of baptism, with its images of transformation or rebirth, the restoration of primal unity, the taking off of the "old human" with the vices thereunto adhering, and the putting on of the "new human" characterized by the virtues that belong to one who is being remade "after the image of the creator," or, in the idiom of 1 Peter, the making of the people of God out of a "nonpeople."

The letters of the New Testament do not contain any outright stories of conversion, however, of the sort that modern converts so often tell as "testimonies" in revival meetings and the like. Such stories were told in antiquity as well, as we have seen—the stories of Polemo, or of the conversions won by Diogenes and other Cynics or by Apollonius of Tyana. Where we do find conversion stories, in John 9, for example, and prominently in the Acts of the Apostles, the functions they serve in their literary contexts are not immediately relevant to our question about moral formation. The stories Justin tells, in the middle of the second century, are more directly to the point.

As we saw earlier, Justin describes his own conversion, in the *Dialogue with Trypho*, in conventional terms as conversion to the best school of philosophy, after having tried others. In his *Apology* he emphasizes the moral qualities of the Christians, rather than their reasoning, as the features that won him over from Platonism (2 *Apol.* 12.1).[39] His brief account of baptism (1 *Apol.* 61.1–3) emphasizes the moral transformation brought about by the "washing" and "rebirth," and elsewhere he expands on this transformation in these words: "Those who once rejoiced in fornication [*porneia*] now delight in continence [*sōphrosynē*] alone; those who made use of magic arts have dedicated themselves to the good and unbegotten God; we who once took most pleasure in the means of increasing our wealth and property now bring what we have into a common fund and share with everyone in need; we who hated and killed one another and would not associate with men of different tribes because of [their different] customs, now after the manifestation of Christ live together and pray for our enemies and try to persuade those who unjustly hate us . . ." (14.2–3).[40]

Here again we see the results of Christian conversion described as the attainment of virtues approved by (at least) the intellectual elite of the larger society, as well as the implication that such virtues are exceedingly rare in the practices of that society. Justin makes both points strongly in his account of the licentious wife of a licentious husband, converted by the Christian teacher Ptolemaeus (2 *Apol.* 2.1–9), whose martyrdom Justin then recounts (2.10–20).[41] These are the emphases we would expect in apologetic literature.

Accounts of conversion in some other kinds of early Christian literature, notably the several apocryphal Acts of apostles, lay much greater emphasis on the radical disjuncture between the morality of the pagan world and that of the Christian groups. Conversion in the apocryphal Acts invariably entails change of moral habits, usually in an ascetic direction, but also more generally. In the *Acts of Peter* a matron is converted after the apostle exposes the theft of her property by Simon Magus. "Eubula having recovered all her property gave it for the care of the poor; she believed in the Lord Jesus Christ and was strengthened [in the faith]; and despising and renouncing this world she gave [alms] to the widows and orphans and clothed the poor . . . ."[42] The conversion of Thecla is typical of the encratite Acts in portraying the central alternation by the convert as the abandoning of sexuality and the connections of family.[43]

The conversion of Mygdonia (*Acts of Thomas* 82–101) is typical of the conversions in the *Acts of Thomas*, though more extended than most, and the encratite requirements for the convert are stated at some length. Thomas's appeal is first addressed to Mygdonia's litter bearers, applying to them literally the saying "Come unto me, all you who labor and are heavy laden" (82). Rich and poor, slave and free are alike before God (83). The first requirement is to "abstain from adultery, for it is the impetus for all vices" (84).[44] The central thing in the story, however, turns out to be the abandonment of sexual behavior of all kinds, not just sexual misconduct like adultery, for Mygdonia leaves the bed of her husband, and Thomas declares that even "intercourse for procreation" is to be condemned (88; Lipsius and Bonnet 1959, 3:203.19–20), thus excluding the one ground for legitimate sex recognized by the most rigorous of pagan moralists, like Musonius, and by more moderate Christian teachers, like Clement of Alexandria.

Conversion stories and conversion rituals thus serve several functions in the attempts of the early Christian groups to form their adherents into moral communities. One was to confirm their sense of having acquired a new, primary reference group. That is, their belonging to the Christian movement itself was strengthened by placing their experience within an explanatory narrative with broad metaphorical power and extended behavioral implications. A second function of talk about conversion was in moral exhortation that reminded the converts of their personal conversion stories within that larger story, urging them to act in a way "worthy" of what had happened to them and to their world. A third was the defense of their practices and values by connecting them with values familiar in the "world" from which they had "turned." A fourth, implicitly in tension with the third, was what Berger and Luckmann call the "nihilation" of that world, in order to secure the convert's singleminded dependence upon the new community as the sole source for guidance and support.[45]

The two major ways of construing conversion, as individual moral reform or as a countercultural formation of "the new human," correspond to two ways of thinking about the formation of a Christian character and two ways in which the Christian communities related to the world around them. These opposing ways sometimes embody themselves in mutually hostile movements within the church, sometimes appear in a dialectic of both thought and institutionalization, sometimes are submerged for a time only to break out in new problems and innovations. Perfectionism and universalism, abhorrence of the world's perversions and longing for the world's wholeness, the mind of the sect and the mind of the church struggle on in the history of Christian moral thought and practice.

CHAPTER 3

City, Household,
People of God

❖ ❖ ❖ ❖ ❖ ❖ ❖ ❖ ❖ ❖

The eloquent exhortation that we know as the Epistle to the Hebrews climaxes with a vision of "the city of the living God, the heavenly Jerusalem" (12:22 in the New Revised Standard Version, hereafter cited as NRSV). Then, returning to the imagery of the Israelites wandering in the desert, the author calls on Christians to go forth to Jesus "outside the camp. . . . For here we have no lasting city, but we are looking for the city that is to come" (13:11,14, NRSV). Yet the specific admonitions that stand between these two flights of metaphor pertain to life not in some desert retreat but in an urban congregation: let brotherly love abide; don't neglect hospitality; remember the prisoners; honor marriage. Early Christianity was an urban phenomenon. Its growth and its shape were very closely entangled with the nature of the Greek-speaking cities of the Roman provinces and the Greek-speaking quarters of Rome itself. And, as the metaphors of Hebrews suggest, Christians felt simultaneously at home and not at home in these cities.

The Polis as Context for Greek Ethics

The morality that we know from the Greek and Roman world is indigenous to the city: the unique polis of the Greeks, now overlaid by Roman power and influence, alongside the Roman city forms, including its colonies outside Italy, all more or less influenced by Greek traditions and theories. In a variety of direct or subtle ways, an idealized concept of the city, a glorified memory of fifth- and fourth-century Athens, was the context that gave meaning to Greek notions of ethics.[1] The "political" context of ethics receives its classical definition from Aristotle, as we saw in chapter 1. For

Aristotle, human flourishing—the "happiness," *eudaimonia,* that all varieties of Greek philosophy took to be the aim of politics and ethics—was conceivable only within a community, and indeed within the specific kind of community that the Greeks called a polis. The polis was not only the arena in which moral responsibility was exercised, it was also the school in which moral habits were learned. Even though popular philosophy of the age of Hellenism and of Rome emphasized the individual "contest" for virtue, as we saw in the case of the *Tablet of Cebes,* the literary and rhetorical moralists of these later ages still assumed the city and its constituent structures as the context of the moral life and of its goal.[2]

The firm hold that the city's forms of life had on the ethical imagination is apparent even in the case of movements that seem on their face to disparage those forms. The Cynics, particularly those of the more flamboyantly ascetic and "shameless" wing of the movement, flaunted their deliberate violation of urbane conventions.[3] Yet the shock therapy they thus sought to administer to any who would listen required the city's public spaces. And the therapy had little point, given the Cynics' own choice of practice over theorizing, apart from some underlying values and goals that the Cynic attacks undertook to shock into wakefulness, and which drew their meaning from the potential of the city. The case of the Epicureans is harder, for Epicurus's motto, "Live privately," entailed a withdrawal from political life and public responsibilities. Indeed, such withdrawal was the occasion for one of the standard complaints against the Epicureans by philosophers of other schools.[4] Nevertheless, the withdrawal from public life was not a retreat into individualism, but into an alternative community. The Garden of Epicurus was, as it were, a countercultural community, an antipolis.[5] Analogies to both the Cynic and the Epicurean ambivalence about the city can be seen among the variety of ways that the early Christians conceived of their existence in the cities.

City and Household

One of the constituent structures of the polis was the household. Indeed the household, as Aristotle and subsequent moralists saw it, was the veritable microcosm of the city, for the governing forms of exchange that constitute friendship and all the relationships of power, protection, submission, honor, and duty that must be properly tuned if a city is to flourish—all these exist between husband and wife, master and slaves, parents and children, householder and dependents, householder and social equals. It is in the household, then, that a member of the decurial class learns to govern—as later the Christian household would serve as training ground for the bishop. A handbook for church governance, written in Paul's name probably early in the second century, mandates that a bishop must be someone who "governs his own household excellently" (1 Tim. 3:4–5). The sign of that excellence singled out by the author is the subordination *(hypotagē)* and sense of dignity *(semnotēs)* shown by the children. Children in a well-governed household, of whatever class, learn what is expected of them. The household is the primary school of morality; the secondary school is the city itself. For boys of citizen class, that higher moral training would begin with father and tutors at home and advance to the gymnasium and palaestra. For others, the larger schoolroom would be the streets and marketplaces. Some schooling was available for girls of aristocratic families. For most girls, however, moral training (including the particular duties of submissiveness and quiet modesty expected of the proper wife: see 1 Tim. 2:9–15) was almost entirely a household matter.

Submission and dignity were, at every stage, the most important lessons to be learned, and they were not simple. Whether to yield or to receive submission, whether to affect that double-edged *dignitas,* at once hauteur and graciousness, prized by the Roman gentleman,[6] and when, and in relationship to whom; or whether one had no choice but always to yield to the dignitas of the powerful: knowing such choices entailed an intricate calculation of one's place in society and the place of those one met. But of course the occasions when one really had consciously to calculate were exceptional. The lessons of appropriate deference or its opposite had to be learned early and so thoroughly as to become intuitive. One learned them within the *familia,* the *oikos,* whether one was a child in that household or a slave. The whole complex of taken-for-granted rankings would be instantly understood when Paul admonished the Roman Christians: "Give to each what is due . . . fear to the one owed fear, honor to the one owed honor" (Rom. 13:7).

Rituals and Morals of Dependence

Fear and honor: the society was ruled by honor and its opposite, shame, and beneath the sanctions of honor and shame were the manifold forms of fear. No one to my knowledge has so vividly described the way this society actually worked, in the period of the high Roman Empire, than Ramsay

MacMullen. In the second chapter of his book *Corruption and the Decline of Rome*, he shows how that society, before it began to disintegrate under the weight of sheer greed in the third century, managed to control the potential for conflict. That potential was enormous, in "a society made up in some sense of only two classes, Haves and Have-nots," and characterized by aggressive competition. "The Roman solution," says MacMullen, "ritual-ized and moralized dependence, and so fixed people in stable relations with each other."[7] Dependence took one form between Haves and Have-nots, another among the Haves. The former is epitomized, and most thoroughly ritualized, in the specifically Roman institution of *clientela*, patronage, but less formal equivalents are visible everywhere, in Greek East no less than in Latin West. The client trades service and submission for the patron's protec-tion and, as it were, honor by association. The links of interdependence among the Haves took the form of "friendship," *amicitia*, *philia*. As Mac-Mullen says, "The higher one was in this society, the more one was owed and the less one owed others. But ties which the most lofty ranks preferred to call friendship, not dependence, united even these in mutual obligation."[8] Even among the Haves, of course, some were more equal than others, so some of the relations called "friendship" were not so very different, struc-turally, from those called "patronage." Someone called by the formal honor-ific "friend of Caesar," for example, was inevitably Caesar's client, though sure to have many clients of his own, and thus a person of great honor and power. (The double edge of the status enables the implicit threat of the Jews to Pilate in John 19:12.) The honor of the patron rubbed off on the client; the freedman of a very important personage was very important himself. Even the slave of Caesar might think the fact something to record with pride on a tombstone.[9]

This story of the intricate ties that bind, in a society of limited goods and a steep social pyramid, has been told many times. It is still familiar in many parts of the world, especially in some lands around the Mediterranean.[10] Yet what has it got to do with morality? The clue may be found in MacMullen's comment that the system functioned smoothly because "it ritualized and moralized dependence." Ritual, that is, public and formal kinds of display, reinforced the values endemic to the system, gave them that force of neces-sity that Clifford Geertz calls "the air of simple realism."[11] Without that sense of the obvious, moral conviction cannot grow and persist. *Moral conviction is at stake*, for a critical number of the participants in the system must somehow believe that the relationships it embodies are not only the way things are, but, at least on average, the way things ought to be, that the way one behaves is not only necessary but also right.

Competition and Harmony

The virtues celebrated in this society were, on the one hand, those that expressed the aggressive competition for honor, summed up in the word *philotimia*.[12] On the other hand, the virtues that make for harmony and peace, which seem just those qualities most likely to be trampled in the eager race for public recognition and prestige, were equally prized. Alföldy, for example, has collected from inscriptions of the principate typical expressions of individual achievement. Superlatives are much loved: one is not just *bonus* but always *optimus vir;* even superlatives of superlatives are coined, in language that sounds like copy by a Hollywood press agent: *carissimissimissimis, adulescens . . . omnium rerum bonarium melior, super omnes incomparabilis,* and the like, and equivalents even more common in Greek inscriptions. People are honored for being the first to do all sorts of thing: first woman to endow banquets for her town; first citizen to donate a hundred thousand sesterces to his town, and so on. Yet the excelling performed by these heroes of self-display is not eccentric or lonely: their epitaphs are crowded in with those of a host of similarly "unique" individuals, and all excel in virtues typical of the community at large. Indeed, the most prized virtues are those that protect the tranquility of the commons.[13] The most frequent epithet on Greek tombstones is "good," *chrēstos,* and the next most frequent is "harmless," *alypos.* More fully, "Friend of all, troubling no one."[14]

The Christians, that movement of converts, who talk so often about turning away from that world to a different order, would have to discover whether the turning implied an alternate conception of honor, of achievement, of goodness. If they were to make any kind of effective morality to match their conversionist talk, they would have to find other rituals to challenge the facticity of the moral order. They would have an uphill struggle, and we should not be surprised if we find them echoing the pervasive order at least as often as they tried to change it.

Polis in Empire

Let us return now to our question about the city as the context of early Christian moral development. The structures of dependence and protection I have just sketched were, to be sure, just as important in village and farm as they were in the city—and indeed constituted the strongest links in the chain that bound the city to its rural territory. Honor and shame were as ubiquitous in the life of a rural clan as in an urban household. Nevertheless, the polis provided the most conspicuous stages on which the daily rituals of patronage and friendship were acted out. It was in the polis that the great man paraded to his bath with crowds of dependents and slaves as his entourage. It was in the polis that statues and steles and inscriptions on public buildings proclaimed the benefactions of the most-honored. It was in the city that seating at a dinner party graphed out the status of those present.

Aliens in the Imperial City

The city in which Christianity discovered its enduring form was not the city of Aristotle. A great deal has been written about the "crisis of the polis" beginning in the fourth century B.C.E. It is obvious that the rise first of the Hellenistic kingdoms, then of Rome as an imperial power, radically altered the political situation of cities. The fiction of the self-governing *poleis* was preserved and cultivated by their new "founders" or re-founders, but those royal patrons controlled as surely as they protected. The limits to the cities' own autonomy, by the turn of the second century C.E., are painfully obvious to any reader of the correspondence between the emperor Trajan and his high commissioner of Bithynia and Pontus, Pliny, or to readers of Dio Chrysostom's speech to the Tarsians. Dio warns them that if they do not settle the complaints of the linen weavers, the Romans will do it for them, and they will have lost their *parrhēsia*, the cherished ideal of republican free speech, altogether.[15]

Not only the political shift brought by the new imperialism, but also the new ease of travel brought by Roman roads and Roman peace altered the face of the city. Resident aliens had already been a significant foreign body in the Athens of the Golden Age. Under Rome, migration becomes a constant fact of urban demography, and with it the growth of large and organized communities of immigrants in every major city. Elsewhere I have tried to describe the importance of this new physical mobility for the early Christian mission.[16] Here I am concerned with its effects on the moral universe of people living in those cities. When people move from a community with one kind of culture into one that is quite different, very often their moral intuitions no longer match the reality around them. The move from countryside into a city often has this effect, and so does immigration. Peasants or rural artisans moving to town might continue to hold onto their old values if they continued to work fields around the city and found neighborhoods made up of other rural people. Immigrants, too, could take the edge off their sense of foreignness by settling in neighborhoods with people who had come from the same area and by forming ethnic clubs and community centers with them. These centers and associations were normally formed around the cult of the gods of the immigrants' homeland. Nevertheless, life in the Mediterranean city was lived in close quarters and in public spaces. Pressures to assimilate to the common culture of the city, with its Greek or Roman constitution, its Greek or Latin language, its common city plan and architecture, and the common expectations of the way public honor or shame was awarded, would be very strong.

The combination of imperialism and migration meant that the world inhabited by urban people in a given place was larger and more diverse than before, but that they tended to have less clarity about the things that were demanded or expected of them and, on the whole, less control. It is generally agreed that the Hellenistic and Roman periods brought increasing social distance between the Haves and Have-nots, though probably accompanied by some slight increase in the opportunities for social mobility—in either direction.[17] It is probably also true, as Eckhard Plümacher has argued, that Roman domination made it more difficult for many people below the ranks of the decurions to find the chief mirrors of their personal identity in the public life of their cities, though the changes were perhaps less one-sided than he represents them.[18] In any case, it is clear that for many residents of the Greco-Roman cities the polis as such was not so obviously the primary reference group for moral judgments as it had been for Aristotle.

The Jews

Among the immigrant communities in the typical Greco-Roman city, the Jews were a special case, interesting in its own right as well as for the light it sheds on the birth of Christianity. Though their organization of local associations followed a pattern that was very common among other immigrant groups, they stood apart in certain ways. To begin with, the prophetic polemic against "idolatry" had shaped in many Jews the conviction that their monotheistic worship was vastly superior to the polytheism and syncretism that surrounded them. For most of them, at least in the early Empire, that conviction was a barrier to participation in many of the civic rituals of the cities in which they lived, and thus strengthened the boundaries around their own community. The ambivalence of their situation as resident aliens led to changed notions about the nature of their own identity—what was "Israel" when it was not a political entity in the land of Judaea or Samaria?— and about the nature of the Torah. The latter came more and more to be understood as a code of laws—and thus deserving Roman recognition and protection like any local and ancestral laws—and indeed as a civic constitution, a *politeia*. Israel was a unique people, constituted by its practices and its traditions. Moses thus comes to be represented, in Greek Jewish writings, preeminently as the "legislator" and moral philosopher of the Jews.[19]

Plato and Zeno had already paved the way, by their writings entitled *Politeiai*, "Republics," both for a utopian vision of the ideal polis and for taking the polis as metaphor for the moral psychology of the self. The soul, they taught, was like a city—with competing forces jostling for dominance, requiring strong government. Both moves were repeated many times by Platonists, Stoics, and eclectic philosophers of the Roman period, and the more sophisticated Jewish authors seized on them with élan. Thus in Philo's allegorical interpretation of the Torah, the Republic founded by Moses is simultaneously the ideal form of Jewish practice, embodied in the life of the Jewish community of Alexandria and elsewhere, and the universal commonwealth of harmony to be realized within the soul of the wise man.[20] One may reasonably doubt that very many Alexandrian Jews were able to follow Philo's high-flown philosophizing. Nevertheless, his commentaries give grand expression to a sense about the relevant moral universe that seems to have been shared by a great many Jews. That is to say, as for many other immigrant groups, their organized *politeuma* (or whatever their immigrants' association might be called in a local instance) was for them an alternative city. Israel, not Alexandria or Antioch, was their ultimate moral reference point, and Israel was both the local embodiment of Moses' ideal polis and the company of God's people that transcended local boundaries and the boundaries of time. Simultaneously, their understanding of Israel itself, and their local embodiment of it, were shot through with ideas, values, attitudes, and relationships that were indigenous to the life of the Hellenistic-Roman city—just as Philo's Moses speaks the metaphysics of Plato and the ethics of the Stoa, inscribing the highest of Greek culture into the very words of the Torah, Israel's constitution. To emphasize either side of this ambivalence to the exclusion of the other, either the Jewish community's assimilation to the encompassing culture of the cities or its sense of distinctiveness and superiority as "the nation that sees [the only true] God," would miss the fundamental tension that shaped the ethos of diaspora Israel.

Christians in the Polis

The Hebrew Bible in a number of places speaks of the tribes of Israel gathered in solemn assembly, the *qahal* of God. *The* assembly par excellence was at Mount Sinai, when the Torah was received (for example, Deut. 9:10; 18:16). For the Greek translation of that word, the Septuagint chose *ekklēsia*, a word that referred to, among other things, the voting assembly of the citizen body, the *dēmos*, of a Greek polis. Did the translators already have some notion of Israel as an ideal republic, or did their choice of words suggest that to Philo, Josephus, and other later writers? We have no way of knowing. No Jewish community in the Hellenistic cities called itself an ekklesia, so far as we know.

It is remarkable that the Christians in those same cities did seize on the term that had been adopted by the Bible translators for the sacral assembly of Israel and applied it to themselves. By the time Paul wrote the letter that is our earliest extant Christian document, "the ekklesia of God" or, as New Englanders would say, "the town meeting of God," was already the preferred self-designation for Christian groups in the cities of the Roman provinces. The irony of addressing the handful of new converts, meeting probably in the dining room or atrium of some modest home, as "the Thessalonians' Assembly," *ekklēsia thessalonikeōn* (1 Thess. 1:1), is probably unintended. Nevertheless, the real irony is an apt expression of the ambiguity of the new cult's relation to its urban environment, as well as a signal of the implicit task of its moral self-formation.

The formation of the Christian groups as house-based communities embodies the physical and social ambiguity of their place in the cities. By depending upon the hospitality *(proxenia)* of a patron-householder, they followed a well-tried pattern by which clubs, guilds, and immigrant cults found space in the cities. These were groups that lacked on their own both the standing that would grant them use of the public spaces of the polis and the means for establishing private facilities. By accepting the patron's protection, such groups are, as it were, grafted into the structure of reciprocity that makes the urban society work.[21] The patron's benefactions add luster to his or her honor and thus enhance the patron's political capacities.[22] In turn, the clients are obliged to respect the conventional values of the system, so as to continue to receive protection while not bringing shame on their patron.

One peculiarity of the patronage the early Christians depended on may have increased the "political" ambiguity in their case. With the possible exception of Erastus of Corinth, the "treasurer of the city" (Rom. 16:23), who may have been identical with the like-named *aedile* of the colony known from an inscription, we do not know a benefactor of the church in the period of our concern who was clearly a member of the decurial class, that is, the aristocracy to whom patronage had traditionally belonged.[23] By and large the persons who played the part of patrons to the Christian groups, in other words, were not regularly engaged in the governance of the polis nor in the liturgies by which the wealthiest citizens were required to support civic amenities while enhancing their own power and prestige. Nevertheless, the pattern of patron-client reciprocity clearly has been imitated by those of relatively ample means and ambition beneath the decurial class, and the civic values displayed in that pattern trickle down, so to speak, to those of more ambiguous status who provide the household bases of the Christians. The Christian groups' engagement with the city is thus in a sense buffered by their distance from the decurial class, but inevitably the morals of reciprocal status, of honor and dependence, are implicit in the very physical spaces those groups occupy.

James S. Jeffers has provided us with a fascinating analysis of two documents from Roman Christianity toward the end of the first century that, if he is correct, exhibit rather vividly the conflict of values that could ensue from this ambiguous social location. The author of the first, a letter from the Roman churches to the Corinthian Christians commonly called *1 Clement*, shows familiarity with the ruling elite and shares many of their moral sensibilities: idealization of civic harmony *(homonoia)* and dislike of strife *(stasis, eris, schisma)*, firm support for the patriarchal household, and approval of the hierarchy of status in the city, with deference due to the patrons. The other document, known as the *Shepherd of Hermas*, is written by someone evidently further down the social scale (a freedman and a failed businessman; ironically Clement, too, is probably a freedman, according to Jeffers, but of the élite Flavian family). Hermas is far harsher toward the wealthy than Clement, though he, too, recognizes that the church must depend upon them. Though it is an exaggeration to say with Jeffers that "Hermas stood the patron-client relationship on its head," Hermas certainly does shift the center of gravity of that relationship quite considerably in his allegory of the vine (the faithful poor) supported by the elm (the strong but otherwise unfruitful rich, *Similitudes* 2). For Hermas, unity of the church will be attained not by practice of the civic virtues, but by isolation and purity.[24]

Pseudo-aliens

Returning now to the time four or five decades earlier when the traveling apostles of the new movement had just begun to adapt the Roman and Greek household and the pattern of patronage to their own needs, we discover further clues in that first letter of Paul's to which we have turned so often already. The converts in Thessalonica, in the interval since Paul last saw them, have been under pressure *(thlipsis)* in the form of hostility from the people in the city formerly closest to them—their *symphyletai,* literally "fellow tribesmen," their kith and kin. Paul compares this experience with that of the Judean Christian groups ("the town meetings of God that are in Judea") at the hands of those Judeans who opposed the Christian movement from the beginning (1 Thess. 2:14). Now the kith and kin of the Thessalonian Christians are not Jews but gentiles, people who still worship those "idols" from which the converts "turned" (1:9). Nevertheless, Paul can write to those converts as if they were Jews, that their sex life should be "not like the nations that do not know God" (4:4). Their conversion has made them into pseudo-aliens: they are on their way to becoming that "third race" that Aristides and other apologists of the next century would celebrate.

The metaphors of immigrant life are taken up more extensively and explicitly later in the century in a letter written in the name of Peter and addressed to "the chosen expatriates of the Diaspora of Pontus, Galatia, Cappadocia, Asia, and Bithynia" (1 Peter 1:1). Like 1 Thessalonians, this letter is written to an audience mostly composed of former pagans, not Jews, and there is no reason to believe (contra John Elliott[25]) that they all really were resident aliens or rural noncitizens in the towns of the four or five provinces named in the address. Rather, we see again the implicit analogy of the *convert* with the immigrant, especially the Jewish immigrant. The all-important Christian household, which Elliott has rightly emphasized, into which these converts are being "built" in the metaphorical language of the letter, is explicitly identified here with the house of Israel. Those who were "no people" have become "God's people," a "chosen race, a royal priesthood, a holy *ethnos*, a people to be [God's] private estate" (2:9–10). The experience of Israel as a self-conscious and organized community of resident aliens in the diaspora cities is here simply commandeered by the new offshoot cult and used to explain their own social and moral situation in those same cities.

Honor to Whom . . . ?

Those metaphors we have looked at so far imply *separation* of the converts, the pseudo-aliens, from the larger life of the city. We will see in a moment that that is only one side of the picture, but it is an important part of the early Christian self-consciousness. Conversion implies a change of reference groups and reference individuals—those groups and persons to whom we look, in fact or in imagination, for standards, for approval or disapproval, for measures of how well we are doing. The admonitory literature of early Christianity attempts, for one thing, to substitute for the reference groups and individuals that were important in the normal life of the city, the Christian group itself and its heroes and leaders.[26]

One way to get a clearer picture of the way this change of reference groups was supposed to work is to ask whether honor and shame, those pervasive sanctions of ancient society, were different for the Christian groups. This is a large question, to which we must return in a later chapter, but a few observations may anticipate that fuller discussion. When Paul tells the Thessalonians about the anxiety he has suffered over them, it is clear that his honor was at stake. Their failure would mean his "labor had been in vain" (3:5). He can call them his "hope and joy and crown of pride," his "glory and joy" (2:19–20)—yet in the context of the specifically Christian belief in Jesus' *parousia* (his future glorious advent) and the final judgment. The "public" before which the apostle's shame or honor will be manifest is not a crowd of citizens in the agora of the polis, but a transcendent company: God and Christ and their "holy ones." The earthly forum is of course the Christian community itself. The shift of effective reference group could go so far as to attempt to stand the larger society's measures of honor and shame on their head, to attempt to "nihilate" the power of those sanctions.[27] It is not surprising that a group who had somehow to deal with the fact that its founding figure had died by the most shameful form of public execution would occasionally take that step: to make the world's honor seem shame and shame, honor. Thus the Book of Acts, for example, depicts the apostles, released after questioning by the Sanhedrin, "rejoicing that they were deemed worthy *to be dishonored* for the Name" (5:41, emphasis added).

Nevertheless, the Christians for the most part continued to give heed to the measures of honor and shame in the larger society. "Give honor to the person owed honor," writes Paul, repeating traditional admonitions about respect for governmental authority (Rom. 13:7), and 1 Peter, in the same tradition, says, "Honor all, love the brotherhood, fear God, honor the Emperor" (2:17). Like any immigrant group, the Christians wanted to be seen as leading a "quiet life," causing no trouble and needing nothing, in short, "behaving decently toward the outsiders" (1 Thess. 4:11–12). If outsiders happened into one of their meetings when tongue-speaking charismatics had the floor, they would accuse them of being mad (1 Cor. 14:23), surely grounds for shame. Rather, the Christians' behavior must be such that even their slanderers will be persuaded by their good works and "give glory to God on the day of visitation" (1 Peter 2:12). That means, of course, that the moral norms of the Christians cannot be so very different from those of the outsiders.

That is not surprising. The urban household, after all, was the microcosm of the city in the ideals of pagan morality and, in a more complicated way, in the realities of power, as I suggested earlier. And that same urban household has been called "the basic cell" of the early Christian movement. All the ambivalence and tensions that we have noticed between this movement of self-described converts and the moral world of the Greek city were focused and concentrated in the very houses where they held their "town meetings of God." The formulas of their baptismal ritual proclaimed that they had taken off their "old human" and put on "the new," that the old connections had been replaced by a new family of the children of God, brothers and sisters, a family in which there was no longer "Jew or Greek, slave or free, male and female" (Gal. 3:28). But life in the house continued. Christian brothers and sisters still had siblings of blood who might or might not also be Christians. Christian slaves had masters and Christian wives had husbands, and a householder incurred obligations to his or her patrons and clients and equals in the social network of the city. True, a prophet of the lowest social class might receive in a trance a "revelation of the Lord" and with it the right to speak and give direction to the household assembly—but everyone still knew to whom the house belonged. True, women sometimes took on exceptional roles of leadership in the new movement—but there were soon strong reactions against that. True, in an exceptional case the apostle could write to a householder that he should welcome back his delinquent slave "no longer as a slave, but more than a slave, a beloved brother . . . both in the flesh and in the Lord" (Philem. 16), but elsewhere he treats slavery as a matter of indifference: "You were a slave when called? Never mind" (1 Cor. 7:21). Soon Paul's disciples and other leaders as well would be repeating the old rules of Greek household management, "Slaves, be submissive in all fear to your masters . . . ; Likewise wives, be submissive to your own husbands . . . ," and so on (1 Peter 2:18–3:7).

Metaphors of Ambivalence

The city loomed large—and ambivalently—in the symbolic language of the early Christians. Motley groups in urban households, they saw themselves as pilgrims questing for a city made by God (Heb. 11:10,16; 12:22; 13:14). Some of them saw the cities around them, and Rome above all, as demonic: Babylon, the harlot-city, drunk on the blood of God's witnesses. Even so, they imagined a different city, a heavenly Jerusalem to come. Only later would some Christians find the city as such and even its basic unit, the family, evil, and they would flee to the desert. The ambivalent middle way that the majority were to go is nowhere expressed more eloquently than in the anonymous apology called the *Letter to Diognetus*, which explains that "Christians differ from other people neither in land nor speech nor custom, for they do not inhabit their own cities somewhere, nor employ an exotic dialect, nor practice an unusual way of life." Paradoxically, the letter continues, the Christians keep all the local customs, whether living "in Greek or barbarian cities," while somehow at the same time demonstrating "the amazing and admittedly strange establishment of their own republic." There follows a list of wonderful paradoxes, too long to quote in full, culminating in the claim that "what the soul is for the body, the Christians are in the world. The soul is distributed through all the organs of the body, and Christians in all the cities of the world" (*Diogn.* 5:1–6:2).

Two great complexes of traditional thinking about the moral community form the horizons of Christian moral discourse: the one focuses on the polis of the Greeks, the other on the people Israel. The long tradition of moralizing discourse in and about the polis continued to echo in the writings of educated Christians. The complex web of dependence and protection, honor and deference that gave location and stability to people in their towns held the Christians fast as well, and they adapted them in more or less subtle ways to their own needs and novel perceptions. The diaspora Jews' special experience and their special sense of themselves as not merely aliens competing with others, but as a unique people of the one and only God, a people parallel to and somehow transcending all the other *ethnē*—all this struck a peculiar resonance in the emerging Christian sensibilities. Yet, unlike the Jews, they had no home*land.* The Christians had been made immigrants, as it were, by their conversion. So where was their constitutional community, the *politeia* to which they were responsible, whose laws they must obey, whose customs would shape their lives? Was it in the sky, as Paul wrote to the Philippians? Or was it an alternative constitution that could be realized in the commonwealths on earth? We can hardly blame the early Christians for not having worked out a clear and satisfying answer to these questions. When St. Augustine three centuries later took up the issue in his greatest treatise, the image of the city still dominated his formulation. Even Augustine only named and did not finally solve the question of how the city of God and the cities of this world intersect. It is an issue that has troubled Christian ethics through the ages: the issue that H. Richard Niebuhr named "Christ and Culture."[28] In ever new ways it faces Christians and their neighbors urgently today.

CHAPTER 4

Loving and Hating the World

❖ ❖ ❖ ❖ ❖ ❖ ❖ ❖ ❖ ❖

Jesus said, 'Whoever has become acquainted with the world has found a corpse, and the world is not worthy of the one who has found the corpse.' "[1] This is not the Jesus of the canonical Gospels, to be sure, but the one called "the living Jesus" of the *Gospel of Thomas*, who utters sayings that the prologue to that Gospel understandably calls "cryptic." The *Gospel of Thomas*, which probably originated in Syria sometime in the second century, was widely disseminated and read among Christians for several centuries thereafter, until authorities of the emerging catholic churches succeeded in suppressing it. It then remained unknown until a Coptic version was discovered in Egypt in 1945.[2]

The *Gospel of Thomas* is only one of several writings that were associated with Judas, the brother of Jesus, in ancient Christianity, beginning with the Epistle of Jude that became part of the canonical New Testament. The Thomas tradition seems to have appealed to morally rigorist Christians especially in eastern Syria and in Egypt; whether it should be identified with some particular sect ("heresy") of the early church is problematic.[3] In any case, it provides a suitable starting point for our consideration of the early Christians' varying perceptions of "the world." We shall see later that cryptic and not-so-cryptic comments disparaging "the world," the *kosmos*, are not infrequent in more "orthodox" literature of the early Christians, including the New Testament. The judgments or attitudes implied by such sayings surely must have moral consequences. If the world is a corpse and, by the fact of our recognizing it for what it is, unworthy of our attention, then we are not going to waste much time laboring for, say, a more just economic order or better housing for the poor.

Becoming a Solitary

Indeed, cryptic though many of the words of the *Gospel of Thomas* remain, it is not hard to imagine some dimensions of the kind of life that would accord with its dark but often witty images. It is a life estranged from the ordinary and threatened by it: like the owner of a rural estate who must fortify it against bandits, the disciples are told, "Be on your guard against the world. Arm yourselves with great power lest the brigands find a way to get to you; for the trouble that you expect will come" (21b, 37:11–15). Perfectly commonsense advice, as archaeologists can show us from the ruins of fortress-villas all over the Empire. But Thomas's Jesus is not talking common sense at all. Common sense found security only in lots of wealth, lots of slaves and other dependents—who could be made into a small private army if need be—and in a wide network of powerful relatives and friends.[4] But "the one who comes to know the world" in Thomas's way rejects all three: wealth, dependents, family. The force with which the disciples arm themselves is interior and counterintuitive. The short dialogue that precedes the saying just quoted uses quite different metaphors to depict the confrontation: "Mary said to Jesus, 'What do your disciples resemble?' He said, 'What they resemble is children living in a plot of land that is not theirs. When the owners of the land come they will say, "Surrender our land to us." They, for their part, strip naked in their presence in order to give it back to them, and they give them their land'" (21a, 36:33–37.5).

Nakedness is an important metaphor in this Gospel. "Jesus said, 'When you strip naked without being ashamed, and take your garments and put them under your feet like little children and tread upon them, then [you] will see the child of the living'" (37, 39:29–40.1). Yet there is no reason to believe that Thomas's first readers had organized a nudist colony. What is to be stripped off is everything that ties one to "the world," that is, to ordinary social structures. The language alludes to baptism. The Christians of the Thomas circle perceive the ritual divestment practiced at baptism as a metaphor for the renunciation that should characterize the Christian life.[5]

Wealth is one such thing: "If you have money, do not lend it out at interest. Rather, give [it] to one from whom you will not get it back" (95, 48:35–49.1). At first hearing, this advice could sound like the standard morality of patronage. By ancient conventions, giving to one who could not repay put the receiver under obligation and created more honor—and another dependent—for the rich person. Thomas's Jesus, however, has a different notion of what constitutes real wealth: "The one who has found the world and become rich should renounce the world" (110, 51:4–5). In Thomas's version of the parable of the Great Supper, what keeps the invited guests from coming is their involvement with trade (merchants are coming to pay me; I have bought a building) and social connections (I am giving a dinner for a friend's wedding). Its moral is, "Buyers and traders [will] not enter the places of my father" (64, 44:10–34). Like the more familiar Jesus of the Sermon on the Mount, this Jesus says, "Blessed are the poor," and means it.

Family is another tie that binds—fatally, for Thomas. The saying we also know from the Synoptic Gospels about hating father and mother and brothers and sisters turns up in two different versions here (55, 42:25–28; 101, 49:32–50.1). Like the Synoptic Jesus, too, this Jesus will have nothing to do with settling a quarrel between brothers over their father's estate (72, 46:1–5); his own true siblings and mother are "those who do the will of the Father" (99, 49:21–26). But he goes further: "Whoever is acquainted with the father and the mother will be called the offspring of a prostitute" (105, 50:16–17). This saying perhaps reports the outside world's jibes against disciples who claim to have an invisible Father and Mother. That heavenly family is not congenial with ties of clan. "Jesus said, 'There are many standing at the door, but it is the solitaries who will enter the bridal chamber' " (75, 46:11–12). The briefest of his maxims to the disciples is, "Be passersby" (42, 40:19). To be saved, one must be disconnected.

For Thomas, the body is the switching point where one meets the world and where one must break the connection. Insofar as the sexual images in this Gospel appear to be negative, what appears to be wrong is not, as usually in ancient moralists, that sexuality entails pleasure or passion and hence impairs rational control, but rather that it connects us. It creates dependency. "Wretched is the body that depends upon a body. And wretched is the soul that depends upon these two" (87, 48:4–6; compare 112, 51:10–11). Yet another variant of the saying with which we began is: "Whoever has become acquainted with the world" has found *the body [to sōma]*, and the world is not worthy of the one who has found the body" (80, 47:12–14, emphasis added). Hence, "Blessed are those who are solitary and superior, for you will find the kingdom" (49, 41:27–29). The good life envisioned here is not a very social one. The saying of Jesus that in the Synoptics refers literally to the destruction of the Temple in Jerusalem and in the Fourth

Gospel to Jesus' death and resurrection, here may very well refer to the dissolution of the world itself, beginning with the structures of society: "Jesus said, 'I shall throw down [this] building, and no one will be able to build it" (71, 45:34).

The kind of ethos suggested by the sayings of Thomas's Jesus receives a more plastic fictional embodiment in a somewhat later text in the same tradition, the *Acts of Thomas*. This narrative, composed around the beginning of the third century in Syria, has come down to us in both a Greek and a Syriac version.[6] In the style of the popular Greco-Roman novel or romance, it recounts a series of marvelous escapades of Judas Thomas, here explicitly identified as Jesus' twin brother ("Thomas" reflects the Aramaic or Syriac word for "twin"; in Greek Judas is also known as Didymos, which means the same thing). In these tales the ascetic, migratory, solitary life that seems in the Thomas tradition to be the road to salvation is displayed by the apostle's adventures after he has been sold by Jesus to a traveling merchant, to serve him as a master builder. While the setting and imagery of the stories is often exotic, the moral implications of the apostle's preaching and actions are often quite earthy. The most striking appeal, repeatedly dramatized in the stories, is for celibacy, but there are also more mundane elements in the apostle's message, including care for slaves and for the poor. The story of Thomas at the court of King Gundaphorus (chaps. 17–29), for example, tells how the apostle takes large sums of money from the king in order to build for him a magnificent palace—only to spend it all on "the poor and afflicted." Apprised of the apparent fraud, the king decrees that Thomas shall be flayed alive and then burned. He is saved when Gundaphorus's brother, who has just died, returns to life to report that he has seen a wonderful palace belonging to the king—in heaven!

Although the emphasis on care for the poor was deeply rooted in the Jewish ethos and, from it and its biblical expression, in early Christianity, the Gundaphorus episode in the *Acts of Thomas* by its melodramatic effects suggests something more: a radical reversal of values. Comparing the apocryphal Acts with popular romances which they in part resemble, Judith Perkins notes that, while the latter with their happy endings reaffirm broadly accepted social values ("true love and lawful marriage"—Chariton), "The *Acts* are rigorously anti-social, unremittingly opting for the dissolution of social categories and relationships. The goal, death, that they present as a transcendence of human society is, in effect, a repudiation of their contemporary society."[7]

Escape by the Knowing Ones

The surviving documents of the Thomas tradition—if indeed they represent a single, coherent body of tradition—fail to explain to us just why the Christians who produced them thought of "the world," meaning principally the web of human society and culture, in such profoundly negative ways. Growing up among the Christians at about the same time, however, were other groups of a more philosophical bent who began to articulate a somewhat similar conception of the world in the form of elaborate myths and speculative interpretation of the early chapters of Genesis. One such group referred to themselves as "Gnostics," the peculiar Greek word *gnōstikoi*, which seems to have been used previously only by Plato and by people who stood in his tradition, but never as a self-designation. It meant something like "tending toward knowledge [or acquaintance]," "cognitive," "promoting knowledge," or "able to know."[8] One of the things the Gnostics claimed to know was the way in which the material and the human worlds had come into being and why they were so unsatisfactory.

Once upon a time, the Gnostics taught, there was only the First Principle, the Parent of the Entirety, pure spirit. But that solitary principle began to project itself outward and downward, as it were, expanding into the multiplicity of a spiritual universe, the Entirety. Then came a fateful error: one of the emanations thus produced, typically a female principle named "Wisdom," asserted her independence, broke through the boundary containing the Entirety, and sought to create on her own. As a result of Wisdom's rash act, some of the power of the spiritual realm was stolen by a nonspiritual being, sometimes called "Ialdabaoth" (a corruption of Yahweh Sabaoth, the "Lord of Hosts" of the Hebrew Bible), who created the physical universe. The spiritual forces contrived then to deceive Ialdabaoth, with the result that human beings were created, some of them possessing the power that had been stolen from above. Eventually the powers of the Entirety would send a heavenly savior, variously named, who would announce a message of salvation that only the specially endowed humans could receive. They were the Gnostics, who would then return with the savior to the heavenly world, leaving the material world bereft of power and reason so that it would collapse into nonbeing, while all rational power would be restored to the unity and "repose" with which everything began.[9]

One of the most learned and imaginative of the Christian thinkers of the second century was a man named Valentinus. Born in Egypt, he had received a philosophical education in Alexandria, where he also apparently became acquainted with the kind of biblical interpretation found in the Jewish intellectual Philo, which was later to be important in the work of other great Alexandrian Christian teachers, Origen and Clement. Sometime before the middle of the second century, Valentinus moved to Rome, where he established a school, alongside other Christian teachers like Justin Martyr and Marcion. Valentinus had taken up the classic myth of the Gnostic group and joined it with the notion of salvation by self-knowledge that was central to the Thomas tradition. Like the Jesus of the *Gospel of Thomas*, Valentinus taught that fully to know one's inner self—that is, the inner self of a person *capable* of such knowledge, for not all had such a soul—was to know the ineffable God. Through his subtle and poetic writings and through his disciples, whom he encouraged to start schools of their own, Valentinus's vision of the world and of Christian salvation spread widely and rapidly, undergoing endless variations as each of his followers introduced new speculations.[10]

It is evident from the myths and commentaries written by the Gnostics and the Valentinians that the goal of a life lived in accord with the truth they proclaimed would not be the salvation of the world but escape from it. Yet it is impossible to say in any detail what kind of everyday behavior this vision of the world produced among them. The only ancient descriptions of Gnostic or Valentinian morals that we have are written by their attackers, the defenders of the catholic party that was slowly gaining dominance in most parts of the Roman Empire. Given the conventions of ancient invective, it is not surprising that these accounts portray the "heretics" as not only mistaken but immoral, unscrupulous, and licentious. Sometimes, however, even the catholic polemicists depict some Valentinians as ascetics rather than libertines. The problem of detecting specific features of their ethos is compounded by our ignorance of the social forms these movements took. Irenaeus called the Gnostics who preceded Valentinus a *hairesis,* which is sometimes taken to mean "sect" in more or less our modern sociological sense. (Describing different parties in first-century Judaism, Josephus speaks of the *haireseis* of the Pharisees, the Saduccees, and the Essenes.) However, *hairesis* frequently referred to a philosophical "school," and we know that the Valentinian version of Christianity was most commonly propagated by schools, each consisting of a teacher to whom individual students attached themselves, like most of the philosophical schools in the Roman period. (Josephus in fact wanted his readers to think of the "sects" he described as philosophical schools.)

On the other hand, some Valentinian documents, such as the *Gospel of Philip*, suggest the institution of several additional sacraments beyond the Baptism and Eucharist of other Christians. The practice of such specific rituals would indeed point to the formation of distinctive groups separated from the other churches. However, scholars are divided over the question whether the texts in question depict actual practice or ideal events that were to occur in the spiritual world above, or even esoteric interpretations of common Christian practice. By the late fourth century, we know of at least one instance of a separate Valentinian building (burned by some orthodox monks, whereupon the Valentinians complained to the emperor).[11] Most likely, the social formation of the Gnostics and of the Valentinians varied from place to place and from time to time, and it is probably beyond our ability to determine, in the absence of new and unanticipated information, the shape of their moral practice. In a world perceived as the result of a mistake and a fraud, one could presumably reason to an ethic either of ascetic detachment from all its lures, much as the Thomas Christians did, or of nonchalant enjoyment of pleasures whose ultimate unreality rendered them indifferent.

Solidarity against the World

The difficulty of our attempt to understand the moral significance of the ways Gnostic and Valentinian myths depicted the world's origin and nature lies in the fact that we have no external or even direct internal descriptions of the ways those groups in fact lived. We are dependent entirely on our deductions from the often cryptic imagery in their writings. The same is true of an earlier body of literature in which "this world" plays a strong and ambivalent role, namely, the Johannine writings of the New Testament. We are on somewhat firmer ground with the Johannine texts, however, because they enable us to get some glimpses of the historical experience of some quite self-conscious communities. Research on the Fourth Gospel in the past two decades has enabled us to see in some detail how these groups had come to retell the story of Jesus in such a way that it incorporated their own history of confrontation with other Jews, leading to hostility and alienation and finally expulsion from the organized Jewish communities. What is remarkable is that the Johannine writings portray this history as the account of a crisis between God's Logos and Son and the world, the *kosmos*, which was made through him and was the object of God's love.[12]

The ambivalence expressed in the prologue of John's Gospel recurs throughout the work. The Savior is one who comes into the world and then returns whence he came. Those whom he chooses, he chooses "out of the world," and thenceforward they are "not of the world" (15:19). Consequently, the world hates them, as it hated Jesus (15:18). Here we see most transparently both the story of Jesus and the community's experience of hostility from neighbor and synagogue transmuted into judgments about the cosmos. Not merely the leaders in Jerusalem, but *the world* rejected Jesus. Not merely the local synagogue authorities, but *the world* hates his disciples.

Though the world grows darker and more sinister as the story progresses, the positive side of the Johannine ambivalence is not entirely submerged. The world is not evil *ab ovo*. It was created through the Logos who has now "become flesh." He is the world's light and its savior (4:42; 12:47); he gives it life (6:33), for God loves it (3:16). Yet what hope this Gospel holds out for the world is paradoxical at best. The climax of the book is the account of Jesus' arrest, trial, and crucifixion, which introduces into the traditional narrative an unparalleled dimension of irony. The moment of Jesus' helplessness before the posse that has come to arrest him is transmuted into an epiphany, as his captors fall to the ground at his simple pronouncement, "I am" (John 18:6). On trial on obscure charges, it is rather he, the reader knows, who judges the world. He faces the prefect who embodies Rome's imperium, but the reader has heard that "now the ruler of this world is cast out" (18:28–19:16; 12:31). Evidently defeated by the world's forces, he has nevertheless assured his disciples and the readers that "I have conquered the world" (16:33). Those who have insisted "we have no king but Caesar" cannot persuade Caesar's representative to erase the declaration "This is the king of the Jews" (19:15,19–22). Thus the incarnate Logos asserts his proprietary rights over the world. And the Spirit he sends will be not only the further teacher of the disciples, but an "attorney" who "will indict the world" (16:8).

For our present purposes, two things about John's ambivalent obsession with "the cosmos" are important to notice. First, the world of the Johannine Christians is in some highly conflicted way a thoroughly Jewish world. When the Logos comes into "his own" world, it is precisely within "his own" people, Israel, and it is in their rejection of him that "the world" rejects him. That rejection and that alienation from the world are something that the Johannine groups themselves have experienced quite tangibly by being removed from the organized Jewish associations, the synagogues, of their towns. Yet they remain convinced that their Christ is also the Prophet and King of the Jews, the Restorer awaited by the Samaritans, the fulfillment of all the hopes of all Israel. Their struggle to endure with confidence and hope in the face of a world grown hostile is centrally a struggle to repossess, by transforming them, the specifically Jewish scriptures and traditions that they still think their own.

The second thing that we must see in the Johannine ambivalence about the world is that their alienation from it is not a flight from the world by individuals. These Christians confront the world in the solidarity of a sect. The central moral imperative that this Gospel conveys to its implied audience is that one must choose between "the world" and the community of disciples. The choice is exhibited in certain characters of the story. On the one side are Nicodemus, who believes in Jesus, but secretly for fear of the Jews, remaining in the night, and the paralytic of chapter 5, who is healed but remains ignorant of Jesus' identity and weakly informs against him. On the other side is the man born blind, who boldly confutes the Pharisees, is expelled from the synagogue, and thus becomes a believer. The "work of God" is "to believe" (6:29), and the one commandment of Jesus is "to love one another" (13:34; 15:12). Both faith and love, in the Johannine vision of life, separate from the world and bind one to the other believers. It is an intensely corporate, sectarian vision.

To some extent we can see this ethos working its way out in the later life in this same circle of early Christianity, for we get glimpses of that life from the Johannine letters. It was an ethos that was becoming more introverted. The confrontation with the other Jews has disappeared from the view of the letters; "the world" that the writer of 1 John views with such suspicion is no longer a Jewish world. It now looks more amorphous, and more unrelievedly evil, though formally the more hopeful side of the Johannine ambivalence occasionally shines through. The writer can still say, for example, that Jesus is the expiation not only "for our sins, but also for the sins of the whole world" (1 John 2:2). But the confident "Be valiant, I have conquered the world" of John 16:33 takes a different turn. Now "conquering the world" becomes a task set before everyone "born of God," that is, every believer, and they conquer precisely by their faith (1 John 5:1–4). Here that seems to mean, by *right belief* (vv. 5–10), in contrast to those who "have gone out from us," against whom the writer polemicizes. The battle against the threatening world is now waged not so much in the public confrontations in synagogues and courts, as the Gospel portrays it, but in the little houses where the Christians meet, by the lines drawn between followers of one charismatic and those of another. Hospitality and the withholding of it become the major weapons (2 and 3 John). On the other hand, the emphasis upon loving one another as the primary imperative of life in the sect takes quite concrete form: sharing one's livelihood with the brother who is lacking (1 John 3:17).

This specific and concrete caring for one another within the brotherhood is the way the Johannine Christians see the love of God being realized among them—both God's love for them and their love for God. They do not imagine, however, that they can dare to manifest God's love for the world, which presumably they still affirm, by themselves engaging the world lovingly. On the contrary: "Do not love the world nor what is in the world," writes the Elder. "If one loves the world, the love of the Father is not in that person" (1 John 2:15). This passage also gives examples of what this author thinks "is in the world": "the desire of the flesh and the desire of the eyes and ostentation of life" (v. 16a). Ingenious lexicography to detect precisely which vices the author has in mind is largely wasted; the intention is a general, not specific,[13] indictment of the temptation to focus one's attention on the things that provide ephemeral pleasure and attract envious attention. Any high-minded Greco-Roman moralist might have said the same thing, and also agreed that "the world passes, and so do its desires" (v. 17a). What is novel about the Johannine vision is that what is set over against this superficial worldliness is not rational high-mindedness, but rather a passionate, sectarian, practical love that binds members of the group exclusively to one another and to the God they believe in.

A World Measured by the Cross

The groups founded by the apostle Paul and his associates appear to have had a broader and more complex experience of the urban society around them than did the Johannine groups. That broader experience may be one of the reasons why the picture of the world we see in the letters written by Paul and his disciples seems somewhat less unrelievedly hostile. Now it is true that Paul, too, could speak of "this world" or "this age" in quite negative language, especially when he refers darkly to "rulers of this age" (1 Cor. 2:6,8), "the god of this age" (2 Cor. 4:4), or "the elements of the cosmos" (Gal. 4:3), who stand in ignorance and hostility to God's purposes. Nevertheless, his letters usually convey an outlook less confined and threatened by "the world" than that of the Johannine writings. Geographically, the world of Paul's letters was a wide one, and socially the groups to which they were addressed included a fairly wide spectrum of men and women of varied status, means, origin, and ethnicity. Questions about practical participation in everyday affairs of the larger society intrude themselves into the issues Paul must write about, even though his primary attention, like the Johannine elder's, is always focused on the internal life of the Christian groups.

Paul talks about "the world" more than any other New Testament writer beside the writers of the Johannine circle. Especially from the Corinthian correspondence, where talk about the *kosmos* is concentrated, we can get a notion about what "the world" meant in the moral discourse of Paul and his followers. For example, the argument in 1 Corinthians starts out (1:18ff.) with a series of sharp contrasts between "the world" and "God." What is foolishness to the one is wisdom to the other, what is weakness to the one is strength to the other, and vice versa. Notice that synonyms of *kosmos* here include "this age" *(houtos ho aiōn,* 1:20), but also "human beings" (v. 25) and perhaps "angels" (4:9) as well. "The world" then does not refer here to the physical universe, but to society, the human world, or, as we might say, "culture." The antitheses that Paul sets out, especially in the rhetorical climax of 1:26–31, assert an opposition between cultural values and the values implicit in God's action. For God has "chosen" the "foolish of the world," the "weak of the world," the "commoners of the world," and the "despised [of the world]" to "shame" their opposites. These phrases are the equivalent, then, of "those things commonly regarded to be foolish, weak, ignoble, despised." The point Paul is making is analogous to the one frequently made by philosophical moralists: that the wise person ought to distinguish between truth and mere opinion, *doxa*. Notice, too, that all the categories have to do with social status; in Roman terms, it is the *humiliores*, the "no-accounts," that God has chosen.

Now the rhetorical point is obviously to shame the Corinthian Christians, though the shaming is merely a tactic incidental to Paul's real purpose, which is to persuade his audience to change their attitudes and behavior. Consequently he says, wrapping up this section of the letter, "It is not to shame you that I am writing this, but . . . to admonish you" (4:14). Clearly he recognizes that what he has said *would shame* the people he is addressing, and certainly that was his intention. The shame consists in equating their behavior with attitudes characteristic of "the world" (both Jewish and gentile: 1:22–24) that stands against God's purpose. Now what behavior exactly does Paul oppose?

The enigmatic verses 4:6–13 hold the answer. Paul writes to counter an incipient factiousness that derives from the kind of competitive jostling for status and esteem, the *philotimia*, that was so characteristic of ancient Greek and Roman society.[14] Paul's argument implies a double irony. At one level, he accuses humble people of acting high and mighty. The spiritual "wisdom" they claim to have received each from their preferred apostle, whether Apollos or Paul, leads them to think of themselves, as Paul's sarcasm describes them, as if they were the Stoic perfected wise man—the only king, who possesses all, who is already filled to satiety (4:8). They are behaving, then, with comic hubris, acting as if they were something when they are nothing, being "inflated" by their comparisons of themselves and their respective teachers (4:6–7). So they might well have been described by a Petronius or a Lucian, the satirists who love to lampoon the pretensions of the low-born arrivistes of Roman society. For Paul, however, there is a more serious second level of irony. These no-accounts really have been made someone special by God's choice of them, but they are in danger of throwing it all away by acting as if the gospel had merely given them a leg up in the old competition for honor and status, now exercised in the microcosm of the Christian household.[15] They have brought the values of "the world" into the Christian brotherhood—and how could they not have done so? For "the world" was part of themselves and the household was an integral part of the structure of that world.

The household, as we have seen, was also essential to the development of urban Christianity. The antihousehold attitude exhibited in the Thomas traditions has no place in the hortatory strategies of the Pauline leaders. Moreover, the notion of withdrawal from the world is something that Paul treats as an absurdity (1 Cor. 5:10). And Paul and subsequent Christian leaders of like persuasion care about the opinions that outsiders have of the Christian groups (for example, 1 Thess. 4:12; 1 Cor. 14:23–25). The attempt by Paul and his coworkers to "nihilate" in the minds and behavior of their converts the commonsense moral world of rigid hierarchies and fierce but closely ordered competition for "honor," while leaving those converts intimately engaged in the daily life of that same world, would require an extremely delicate balance. Perhaps it was doomed to fail. We have seen how the Johannine notion of being "in, but not of, the world" declined into a more and more defensive and suspicious posture against the world, paired with internal dissension and schism, relieved only by the continuing ideal of an active and material "love" for those who remained within the narrowing sect.

Among the later generations who evoked the name of Paul as model, there seems to have been a division. On the one hand were those who found in Paul's letters the grounds for an individualistic asceticism, at war with the world, not unlike that which we saw in the Thomas tradition. On the other, exemplified in the writings of those disciples very close to Paul, the authors of Colossians and Ephesians, and then in the more distant and formal imitator in the so-called Pastoral Epistles, we see an attempt to maintain the ambiguity of Paul's worldly/unworldly position, but tipping more and more in the direction of adopting the commonsense universe of popular morality.

The strategies the leaders used in trying to effect a novel set of moral dispositions must occupy us in later chapters. Before leaving Paul's special rhetoric about the world, however, there are some further innovations to be noticed, which will point us toward some of those later questions. The most important observation is that at the center of Paul's hortatory rhetoric is an expandable set of analogies, some explicit, more often implicit in metaphorical speech, between the story of Jesus' crucifixion and resurrection and the desired dispositions and behavior of believers. This transformation of what was for Paul the basic message of Christian faith into a malleable, polysemic trope was perhaps the profoundest and most enduring contribution that Paul made to Christian speech and thought.

The implications of this trope for life in "the world" are summed up most tersely in the peroration of Paul's sharp rebuke of the Galatian Christians: "Far be it from me to boast except in the cross of our Lord Jesus Christ, through whom the world was crucified to me and I to the world" (Gal. 6:14). We can see at once how the ascetic could find here warrant for treating the world (and one's own body) as a corpse. But for Paul to speak of the crucifixion is always to imply the resurrection. Therefore, a Kierkegaardian "repetition," in which faith simultaneously gives up and gets back—transformed—the desired object, catches better the double movement of Paul's concern. Still, Paul is far from advocating a Kierkegaardian subjectivism and individualism. On the contrary, the point of the letter is the integrity of a community; his theological concern is simultaneously a social concern, as his next sentence makes clear: "For neither circumcision nor a whole foreskin is anything; what counts is a new creation" (v. 15). The trope, crucifixion of and to the world, declares that the social and religious division that for the Jew was utterly fundamental, between those who were circumcised and those who were not, can divide no longer among those who belong to the community that has been initiated into Christ's death and resurrection.

In the Corinthian letters, too, Paul uses the trope of crucifixion to relativize social divisions within the Christian groups. Such divisions belong to a world for which the proclamation of "Christ crucified" is foolishness and a stumbling block. Yet in that same letter, when Paul answers explicit questions about sexual asceticism, he relativizes Christian asceticism just as much as the world's values. Just because "the structure of the world is passing away," the Christian, married or unmarried, virgin or sexually active, is to participate in that world, yet without being defined by it. Paul thus advises "that those who have wives be as if they had none, and those who weep as if they did not weep, and those who rejoice as if they did not rejoice, and those who trade in the market as if they owned nothing, and those who make use of the world as if they did not exploit it" (1 Cor. 7:29–31). As we saw in chapter 3, elsewhere Paul, and other Christian writers after him, could compare this amphibious engagement of the Christians in the cultural world around them with the experience of resident aliens in a city. They are surely engaged on a daily basis with the city where they reside, but as if their *politeuma*, the quasiconstitutional organization of immigrants, were somewhere in the sky (Phil. 3:20).

CHAPTER 5

The Language of Obligation

❖ ❖ ❖ ❖ ❖ ❖ ❖ ❖ ❖ ❖

It is time now to examine some of the specific ways in which early Christians gave moral directives to one another. In this chapter we will sample some of the typical patterns of language by which they expressed moral obligations. The study of early Christian ethics would benefit from a complete catalogue of such action guides, but that task would exceed the bounds of this book, not to mention the reader's patience. The samples we shall consider begin with some of the simplest forms and move toward more complex compositions. That progression will also take us from forms of language that the early Christians shared with the larger culture of Greco-Roman society to modifications of those forms and novel patterns peculiar to Jews and Christians or to Christians alone.

Virtues and Vices

Early in the second century the Roman governor of Bithynia and Pontus interrogated some people who had once been Christians. From them he learned that Christian practices included predawn meetings at which the initiates took an oath to abstain from a series of vices: theft, robbery, adultery, breach of trust, and embezzlement. Pliny's report is anticlimactic. The line of questioning implies suspicion of some conspiratorial club or some insidious superstition dangerous to public morals.[1] In fact, Pliny was not able to turn up anything much out of the ordinary. The Christian language of virtue and vice *is* ordinary, so much so that it is sometimes hard to see what all the fuss was about on the part of its attackers or its defenders. Apparently, context was everything.

Listing the Good and the Bad

Now we can hardly suppose that the Christians of Bithynia thought abstention from theft, robbery, adultery, breach of trust, and embezzlement was
the essence of Christian morality, or that a solemn oath to avoid these things
was an adequate introduction to the Christian life. Nevertheless, such lists
and their counterparts, lists of virtues, abound in early Christian literature.
It is hard to assess the weight of such catalogues of things naughty and nice,
because they appear in such variety of form, content, and context, and
because they are ubiquitous in the discourse of popular morality and even of
philosophical morality of antiquity. Most of the research on such lists by
students of early Christianity has focused on questions of origin. Did the
Christians borrow their lists of virtues from the Stoics, or from the Cynics,
or from Jewish "wisdom," or from "apocalypticism"? The question is probably unanswerable as posed, and perhaps not really so interesting. We would
be further along toward understanding the early Christian senses of vice and
virtue if we knew exactly how they *used* lists like these.[2]

Pliny has given us one specific instance: a list of vices might be used in a
vow, probably taken at the point of entry into the Christian community.
Most commentators think that the occasion of the meeting described by
Pliny's defendants, with its hymns "to Christ as to a god" as well as the
aforementioned "oath," was baptism. A few decades later Justin says that
baptism included an "undertaking" to live a moral life, and he depicts
conversion to Christianity as an about-face from vice to virtue (*1 Apol.* 61.1–
3; 14–17). There are several passages in the New Testament letters, all filled
with allusions to baptism, that speak of "putting to death" or "taking off"
vices and "putting on" virtues (Col. 3:5–15; Eph. 4:20–32; 1 Pet. 2:1).
Here a common metaphor about vice and virtue has been made to interpret
the disrobing and reclothing in the ritual of baptism. Note that here, at least
in the letters from Paul's disciples, "taking off vices" corresponds with
"taking off the old human," who dies in baptism, while "putting on virtues"
corresponds with "putting on Christ," the "new human."[3]

Usually, however, when vices or virtues are listed, there is no explicit
reference in our texts to a christological connection. Rather, the abominations or the desired traits stand on their own, as self-evident marks of the
wrong or right way to live. The lists are variable almost without limit, both
in the particular traits named and in the number of them. Often the choice

seems to depend more on rhetorical effect than on logical progression. For example in the Greek of Rom. 1:29–31, a description of the universal wickedness of the humanity that has failed to acknowledge the Creator, we hear a series of elegant assonances: "peplērōmenous pasē adikia ponēria pleonexia kakia, mestous phthonou phonou eridos dolou kakoētheias, psithyristas katalalous theostygeis hybristas hyperēphanous alazonas, epheuretas kakōn goneusin apeitheis, asynetous asynthetous astorgous aneleēmonas."

There is nothing in the enumerated vices that marks this list as peculiarly Christian. The same is true of most of the others, though there are a few peculiarities. Here are the individual vices found in eighteen lists in various parts of the New Testament; note that the precise formulation varies between abstract nouns and adjectives or nouns defining types of wrongdoers:

abusive language *(aischrologia)*, adulteries *(moicheiai)*, anger *(thymoi)*, boastful *(alazonai)*, carousing *(kōmoi, potoi)*, cowardly *(deiloi)*, craftiness *(kakoētheia)*, dissensions *(dichostasiai)*, drunkenness *(methoi, oinophlygiai)*, enmities *(echthrai)*, envy *(phthonoi)*, evil *(ponēria)*, factions *(haireseis)*, faithless *(apistoi, asynthetoi)*, false witness *(pseudomartyriai)*, foolish *(asynetoi)*, fornication *(porneia, pornos)*, God haters *(theostygeis)*, gossips *(psithyristai)*, greed *(pleonexia, pleonektēs)*, guile *(dolos)*, haughty *(hyperēphanoi)*, heartless *(astorgoi)*, idolatry *(eidōlolatria, eidōlolatrēs)*, impurity *(akatharsia)*, insincerity *(hypokriseis)*, insolent *(hybristai)*, inventors of evil *(epheretai kakōn)*, jealousy *(zēlos)*, liars *(pseudeis)*, licentiousness *(aselgeia)*, male prostitutes *(malakoi)*, malice *(kakia)*, mischief maker *(allotriepiskopos)*, murder *(phonos, phoneus)*, polluted *(ebdelugmenoi)*, quarrels *(eritheiai)*, rebellious toward parents *(goneusin apeitheis)*, revels *(kōmoi)*, revilers *(loidoroi)*, robbers *(harpax)*, ruthless *(aneleēmonai)*, silly talk *(mōrologia)*, slander *(blasphēmiai, katalaliai)*, sodomites *(arsenokoitai)*, sorcery *(pharmakeia, pharmakoi)*, strife *(eris)*, thieves *(kleptai)*, vulgar talk *(eutrapelia)*, wickedness *(adikia)*.[4]

Words on the root *porn-* and perhaps in general references to sexual misdeeds are more common in the Christian lists than in the ordinary ones. The word "idolatry" appears where, in pagan lists, one would expect "desecration" or the like. Both peculiarities are shared by Christian lists with Jewish ones of the same period. Otherwise, Christian and Jewish lists are interchangeable with those of other moralists of the time.

On the whole, the earliest Christian lists are neither systematic nor comprehensive. Clearly their function is not to name *all* the wicked things one should eschew or *all* the good traits one ought to cultivate. Neither do they suggest a rationale of interconnectedness among the virtues or the vices—only later do Christian writers of more philsophical bent begin to use such ordering schemes as the Stoic notion of four cardinal virtues. The logic of the early lists is like their syntax, which grammarians call asyndetic— words set out side by side without connections.

Boundaries and Paths

While lists are often random, there is one obvious ordering principle: vice is the opposite of virtue. Hence double lists frequently are paired to represent a dichotomous view of life. The "works of the flesh," in the specifically Pauline use of the term, are set over against "the fruit of the spirit," in Gal. 5:19–23. The vices of the "old human" are replaced by the virtues of "the new human" who is being remodeled "after the image of the creator" (Col. 3:5– 15). Vices characterize the old life of those who have now been "washed, made holy, justified" (1 Cor. 6:11). "Those who do such things," according to a formula we meet several times in the letters, "will not inherit the kingdom of God" (1 Cor. 6:9–10; Gal. 5:21; Eph. 5:3–5).

It is a short step from marking life before conversion as vicious and that after conversion as virtuous to branding "outsiders" as wicked and initiates in the holy community as virtuous. In the eschatological visions of John of Patmos, "the one who conquers" and who therefore partakes in the divine inheritance is separated from those doers of assorted vices who have their final place in the "lake of fire," the "second death" (Rev. 21:8). The pure are given access to the heavenly city; "outside are the dogs and the poisoners and the sexual deviants [*pornoi:* male prostitutes?] and the murderers and the idolaters and everyone who loves and practices falsehood" (22:15).

Not only do the dichotomous lists signal the boundaries between the unconverted and the converted, they also reinforce them by warning the ostensibly converted. Transgressions by insiders are dangerous anomalies in a world divided simply between the wicked and the good: the offenders must be corrected, shunned, or expelled (1 Cor. 5; Matt. 18:15–18). A public expulsion by the community, such as both these passages envision, would be a sobering piece of didactic theater, simultaneously reminding members of the difference between "them" and "us" and, as we sometimes say, putting the fear of God into those lucky enough to be mere spectators to the proceedings.

Rigoristic communities like the early Christian groups or like the Qumran branch of the Essenes readily adapted to such communal settings the venerable metaphor of the fork in the road, which sounds on the face of it rather individualistic. The metaphor of "the two paths," one of vice, the other of virtue, one leading to life and flourishing, the other to death or misery, was common coin in antiquity. Often the two paths are described by simple lists, respectively, of vices and virtues, though there are many variations. The classic formulation was a fable attibuted to Prodicus, depicting Heracles encountering two women at a road fork. One is superficially beautiful and stunningly dressed and cosmeticked as a courtesan. Her name is Vice, and she beckons to a broad and easy way. The other is rather plain and leads the traveler to a steep and rocky path; she is Virtue.[5] Readers of Jewish scriptures would have found something similar in passages like Jeremiah 21:8, "Thus says the Lord: Behold, I set before you the way of life and the way of death," or Deuteronomy 30:19, "I have set before you life and death, blessing and curse; therefore choose life." We saw a variation of the fable in the depiction of the road of Life in the *Tablet of Cebes*, discussed in chapter 2. There we saw images that stressed the loneliness of the daily choice between vice and virtue in the wise person's struggle toward happiness, an individualism implicit in the Heracles fable. It was not by chance that among the philosophers it was especially the Cynics who made Heracles their hero.[6] In a community that defined itself to some extent over against the dominant culture and the dominant social structures, however, the individualism implicit in the figure would be transformed or, at the least, redirected. In a communal context, taking the correct fork of the road is identical with becoming a faithful member of the holy community.

The road fork was a pretty obvious figure, and not everyone who thought of it had necessarily read either Deuteronomy or Prodicus's parable about Heracles. But in the Jewish and Christian examples from the period on which we are focusing, biblical imagery and the commonplace lists of virtues and vices are equally prominent. Of Christian examples, the best known is the one found with slight variations in the *Didache*, the *Epistle of Barnabas*, and a third-century Latin text called *Doctrina XII Apostolorum*. The *Didache* begins, "There are two ways, one of life and one of death; and between the two ways there is a great difference." In *Barnabas* and the *Doctrina*, as in the *Rule* of the Essene community, they are called "the way of light and the way of darkness." The description of the way of death/darkness consists principally in lists of vices: "It is evil and full of curses—murders, adulteries, passions, sexual sins, thefts, idolatries, magical charms, sorceries, robberies, false witnesses, insincereties, duplicity of heart, deceit, haughtiness, malice, stubbornness, greed, shameful speech, jealousy, impudence, arrogance, boastfulness," and so on (*Didache* 5:1; compare *Barnabas* 20:1). The way of life/light, on the other hand, is developed with a greater variety of hortatory forms, mostly commandments and precepts: "First, you shall love the God who made you; second, your neighbor as yourself." "My child, flee from every evil person and from everyone like him." Many of these are formulated negatively, so that in effect they, too, are elaborations of a vice catalogue: "Do not be angry, for anger leads to murder, nor jealous nor quarrelsome nor irascible."[7]

Other ways of expanding lists of virtues and vices include small essays that define or describe individual traits, or citation of examples from the canons of literature or scripture or from history or fable. Before considering these more complex kinds of moralizing composition, however, we need to consider one or two other simple forms that Christian groups picked up from the rhetorical, literary, and religious cultures around them.

Gnomic Discourse

Only slightly more elaborate than the lists of vices and virtues are the collected maxims, moral aphorisms, clever similitudes, and rules of thumb that were also evidently a major part of early Christianity's moral discourse. The Greeks called such sayings *gnōmai*, the Latins *sententiae*. Collections of such wise moral sayings, sometimes culled from various poets and philosophers of the past, sometimes adapted for a particular school of thought, were much in vogue in the Hellenistic age. Many of the *gnōmai monostichoi*, the "one-liners," gathered from the comic poet Menander have survived. So have the *kyriai doxai*, "Principal Doctrines," of Epicurus, another unnamed collection of Epicurus's gnomes known from the library that preserves it as *Gnomologium vaticanum*, and many of the sayings of Pythagoras that, Iamblichus tells us, novices wishing to join the Pythagorean communities had to memorize.[8] Very similar forms existed in other languages in the ancient Near East; what we have come to call Jewish wisdom literature is replete with examples. The grandson of Jesus ben Sira will not have thought he was adopting an alien genre when he translated Jesus' wisdom into Greek. Sometime around the turn of the eras a Jewish author composed in Greek a *gnomologion* in the form of a didactic poem. Unlike Ben Sira, he put it out not in his own name but in that of the ancient Ionian poet Phocylides. Moreover, according to the leading student of this work, "more than half of the verses in Ps-Phoc. have parallels in Greek gnomic literature."[9]

No wonder that the Christians, too, found a place for gnomes in their moral guidance. A classic instance is the collection attributed to a certain Sextus, sometimes identified with the third-century pope Xystus, but wrongly, for the collection is now thought to have been made in the second century. Here, too, there is much that belongs to the common morality of the age, with some philosophical coloring: "Luxurious living results in ruin." "Let reason guide your actions." "It is terrible to be a slave to passion." "The soul has as many masters as it has passions." "Consider only the good as your own."[10] Many of the gnomes have to do with piety, but only occasionally does specifically Christian language echo in them, and even in those instances there is seldom anything surprising or offensive to pagan piety. For example, "God needs no one; the faithful man needs only God" (49). "You call God 'Father': remember this in your actions" (59,222). "God does not heed the prayer of a man who does not listen to the needy" (217). "Know that you are an adulterer even if you merely think of committing adultery" (233).

The last-quoted gnome from Sextus reminds us that at an earlier time maxims of this kind were being repeated and collected as sayings of Jesus. Some of the sayings shared by Matthew and Luke, which modern scholars attribute to a lost collection we call "Q," are of this kind, and so are many of those found in the *Gospel of Thomas* and the many other extracanonical quotations of words of Jesus that we find in ancient Christian literature. In his *First Apology* Justin collects examples of Christ's teachings in the form of a gnomologium (chaps. 15–17). His introduction to the section emphasizes their gnomic form: "His sayings were short and concise, for he was no sophist, but his word was the power of God" (14.5, trans. Hardy).[11]

Even as these collections of Jesus' wise sayings were being made, and before, similar and sometimes even the same sayings were being used by the early Christians without attributing them to Jesus. Many of them were doubtless part of the common stock of popular wisdom that had been cultivated by many circles in the Mediterranean cultures for centuries. Walter Wilson, in the first full scholarly exploration of early Christian uses of gnomes, has recently shown how widespread was the use of this and related forms. To illustrate the Christian adaptation of the gnome, Wilson analyzes Paul's construction of a "sapiential discourse on Christian ethics" at a key point in the Letter to the Romans (chap. 12). In this composition Paul incorporates several gnomes, including one that would later be attributed to Jesus. Wilson makes a number of interesting observations about the kind of moral reasoning that is implicitly evoked by the use of gnomes and kindred forms. On the one hand, "Maxims normally purport to embody the forever and universally valid findings of common human experience; they are ethical conclusions which, through their literary formulation, become available for future edification and manipulation. As a practical conclusion, a gnomic saying is 'self-confirming, commending itself to empirical validation or to disconfirmation' in various ethical situations. In this way it may operate as a principle of ethical decision-making, or as a means of categorizing human actions and their consequences. Generally, gnomic utterances endeavor to create models of thought and behavior that will guide and correct the lives of those who use and adhere to them." On the other hand, "Although gnomic anthologies are conservative, in so far as they transmit established ideas and preserve the ethical agendas of previous generations, they are at the same time self-generating and self-correcting, in that they continually promote critical reevaluation as well as personal additions and adaptations."[12]

One well-attested use of gnomologia was in schools. Children learned to read and write by copying out and memorizing *gnōmai* culled from the poets; along the way, it was hoped, they absorbed the prudential morality represented by the maxims. But collections of gnomes were also used for more advanced education—the Stoic philosopher Chrysippus, for example, is said to have made a collection to reinforce his own lectures and for use by his students. The sayings of Pythagoras and those of Epicurus, many in gnomic form, were used in the instruction of converts to their respective schools of philosophy. It is plausible, though for the earliest period we have no specific evidence, that the Christians used gnomes in the instruction of new believers, sometimes attributing them to Jesus or to some other figure, sometimes anonymously.[13]

There were a number of similar forms that the Christians seem to have used in the same ways as the gnomes; it is not always possible to make strict distinctions among them.[14] Among these forms, two, the *chreia* and the precept, deserve at least our brief attention, for they are thickly strewn through early Christian literature.

Chreiai

When a pointed and witty saying or symbolic action attributed to a wise person was given a brief narrative setting, ancient teachers of rhetoric called it a chreia, connecting it with the Greek word meaning "useful."[15] The chreia's uses were several. Biographers of noted persons used collections of chreiai to characterize their subjects; the well-known third-century work *Lives of Eminent Philosophers*, by Diogenes Laertius, provides abundant examples, especially in his account of Diogenes of Sinope. The memory of Diogenes' acid wit made him an apt subject of the anecdotal art, and scores of chreiai were attributed to him. "Once, observing the temple officials leading away someone who had stolen a bowl from the treasuries, he said, 'The big thieves are leading away the little thief.' "[16] Chreiai could also be gathered from various sources to use in both rhetorical and moral instruction; for such purposes one might prefer more edifying sentiments: "Diogenes the philosopher, on being asked by someone how he could become famous, responded: 'By worrying about fame as little as possible.' "[17]

Obviously, a great many of the sayings attributed to Jesus in both the canonical Gospels and other compositions, such as the *Gospel of Thomas*, are of the chreia type: "Being asked by the Pharisees when the kingdom of God was coming, he answered, 'The kingdom of God does not come in such a way that you can set a watch for it, nor will they say, "Look here!" or "There!" For, see, the kingdom of God is in your midst' " (Luke 17:20–21).

The writers of the Gospels have used such anecdotes biographically, that is, to evoke in the reader a sense of Jesus' character and identity, but both in the completed Gospels and in the older traditions and collections they incorporate, the chreiai attributed to Jesus also exemplify the moral attitudes a follower of Jesus ought to have. Naturally, the common pedagogical use of chreiai, in exercises for learning beginners' skills in rhetoric, will not have held much interest for the earliest Christian teachers. Even so, variations in the forms of certain chreiai handed down in the Jesus tradition resemble the results of some of the common exercises. For example, pupils were taught both to compress and to expand traditional chreiai.[18] Compare these two versions of Jesus' saying about paying taxes:

> They showed Jesus a gold coin and said to him, "Caesar's men demand taxes from us." He said to them, "Give Caesar what belongs to Caesar, give God what belongs to God, and give me what is mine." (*Gospel of Thomas*, 100)[19]

Then they sent to him some Pharisees and some Herodians to trap him in what he said. And they came and said to him, "Teacher, we know that you are sincere, and show deference to no one; for you do not regard people with partiality, but teach the way of God in accordance with truth. Is it lawful to pay taxes to the emperor, or not? Should we pay them, or should we not?" But knowing their hypocrisy, he said to them, "Why are you putting me to the test? Bring me a denarius and let me see it." And they brought one. Then he said to them, "Whose image is this, and whose title?" They answered, "The emperor's." Jesus said to them, "Give to the emperor the things that are the emperor's, and to God the things that are God's." And they were utterly amazed at him. (Mark 12:13–17, NRSV, translation slightly altered)[20]

Conventional ways of elaborating or modifying anecdotes gave to the Christian apostles, teachers, and prophets who handed on sayings attributed to Jesus simple ways of adapting them to a variety of occasions in the life of the early communities.

Precepts and Commands

Many of the action guides for the early Christian groups were cast in simple rule language: direct imperatives or the equivalent, such as chains of participles expressing actions to be taken or avoided or, imitating the apodictic style of Hebrew scriptures, the future indicative: "You shall (not) . . . ." For example, the *Didache* defines the Way of Life thus: "First, you shall love the God who made you; second, your neighbor as yourself—and anything you would not want to happen to you, do not do to another." A similar style dominates the succeeding chapters. The central section of the *Shepherd of Hermas*, a sprawling visionary and hortatory work written in Rome toward the end of the first century (or, according to some, a half-century later), consists in a series of "commandments" (*entolai*, conventionally known, from the Latin, as "mandates"). These, says Hermas, were delivered to him by "the Shepherd," who is "the Angel of Repentance." They are such rules as, "First of all, believe that God is one, who created and ordered all things . . . ; Have simplicity [*haplotēs*] and be innocent . . . ; Love truth, and let all truth go forth from your mouth . . . ; I command you . . . to keep purity, and let no thought arise in your heart about someone else's wife, or any sexual deviance, or any similar evil things"; and so on.[21] In each case, elaboration follows.

Similar language was used in the instruction of converts to the new movement from its earliest days. In our earliest document, Paul's first letter to the Thessalonian Christians, he reminds them that "we gave you certain precepts [parangeliai] through the Lord Jesus" (1 Thess. 4:2). He then quotes an example, beginning, "This is the will of God, your holiness, to avoid sexual deviance [porneia]; each of you to know how to acquire his own 'vessel' in holiness and honor, not in the passion of lust like the gentiles who do not know God . . ." (4:3–5). Paul explicitly identifies this as tradition (4:1), and he quotes the same precept in 1 Cor. 7:2–3—freely adapting it now to emphasize the equivalent obligations on wife *and* husband. In the same context he can speak of a precept directly from "the Lord" (Jesus) forbidding divorce (7:10, using the verb *parangellein*), but he also confidently gives a ruling *(gnōmē)* on a matter for which "I have no injunction [epitagē] of the Lord" (7:25). In the Johannine circle, the commandments of Jesus, which were the commandments of God, could be summed up in the "new commandment [entolē], that you love one another" (John 13:34; compare 14:15–21; 15:9–17; 1 John 4:11–21; 2 John 5). The heavenly and imperial Jesus seen by John of Patmos naturally gives directives to his churches in the province of Asia, backed by threats and promises, though these are woven into a literary complex that overshadows their preceptual nature.

"Precept" was a broad category, as the various nouns and verbs cited above suggest. Wilson defines precepts well as "practical rules that counsel proper behavior in typical ethical situations."[22] The Roman Stoic Seneca, advisor of Nero and contemporary to our earliest New Testament writers, devoted two of his "Moral Epistles" to the usefulness of precepts, which he identifies as the basic tool of that "department of philosophy which the Greeks call *paraenetic* and we Romans call the 'preceptorial.' "[23] Seneca is concerned to clarify the relationship between such practical rules of thumb and more theoretical ways of grounding moral behavior: with philosophy's "doctrines" *(dogmata, doctrinae)*, "tenets" *(scita)*, or "adopted principles" *(placita) (Ep. 95.10)*. This issue seldom arises explicitly in our early Christian texts. More often, the notion of personal command rather than theoretically derived precept, implicit in much of the language quoted above, is brought to the surface by the context or by explicit identification of the commanding voice as God's or Jesus'.

For example, the introduction and conclusion to the Way of Life in the *Didache* suggest that the commanding voice speaking in its rules is God's, and the fact that some of the commandments are taken straight from the Bible, including the Decalogue (*Did.* 2) reinforces that reading. Yet the form of address "My child" (at 3:1,3,4,6; 4:1) is in the style of the wise teacher addressing his pupil. Perhaps we are to hear Jesus as this sage; perhaps he is "the Lord" who teaches God's commandments throughout. The subtitle of the eleventh-century manuscript takes it this way: "The Lord's teaching, through the twelve apostles, to the gentiles." The latest of the editors who reworked the compilation in the second century understood the two commandments at the head of the Way of Life as Jesus' commandments (Matt. 22:37–39 and parallels) and interpreted them ("What these maxims teach is this") by composing and inserting here a harmony of sayings of the Lord from various sources, mostly Matthew and Luke (1:3b–6).[24] This tendency of the early Christian moralists to put injunctions with common and familiar forms into a theological or christological context is obviously an important factor in the development of their special language of moral discourse, and we will return to it in greater detail later.

Topics and Commonplaces

In the era when Christianity was beginning, philosophers and orators commonly addressed their audiences on a variety of familiar themes or topics (Greek *topoi*, Latin *loci*). For example, we find discourses "On friendship," "On civic concord," "On household management," "On Exile," "On sexual conduct," "On anger," "On brotherly love." The outline of the subtopics to be covered in a given topos had become conventional, too, and often a speaker would develop the outline by using common clichés, maxims, chreiai, definitions, and the like. Nevertheless, each speaker was free to adapt all this traditional material to suit a particular school of thought or individual point of view. We see this happening often in early Christian literature as well, for example, when Paul addresses the Thessalonian Christians "on brotherly love," but proceeds to talk about the family of converts rather than the natural family (1 Thess. 4:9–10). Again, Paul's letter to the Philippians exploits many of the conventions of the topos "On friendship," but subsumes friendship under the peculiar notion of "partnership for the gospel."[25]

Seneca cites the common topic "On household management" to give an example of "the paraenetic department of philosophy": "how a husband should conduct himself towards his wife, or how a father should bring up his children, or how a master should rule his slaves."[26] This is a topic familiar to readers of the New Testament:

> Wives, be subject to your husbands, as is fitting in the Lord. Husbands, love your wives and never treat them harshly.
>
> Children, obey your parents in everything, for this is your acceptable duty in the Lord. Fathers, do not provoke your children, or they may lose heart.
>
> Slaves, obey your earthly masters in everything, not only while being watched and in order to please them, but wholeheartedly, fearing the Lord. Whatever your task, put yourselves into it, as done for the Lord and not for your masters, since you know that from the Lord you will receive the inheritance as your reward; you serve the Lord Christ. For the wrongdoer will be paid back for whatever wrong has been done, and there is no partiality.
>
> Masters, treat your slaves justly and fairly, for you know that you also have a Master in heaven. (Col. 3:18–4:1, NRSV)[27]

This topos "On household management" *(peri oikonomias)* was frequently discussed by philosophers and rhetoricians from the time of Plato and Aristotle until centuries later than the New Testament.[28] Given the importance of the household as the shelter and basic unit for early Christian groups in the Greco-Roman cities, it is not surprising that this topos figures frequently in the hortatory literature of those groups, beginning with the second generation of the Pauline circle.[29] Early in the second century, in writings like the Pastoral Epistles and the Letter of Polycarp to Philippians, the topos is adapted to speak of the responsibilities and organizational structure of the communities themselves: "overseers" ("bishops"), "deacons," "elders," "youths," "young women," "widows," and so on take the place of the more familiar hierarchy of the home.

The household rules quoted above from Colossians illustrate well the tension between the preservation of traditional values and innovative adaptation for new situations. That tension was characteristic of the paraenetic style; when highly self-conscious groups like the Jews or Christians adapted the style for their own, the tension sometimes became acute. Note, for example, the modification of the typical Stoic concern for what is "fitting" by the phrase "in the Lord," the introduction of the Jewish principle of God's impartiality, the limiting implications of the reminder to the masters that they, too, have "a Master in heaven." Moreover, the Colossians code differs from most discussions of household duties in addressing the slaves, and indeed all the "subordinate" groups, directly. Some of the Christian adaptations of the pattern were more conventional, others more innovative; how much difference resulted in practice is a debated question.[30]

Larger Paraenetic Compositions

The elementary forms of popular moral discourse tended to cluster together, as we have seen, around some organizing patterns, such as the "two paths," or under the headings of some commonly discussed topic, such as "On household management." The Christian prophets and apostles, like their pagan and Jewish contemporaries, also developed larger speeches, sermons, letters, and tracts to guide the conduct of the growing communities. There will be space to mention only a few of these.

Epitomes

We saw earlier, following the analysis of Walter Wilson, how Paul had constructed a "gnomic anthology" to introduce the admonitory section of his letter to the Romans. In effect, this anthology (Rom. 12) provides a summary or *epitomē* of Paul's ethical teaching. The epitome is followed by a series of examples of that teaching, several of them generalized from Paul's recent experiences in Corinth. All this forms an integral part of the letter that introduces his "gospel" as a whole, in the style of a philosophical protreptic speech, to Christian groups he had not founded or seen.[31] Epitomes were widely used in antiquity to introduce students or lay people to all kinds of topics, including the philosophical or scientific or ethical teachings of a particular school or teacher or larger work.[32] In the Gospels of Matthew (chaps. 5–7) and Luke (6:20–49), sayings of Jesus have been woven together to provide epitomes of his teaching; perhaps groups of sayings in the collection "Q" were already arranged to serve a similar purpose.[33] It would be possible to construe an entire Gospel composed in gnomic style, for example the *Gospel of Thomas* or the more enigmatic collection called the *Gospel of Philip*, used by Valentinian Christians, as an epitome. These compositions seem less systematic than typical philosophical epitomes; the maxims, anecdotes, parables, and injunctions they contain are exemplary or symptomatic of the whole way of life being advocated, rather than analytic. They would require personal instruction and guidance to be effective.

Letters

In many ways the most important, as well as the most flexible and variously used, of the literary genres adopted by the early Christians was the letter. Several factors made the letter ideally suited for communication among the individuals and groups in the new movement: the rapid spread of small household groups along the trade routes to cities of the Mediterranean basin, the relative ease and speed of travel under the Roman principate, the missionary strategy that evolved under the leadership of numerous traveling apostles, the peculiar sense of identity as a single "people of God" by converts instructed in the scriptures and communal sensibilities of Israel. Yet there was another factor that for the future was perhaps even more decisive in securing for the letter a central position in Christian literature: the extraordinary versatility and rhetorical uniqueness of the letters of one of those early missionaries, the apostle Paul.[34]

It is not accidental that the very first of the surviving Pauline letters has figured so often already in our discussion. First Thessalonians is a typical paraenetic composition, freely using the conventions and topics of Greco-Roman moral advice and adapting them to the unique circumstances of a group of new converts.[35] Significant portions of all Paul's letters are given over to exhortation and moral advice. The Corinthian correspondence is particularly rich in both the quantity and variety of paraenetic language. There we can see how flexible were the strategies offered by ancient rhetoric, and how versatile was Paul's deployment of the resources he had received from Greco-Roman conventions, Jewish tradition, and the special new practices and forms of speech of the Christians.[36]

The disciple of Paul who wrote the Letter to Colossians also constructed a letter that is a mixture of paraenetic and deliberative rhetoric, following the example of Paul and at the same time, in style noticeably different from Paul's, beginning the process of idealization of Paul *as* example. In his own letters, Paul had of course already presented himself as an example, with words such as "Be imitators of me, as I am of Christ" (1 Cor. 11:1; compare 4:16 and 1 Thess. 1:6). Personal examples were a regular feature of paraenetic speech. The later Pastoral Epistles (1, 2 Timothy, Titus), written by an unknown author, probably early in the second century, elaborate the Pauline example into a fictional portrait and, as it were, a hortatory bequest to the next generation. The style is very similar to that of fictional letters from such past philosophical worthies as Socrates, Antisthenes, Diogenes, and

Crates, which were also being widely produced and circulated, especially by Cynics, in the era when Christianity began.[37]

Sometime early in the second century, at latest, Paul's letters began to be collected and circulated, being found useful for instruction of Christians beyond those particular communities and specific circumstances to which they had been addressed. The Pastoral Epistles show that letters could be composed for such general purposes from the outset; such letters could be attributed to other prominent figures as well. At least two of the letters of the canonical collection, James and 1 Peter, display their general purposes in their form, beginning with their addresses (Jude and 2 Peter can probably be put in the same category; Hebrews is a special case, to be discussed shortly). Both the Letter of James and the First Letter of Peter adopt the convention of addressing Israel's Diaspora, with which they identify the Christian churches. First Peter further specifies that the groups addressed are in the Roman provinces of western Asia Minor and that they are made up of gentile converts. James does not further identify the "twelve tribes in the Diaspora," but the letter is evidently intended for all Christians to whom it may come. First Peter resembles the letters of the Pauline school particularly in basing its admonitions on reminders of the conversion and baptism of the audience, in the interweaving of didactic sections (in the style rhetorical handbooks call "epideictic") with direct exhortations, and in the unity of the total composition. James organizes his material in short essays, loosely set together, using mostly a gnomic style. James and Peter have in common a better-than-average Greek style, in comparison with most early Christian literature, and the art of combining echoes or direct quotations from scripture and Jewish tradition with commonplaces and conventions of Hellenistic moral discourse.[38]

The Letter to Hebrews is an example of a more elaborate, even elegant composition. The author calls it a "hortatory speech" ("word of exhortation," *logos tēs paraklēseōs*, 13:22), and indeed it displays some of the finest rhetorical language to be found in Christian writings of the first two centuries. Like 1 Peter and James, it invites a Christian audience (they are certainly not "Hebrews" in an ethnic or linguistic sense) to hear great parts of the Jewish scripture as a message addressed now to themselves. Its point is not to introduce new rules of behavior. The precepts that are strung together at the end (13:1–17) are examples rather than a code; they are scarcely more than a list of topoi—"brotherly love" (*philadelphia*), "hospitality" (*philoxenia*), care for prisoners, marriage, money, obedience to leaders, avoidance of heresies—into which is inserted a brief reprise of the motif that has dominated most of the letter, Jesus' high priesthood and self-sacrifice. Rather, the whole composition is an elegant sort of pep talk, addressed to second-generation Christians who, the writer thinks, are at risk of losing their enthusiasm. To counter that tendency, the writer arranges his scripture-based lessons around two broad schemes of comparison, the one temporal and eschatological, the other spatial and ontological. That is, one takes up a theme common in many circles of early Christianity, declaring that the events Christians proclaim inaugurate the time of "the End" and are qualitatively superior to earlier events and prophecies in the sacred history, which merely pointed forward to them. The other takes up a schema developed by earlier Jewish authors, who used popular forms of middle Platonism to interpret scriptural passages. In this conception, things in heaven are the real, of which earthly countertypes are only "copies" or "shadows." The writer of Hebrews announces the eschatological theme in the speech's first sentence (wonderfully sonorous in the Greek): "God, having spoken of old in manifold and pluriform ways to our ancestors by the prophets, at these last of days has spoken to us by a Son, whom he established as heir of all things, through whom moreover he made the aeons" (1:1–2). The hortatory point of the comparisons is stated near the beginning in a complex and threatening rhetorical question: "For if the message spoken *through angels* was firmly set, and every transgression and disobedience received its just retribution, how will we escape, if we neglect a salvation so great, which at the start was spoken *through the Lord* and then confirmed to us by those who heard him, while God himself joined in witnessing to it by signs and wonders and all kinds of acts of power and [manifestations] of the Holy Spirit apportioned according to his will?" (2:2–4).[39]

One further example of the letter of advice or exhortation will suffice to show the broad range of circumstances in which it could be employed. From "the church of God that lives as a resident alien in Rome to the church of God that lives as a resident alien in Corinth," the letter is commonly called *First Clement* from its supposed author. We see at once from the address that the imagery of the Christians as "pseudo-aliens," as I have called them in chapter 2, remains an important element in their identity. Ironically, however, the central theme of the exhortation is the opposite of countercultural. If the specifically Christian and Jewish illustrations were taken away, the letter would be quite like one of the speeches "on civic concord" that were addressed by moralizing philosophers and orators to assemblies of Greek cities. One of the most famous is the second speech by Dio of Prusa to the city of Tarsus, delivered not many years later than Clement's writing.[40] The great danger is *stasis*, civil disturbance or rebellion. In the Corinthian house churches, stasis has appeared, at least in the eyes of the Roman Christians, by removal from office of some of the elder-bishops, apparently by a younger faction. By heaping up examples chosen mostly from scripture, Clement warns of the dangers to a community of jealousy, envy, and strife and demonstrates the value of faith, hospitality, humility, and obedience. The dissidents are urged to heed these examples, to humble themselves, "each in one's own rank [*tagma*]" (41:1), that "peace and concord" may be restored to the commonwealth of the church.[41]

Testaments

It was a widespread notion in antiquity, not completely lost even today, that the words conveyed by an important person at the point of death to his or, more rarely, her progeny or friends carried special significance. Accordingly, the literary genre of the testament became a common vehicle for handing on the purported wisdom of past generations; for example, prophecies of the future or advice and warnings about appropriate behavior. In the Hebrew Bible, the last words of Jacob (Gen. 49) and of Moses (Deut., especially 31–33) are vivid examples. The eschatological discourses of Jesus in the Synoptic Gospels (Mark 13 and parallels) belong to the general pattern, as does the quite different collection of homilies and prayer that make up chapters 14–17 of the Fourth Gospel. The Second Epistle of Timothy presents itself as a testament of Paul (note especially 1:6–14), as does the speech in Acts 20:18–35,[42] while 2 Peter is composed as the admonitory and prophetic will of that apostle. The most elaborate example of moral testament that we have, however, is a collection that came into Christian use in the late second century and remained popular until the medieval period, the *Testaments of the Twelve Patriarchs*. What is interesting for our present purposes is the way in which each of the sons of Jacob, on his deathbed, delivers a speech that centers on a topos defined by one or two virtues or vices: "Reuben concerning thoughts," "Simeon concerning envy," "Levi concerning priesthood and arrogance," "Judah concerning courage and love of money and impurity," "Issachar concerning simplicity," "Zebulun concerning compassion and mercy," "Dan concerning anger and lying," "Naphtali concerning natural goodness," "Gad concerning hatred," "Asher concerning the two faces of vice and virture," "Joseph concerning chastity," "Benjamin concerning a pure mind."[43] Thus once again we see the blending of biblical examples, Jewish and Christian theology, and the moral commonplaces of Greco-Roman philosophy and rhetoric.

Differences

Perhaps the chief point that emerges from our survey of some of the commonest forms of early Christian moral speech is how ordinary this morality seems to have been, in both form and content. Yet the Christians clearly throught that there was something quite distinctive about their way of life, and outsiders seem to have thought so too, else Christians would not have been treated with such suspicion when people began to learn about them. As I suggested at the beginning of this chapter, what made the difference must have been principally the context. A major dimension of the special Christian context was the set of social practices within which the action guides were embedded; in the next chapter, we shall look more systematically at those. But we have noticed at several points that the ideational and rhetorical contexts of the forms of language we have been investigating also had certain peculiarities. The most important of those peculiarities can be classified under three headings that deserve brief mention now, though they will each be the subject of more detailed discussion in later chapters. The three are references to God, references to Christ, and reference to Scripture.

God's Will

"To do the will of God" is a phrase found often in the Bible, and the early Christians often use it to summarize the goal of life.[44] Indeed, in the Gospel of John, it is the summary of the life of Jesus, who says "I came down from heaven not to do my own will, but the will of the one who sent me" (6:38; compare 5:30). The disciples are taught to pray, "Thy will be done," and in Matthew, Jesus echoes that prayer in Gethsemane (Matt. 6:10; 26:42). Where a pagan moralist might set life according to reason or according to nature over against life following pleasure or desire (*epithymia*), the antithesis to epithymia in 1 Peter 4:2 and in 1 John 2:17 is "the will of God."

But how does one know what "the will of God" is? To paraphrase Freud, What does God want? Answering that requires discernment, and Christian discernment may require, in the famous words of Paul's letter to the Romans, a certain "metamorphosis," a "renovation" of the way one thinks (Rom. 12:2). Paul could also write to the Thessalonian belivers that they were "God-taught" to love one another (1 Thess. 4:9). Practically, how had God taught them? We are left to infer or to guess, but we get a few clues from this context and others. Here and there we find sentences in the form of definitions: "This is the will of God," says the introduction to certain rules about sex and marriage in 1 Thess. 4:3: "your holiness." And this statement stands within a reminder of "certain precepts" that Paul says he gave earlier to the new converts. In 1 Peter 2:15 a similar sentence defines God's will as "by doing good to silence the ignorance of foolish people," again within a citation of traditional directives about behavior. "God's will" seems to have been spelled out for the new members of the Christian groups by all the means of moral instruction that were at the disposal of their leaders.

The same context in 1 Thessalonians 4 shows us another of the most common ways in which talk about God is introduced into the moral discourse of the first Christians: "Because the Lord is an avenger in all these things" (v. 6, NRSV). The notion of God as the ultimate judge of the whole world, who would finally right wrongs by rewarding the good and punishing the wicked, was a belief that the early Christians shared with many other circles of contemporary Judaism. The idea of divine punishment of evil was not unknown in paganism, of course. It was a point of dispute between Platonists and Stoics, according to Plutarch, who accuses Chrysippus of inconsistency for attacking the idea in Plato's *Republic* while stating it himself elsewhere (*Stoic. rep.* 16, 1040C; 35, 1050E). The point at issue, however, was nothing like the conception of an eschatological *world*-judgment that the Christians held. Tertullian reports that Christians were "laughed at for proclaiming that God will be judge" (*Apol.* 47.12, trans. T. R. Glover, Loeb Classical Library).

In Tertullian's time, there were Christians, too, who would laugh at the kind of world-judgment that Tertullian believed in. There were varieties of eschatological belief among the Christians, and the restoration of a just world ruled by its Creator was the very opposite of what some hoped for, especially those various groups that modern scholars have lumped together under the name "Gnostics." The specifically apocalyptic conception of a world made right again by the Creator was nevertheless the view that was or became dominant, and it defined the final chapter of the great Christian moral drama that eventually was to shape so profoundly the sensibilities of Western culture. That is a topic to which we shall return in chapter 10.

The Christian writers frequently transpose to the scene of God's judgment the sanctions of honor and shame that were so all-pervasive in antiquity. People in ancient Mediterranean societies seem to have relished public praise much more openly than we are taught to think nice, and there is no reason to believe that the Christians were exceptions. However, they were instructed that the honor that really counts is the praise and "glory" that the faithful servant will receive from God at the end of days. Moreover, they might have to trade dishonor in the world, in this present evil age, for that glory to come.[45] It is in this context that "humility" becomes a virtue, a notion that was quite strange to most Greeks and Romans.[46]

A Cruciform Style

The Christian notion of proper humility was bound to look peculiar, because it was defined from the earliest days of the Christian movement by a startling event that the Christian moralists transformed quickly into a trope with multiple applications: the crucifixion of Jesus. Martin Hengel, among others, has reminded us how absolutely odd it was that the early Christians were prepared not only to talk about, but even to sing hymns about a death by the mode of execution that was calculated to be the most shaming available.[47] In order for there to be a Christian movement, they had to make sense of a central figure who, as the Letter to Hebrews puts it, "endured the cross, despising the *shame*" (12:2). For those who believed that God had trumped this ultimate official shaming of his Messiah and Son by raising him from the dead and enthroning him in the sky, common notions of shame and honor would have to be rethought.

We do not know whether it was Paul who first made the report of Jesus' crucifixion and subsequent resurrection into the center of missionary preaching. Probably not, for Paul identifies this "gospel" as something he received and passed on as tradition (1 Cor. 15:1–8). However, it was Paul more clearly than any other who transformed this report into a metaphorical complex capable of shaping moral discourse. The example that will be most familiar is in his letter to the Christians at Philippi. There, to reinforce his appeal for unity, other-regarding love, and humility in the place of "empty glory," Paul calls on the readers to fix their minds on the paradigm of Christ, who, though he was "in the form of God," "emptied himself, taking the form of a slave."[48] It was in the poetry of the early churches, like this "Christ-hymn" quoted by Paul, that the antitheses of Christ's humiliation and exaltation were most dramatically displayed. It was in the prose of letters, by Paul and his imitators, that the polarities of Christ's career were made into a model for the Christian life.

Not only in letters, of course. The Gospel of John begins with another of those antithetical poems, and it sets the cosmic stage that surrounds the whole narrative of Jesus' career, a stage that becomes visible to the Gospel's audience through the medium of Jesus' own speeches. Those speeches, and the reaction by disbelievers and even many believers among the characters of the story, illustrate an important point about what the Christians deemed "humility." To outsiders, it often looked like the opposite. Jesus is therefore accused of the worst of hubris, of blasphemy—of making himself equal to God, indeed, of making himself a god. For the implied audience of the book, those in the know, such charges reveal the deep irony that permeates the story, since Jesus has in fact come from heaven in humble obedience to the Father who sent him. To Pliny, too, the Christians who appeared before him were anything but humble when they refused to recant their faith, and he wrote to Trajan that he was sure they ought to be punished for their "inflexible obstinacy" if nothing else. They were not "humbling themselves." On the contrary, they seemed to this governor—himself newly risen into the senatorial class by inheritance, adoption, and hard work—to be acting with a boldness wholly inappropriate to people of their truly humble status and situation.

The specifically Christian beliefs about Jesus' actions and God's actions through him affected the shape of their moral discourse in a number of other ways. For example, Nils Dahl has described several patterns of "early Christian preaching" that can equally well be called patterns of moral instruction. Among them are "the soteriological contrast pattern," examples of which we looked at when we considered the early Christian notions of conversion in chapter 2. For instance: "And this is what some of you used to be [fornicators, idolaters, adulterers, male prostitutes, sodomites, thieves, greedy, drunkards, revilers, robbers]. But you were washed, you were sanctified, you were justified in the name of the Lord Jesus Christ and in the Spirit of our God" (1 Cor. 6:10–22, NRSV). Another of the patterns is the "teleological," stating the consequences of Christ's actions for believers. For example, "He died for all, that those who live should no longer live for themselves, but for the other who died and was raised for them" (2 Cor. 5:15). Again, "You know the grace of our Lord Jesus Christ, that, though he was rich, for your sakes he impoverished himself, so that through his poverty you would become rich" (2 Cor. 8:9). In each case, the consequence for Christian behavior is drawn by the apostle; in the latter case, the Corinthian Christians ought to share *their* wealth with poor Christians in Jerusalem. That imitative or analogic way of moral thinking could be stated succinctly in a third of the patterns Dahl identified, "the conformity pattern": "Put up with one another and forgive one another if anyone has some complaint; as the Lord forgave us, so you ought to do" (Col. 3:13). Or, "By this we know love, that he laid down his life for us; and we ought to lay down our lives for the brothers and sisters" (1 John 3:16). The same author uses this pattern to state what many have taken to be the leitmotif of early Christian morality: "Beloved, if God loved us in such a way, we too must love one another" (4:11, compare Eph. 5:2).[49]

The Christians who modeled their lives—and their deaths—on the example of Christ often engaged in what one might call militant suffering. Militant suffering, in defiance of the power of Rome, is dramatically and elaborately advocated by the visions of John's Apocalypse. In the letters of Ignatius of Antioch, militancy and humility receive a startlingly personal voice as the bishop plans and interprets his own path toward martyrdom. Shortly a whole new literature would be added to the Christian repertory, the acts of martyrs. These stories exhibit the triumphs of suffering stubbornness for the faith. It is hard to discover exactly what role in the moral formation of Christians in the second and third centuries this martyr literature played. We may guess, however, that its principal impact is to be found not in the handful who thrust themselves before the tribunals demanding to be added to the martyrs, but in the comprehensive imagery of cosmic warfare that these stories, like the apocalypses, taught to their audiences. The simplest virtues—sexual purity, a quiet life, regular attendance on the rituals of the group, obedience to leaders—become heroic in a world where the devil plots to destroy the faith and employs the very pillars of the dominant society in his ultimately futile attack upon the people of God.

Scripture Teaches

In the early Christian language of obligation, one further accent recurs frequently, though not uniformly. It is the voice of scripture, which we have heard many times in the examples quoted above. The first Christians were

Jews and, like all the other Jews we know anything about in that age and for a long time to come, they thought that what one could know and needed to know of God and his will was peculiarly mediated by the scriptures of Israel. Even as the majority of Christians came to be converted gentiles, they were instructed in those same scriptures. The church of Rome, by this time predominantly gentile, could write to the church of Corinth, mostly gentile from the beginning, "For you have understanding, you have a good understanding of the sacred Scriptures, beloved, and you have studied the oracles of God" (1 *Clement* 53:1, trans. Lake). It would be a worthwhile pursuit to catalogue all the ways in which scripture informs the moral discourse of the first Christians. This has not been done systematically, but it is too large a task to take up here. A few examples will illustrate the variety.

First, scripture offers rules. The Torah is full of rules, and there are imperative sentences in all parts of scripture that could be used as rules. Further, there are innumerable statements that could be used as warrants for rules, or as principles from which rules could be derived. These are the most obvious ways in which scripture could contribute to the formation of ethos. Even in the Pauline circles, who learned from Paul that the Law is not the means to God's righteousness in the age of the Messiah, the Decalogue could be used in paraenesis. "Honor your father and your mother," quotes Paul's pupil in the encyclical letter we call Ephesians. Among the sayings of Jesus we find, in Mark 10:2–9, scriptural verses cited as a principle from which to derive a new rule: "God made them male and female. For this reason a man shall leave his father and his mother and be joined to his wife, and the two shall become one." Note that even simple rules of scripture are not necessarily used simply. Rules can be used against other rules; they can serve as warrants or backing for other rules; they can be assimilated to rules from other cultural spheres. None of this is surprising; we see similar things happening in many circles of ancient Judaism.

Another simple and familiar way of using scripture to model morality was by means of personal examples. A classic instance is the lists of examples of jealousy and of hospitality in the letter written from the church at Rome to that in Corinth. Even better known are the *exempla* of faith in Hebrews 11. The *Testaments of the Twelve Patriarchs* make episodes from the lives of the Patriarchs, as told in the Bible and tradition, into paradigms of vice or virtue. Not merely individuals in the sacred histories, but also Israel as a whole could serve as an example, both good and bad, as we see quite vividly in the homily used by Paul in 1 Cor. 10:1–22.[50] Or paradigmatic events in the biblical narratives could be held up to exhibit virtue or vice, or to serve as cautionary tales. This, too, was hardly a new approach. The Deuteronomistic historians, within the Bible itself, had already made the rise and fall of Israel's and Judah's monarchies into a moralizing history, and in a different manner the Chronicler followed suit, as did Josephus later.[51] Eventually, as we shall see in more detail in chapter 11, Irenaeus and nameless other Christians of his time incorporated this exemplary history of Israel into the universal narrative under whose aspect the emerging Christian Bible would be read.

On a smaller scale we can see this manner of reading already at work in many places in the New Testament. We also see some of the techniques of actualizing exegesis that we often call by the term borrowed from the rabbis, midrash, as well as instances of freer kinds of reinterpretation including the allegory that pagan philosophers and Alexandrian Jews had already exploited. Sometimes such modes of interpretation could serve the purposes of the emerging, dominant moral narrative of the world and humanity. But these techniques could serve other kinds of narratives, with very different accents. Thus the way of reading the creation stories that Valentinus learned from the groups that Irenaeus calls "the Gnostic sect" stand on their heads the values that Irenaeus would find in the same stories. A Christian sense of a moral universe was not to be achieved without severe conflict.

This observation brings us back to the question of social context. The moral language of the first Christians was evidently a mixture of many accents and many traditions. It was a language that was multiform and malleable. It therefore becomes all the more necessary for us to pursue the question, within what kinds of social practice was Christian language of obligation at home? That is the topic of our next chapter.

CHAPTER 6

The Grammar of Christian Practice

❖   ❖   ❖   ❖   ❖   ❖   ❖   ❖   ❖   ❖

Alasdair MacIntyre, seeking to rehabilitate the concept of virtue as the center of ethical discussion, first had to define in a special sense the notion of *social practice*, "as providing the arena in which the virtues are exhibited and in terms of which they are to receive their primary, if incomplete, definition."[1] MacIntyre gives strong reasons for believing that virtues are embedded in social practices and that they point toward ways of achieving goods that are internal to those practices. That viewpoint coincides nicely with the perspective from which we began our observations of early Christian morality, and it is reinforced by the cases we have examined so far.

MacIntyre's careful definition of "practice" is more complicated than we need for present purposes, which are not concerned with general definitions but with a specific historical development. A commonsense definition will suffice to get us started, and the range of the relevant kinds of practice will become clearer as we go along. We want to know what kinds of social practice shaped and reinforced and gave meaning to the moral sensibilities of the early Christians. Here again we shall feel acutely the fragmentary quality of our evidence. We have only occasional glimpses of the sorts of practice that must have counted, and we do not know how widespread the ones we see may have been, nor can we very often trace exactly how they developed over time. Nevertheless, it is important that we describe as much as we can.

Ritual

Ritual is the appropriate form of practice with which to begin, for ritual, within a functioning religious community, is paradigmatic practice. Does it seem surprising to call ritual a social practice? In our spectator society, any regular and stylized actions in which *we* participate have become so banal that the word ritual would hardly be appropriate; what we call "ritual" is something someone else does at a distance—especially some exotic tribe far away—something we watch on television or study in cultural anthropology, but far removed from any community of which we are a part. Yet this condition is surely exceptional in the broad history of human society. Where ritual is still alive, it is quintessentially social. To be sure, it is a kind of second-order social practice. That is, it has its proper function in relation to other kinds of social practice, the ordinary practices of the community for which it is meaningful. Ritual is a condensed action that is intended to focus and concentrate meaning so that what is done in this nexus of sacred time and place ripples out onto all prior and subsequent doings, the doings that take place in the "profane" or outside world, resonating in those ordinary affairs with interpretive possibilities. When ritual is working, it helps us to make sense—a special kind of sense—of the other things we do.

Baptism and Behavior

In the earliest documents of the Christian movement, baptism is the ritual most often mentioned, and it is mentioned most often in paraenetic or hortatory contexts. That is, the writers remind their audience of baptism when they want to encourage certain kinds of behavior.[2] We do not know how much baptism really changed the behavior of people who were baptized. It is not possible for us to interview them before and after, and no Christian in the period we are considering has left us an autobiography. What we do have are idealized descriptions of the moral results of baptism, like those written by Aristides and Justin that were quoted in chapters 1 and 2, and the exhortations of leaders, which describe the results that *ought* to follow. Such evidence is obviously quite unsatisfactory if we are looking for an objective index of what really happened, but it does at least help us to understand the horizons of expectation that baptism established.

The first of the letters attributed to the apostle Peter in the New Testament is so filled with allusions to conversion and baptism that some scholars have thought it might originally have been part of a baptismal liturgy or a homily delivered to new converts.[3] It is better understood as a "baptismal anamnesis" or reminder of baptism, to use Nils Dahl's phrase, an exhortation sent as an encyclical letter to Christian groups in parts of western Asia

Minor, calling on them to realize in their daily conduct the implications of their conversion. For example, chapter 2 begins with an allusion to baptism as "rebirth" and with a typical exhortation to "take off" vices (like one's clothing before baptism): "Taking off then all malice and all guile and hypocrisy and envy and all slander, yearn like newborn babies for the rational, undiluted milk, so that you may grow up to salvation, if you 'taste that the Lord is good.'"

Then follows the figure of the converts being built "as living stones" into "a spiritual house," on the "cornerstone" of Christ, who is at the same time a "stumbling block" for disbelievers. The figure is backed by quotations from scripture. The "house" is further identified by echoes and quotations of biblical verses that referred originally to Israel:

> But you are a chosen family, a royal priesthood, a holy nation, a people to be God's private property, so that you may announce the virtues of the One who called you out of darkness into his marvelous light—who once were no people but now are the people of God, who were outside his mercy but now have received it.
>
> Beloved, I appeal to you as aliens and immigrants to avoid the fleshly passions that battle against the soul, maintaining fine moral behavior among the gentiles so that, although they malign you as criminals, when they see your good actions they will glorify God on the day of his visitation. (1 Peter 2:1–2,9–10)

Here again we see the tension that we have observed many times in the exhortations of the early Christians, between a sense of sharp separation from the prior life of the convert and the larger society of the city, on the one hand, and on the other a tacit acceptance of the moral values espoused by that society—which is expected after all to recognize the "fine moral behavior" of the Christians. Thus, though the letter's recipients are to think of themselves as "aliens and immigrants" because they are God's unique people in the world, yet they are to "submit to every human establishment," beginning with the emperor and the provincial governors (2:13–17). They are to maintain the good order of the household through the dutiful submission of wives to husbands and of slaves to masters (2:18–3:7), and in general to behave in such fashion that all will see that they are innocent of wrongdoing. If they nevertheless suffer, they will be following the model of Christ, who also suffered unjustly (3:13–23).[4]

Two of the letters attributed to Paul, Colossians and Ephesians, exhibit characteristics like those of 1 Peter. In both, the reminders of the actions by God and Christ that led to the audience's conversion and baptism become the basis for exhortations to the audience to maintain a standard of belief and behavior that they have previously been taught. This pattern of exhortation seems to have been well developed in the Pauline school, and it had strong roots in Paul's own approach to paraenesis, as we have seen in 1 Thessalonians.

One of the most elaborate discussions of baptism's moral implications is in the sixth chapter of Paul's letter to the Romans. The chapter is difficult, because it forms a key part of an exceedingly complex argument that Paul unfolds as he endeavors to introduce "his gospel" to groups of Christians he has not met, in a city he hopes to visit soon. In this chapter Paul at last takes up the objection he recognized already in chapter 3, one that any careful reader of the letter is bound to raise. If there is now no distinction between Jew and gentile, so that both stand equal before the impartial judgment of God; if that equality arises only by the manifestation of God's righteousness apart from Law; if the Law is now seen as only having magnified transgression in order that God's grace to Jew and gentile alike could superabound— then is the Christian faith not utterly amoral? If the structure of commandments no longer shapes the way of doing God's righteousness, then has the moral life no shape at all? As Paul says at the pivotal points in this chapter, "What shall we say? Shall we persist in sin that grace may abound?" (v. 1). "What then? Shall we go on sinning, because we are not under law but under grace?" (v. 15). *Mē genoito*, he says, "Unthinkable"—but he knows that is not quite enough.

The web of metaphors that Paul weaves in this chapter is remarkable, but a detailed exegesis would take us too far afield. We need only to fix our attention on one fact: for Paul's argument to work, his audience must have experienced their initiation into the Christian community in a way that is at least open to Paul's symbolization of it. He recalls and trades upon a beginning common to all who have been baptized. "Don't you know," he reminds them, "we who have been baptized into Christ Jesus were baptized into his death? We were buried then with him in baptism into death, in order that, just as Christ was raised from the dead through the Father's glory, so we ourselves should walk in newness of life" (vv. 3–4). Baptism represents a dying and rising, and the rising entails a new life. The ritual of initiation dramatized as sharply as possible the discontinuity between the old and the new, between the world the convert was leaving and the world he or she now entered, between the "old human" and the new.

The shape of the new life, however, is open-ended, not spelled out in the ritual itself. In their reminders of baptism, the early Christian writers connect life and ritual in various ways. Take, for example, the several ways Paul uses the word "walk," *peripatein*. The intended effect of our rising with Christ from the baptismal death of our past, he says, is that we should "walk in newness of life." That is his common metaphor for moral behavior, as it is for other Jewish teachers of his time and later. In later usage the metaphor congeals into a standard designation for a code of rules, of the type found in the Mishnah or Tosefta, as *halakah*; that is not what Paul refers to. This does not mean that the rabbinic way of shaping behavior was inherently less flexible than Paul's, but the rabbis achieved adaptability by a process of application and reinterpretation within certain specific legal traditions. Typical for Paul is rather 1 Thess. 2:12, where he reminds recent converts of the process by which he instructed and exhorted them, to the end that "you should walk in a way worthy of the God who called you into his own kingdom and glory." Again, a vague expression, but not contourless. God has a character, about which the convert has been instructed. "Conversion," indeed was specifically a "turning" "from idols to serve the God living and true" (1 Thess. 1:10). To behave worthily of this God meant to behave in accord with his character and, more, in accord with his summoning action, the same action celebrated in baptism.

Moreover, the absence of halakah does not mean that there were no rules for Christian behavior. We saw numerous examples in the previous chapter, and even in 1 Thessalonians Paul reminds the converts of specific "precepts" *(parangeliai)* which are taught to those who are baptized (4:1–2). But these precepts and those of other letters are placed within the framework of reminders of baptism. Each of these admonitions recalls the shape of the experience and the learning that were focused by baptism. The appeal is to make one's behavior conform somehow to that shape, but there is a certain openness as to *how* that conformity will look.

It was not only in letters and exhortations that reminders of baptism occurred. Every new baptism reenacted for all the believers who were present their own original experience, re-presenting to them the passage from death to new life and reminding them of the obligations undertaken under those solemn circumstances. The *Apostolic Tradition* of Hippolytus shows us what an elaborate practice for the admission of new converts had developed in the Roman churches by the end of the second century. At the beginning of their period of instruction, candidates were presented by sponsors who had to give testimonials on their behalf, followed by interrogation about their occupations and their social status. At the end of their catechumenate, "their life" was to be examined (§§15–16,20).[5] These examinations as well as the instruction that came in between would impress not only on the catechumens themselves, but also on their sponsors and on the whole community, the manner of life that was expected of the baptized.[6]

Eucharist and Group Integration

The other major ritual that reinforced for the early Christians a special sense of identity was the Lord's Supper or Eucharist ("Thanksgiving"). Because it was celebrated more frequently than baptism, it provided more occasions on which the implications of that special identity for appropriate modes of behavior could be impressed on the participants. As in the case of baptism, the Supper was an occasion for recalling to memory the sacred events it symbolized: "This do in memory of me" (1 Cor. 11:24,25).

Gerd Theißen has shown how Paul refers in 1 Cor. 11:17–34 to the tradition of the Lord's Supper in order to upset the "status-specific expectations" of the Corinthian Christians. In ordinary society any occasion on which people of different social levels ate together was likely to become an occasion for exhibiting the distance between them. The younger Pliny, for example, recounts in a letter to a friend how, at a dinner to which he was invited, the host and people of his social level reclined at one table with a fine series of wines accompanying several courses of elegant cuisine, while freedmen were separately served quite ordinary food and barely drinkable wine. While Pliny disapproves ("When I invite guests it is for a meal," he says, "not to make class distinctions"), the practice he describes was common.[7] When in Corinth "each goes ahead with his own supper at the meal, and one goes hungry and another is drunk," few apparently thought this remarkable. Paul, however, insists that such behavior amounts to "despising the church of God, putting to shame the have-nots." Such behavior followed from "eating and drinking without discerning the Body," and it would have dire consequences: sickness and death.[8]

The second-century church handbook called the *Didache* decrees that any Christians who have quarreled must first patch up their differences before they come to the Eucharist, "lest your sacrifice be profaned" (14:2). The prayers that the *Didache* prescribes for the eucharistic liturgy emphasize the integrative implications of the ritual, but less in social terms than in geographical and eschatological dimensions: "As this broken bread was scattered upon the mountains, but was brought together [compare John 6:12–13] and became one, so let thy Church be gathered together from the ends of the earth into thy kingdom. . . . Remember, Lord, thy Church, to deliver it from all evil and to make it perfect in thy love, and gather it together in its holiness from the four winds to thy kingdom which thou hast prepared for it" (*Didache* 9:3; 10:5, trans. Lake).

There is, of course, a certain ambiguity about the ritual—about every ritual. It lends itself to a variety of interpretations, and the wealthier members of the Corinthian house-churches evidently did not recognize the same implications that Paul saw. Nor does Paul's interpretation necessarily entail a program of social transformation. That some "have houses in which to eat and drink" and others do not is taken for granted. What counts for Paul is that the "coming together in assembly" of the haves and have-nots must not become an occasion for putting the latter to shame. That happened when "the Lord's Supper" was treated as "one's own supper," just another occasion "to eat and drink," as the better-off might do at home, rather than an occasion for memorializing the death of the Lord. Earlier in the same letter Paul has used an allusion to the death of Jesus to admonish those who boasted of religious knowledge that made them superior to those "weak" Christians who superstitiously shunned meat as "idol-sacrifice." "For the weak person is being destroyed by this knowledge of yours—the brother for whose sake Christ died" (1 Cor. 8:11). An analogous chain of moral reasoning is being suggested in 1 Cor. 11:17–34: the death of Christ for all, symbolized in the Supper, implies that participants in the Supper ought to put the needs and feelings of one another ahead of their private honor. That connection evidently had not been obvious to the Christians in Corinth. The rituals provide a dramatic structure within and on which a pattern of moral reasoning may be erected and an interpretive dialectic begun between ritual and common life experience.

A direct link between ritual and behavior was made on occasions when exclusion from the ritual became a disciplinary sanction. We saw above how the Roman churches developed a formal practice for screening candidates for baptism, excluding those who persisted in unacceptable occupations or other activities regarded as unholy. In his first, now lost, letter to Corinth, Paul had admonished the Christians to shun anyone claiming the name "brother" who was guilty of any of a series of vices, "not even to eat with such a person" (1 Cor. 5:11); in the extant 1 Corinthians he applies that dictum by ordering the formal expulsion of a man living in flagrant immorality (5:1–13). Shunning is prescribed in 2 Thess. 3:14–15 for persons behaving in a "disorderly" fashion, but within limits, so that the disciplined people would be "shamed" and "admonished" but not treated "as an enemy." Exclusion from the common meals would be one of the most visible instances of this sanction.

Lesser Rituals

Not only the rituals that were becoming the pivotal sacraments of the church helped to shape moral sensibilities. Also smaller practices and habits, repeated either within the great rituals or on lesser occasions and even privately, could have their cumulative effect. For example, Martin Hengel has called attention to the importance of early Christian hymns as simultaneously shaping the communities' christology and shaping the communities themselves.[9] The Letter to Colossians may allude to this function of charismatic poetry in the early Christian gatherings, for it speaks of "psalms, hymns, and spiritual odes" in the context of "teaching and admonishing one another" (3:16–17). Form critics have identified several stylized compositions incorporated into Christian letters that may be examples of this liturgical poetry. Most firmly established is the "hymn" quoted by Paul in Philippians 2:6–11. Colossians 1:15–20 may be another, quoted by a disciple of Paul. In both cases it is quite clear that the letter uses the poem as a basis for moral exhortation. In Philippians, Christ's self-humbling obedience is both basis and model for the practice of "humility" and other-regarding love in the church. In Colossians the reconciliation performed by the heavenly Christ is to be enacted in the peace and harmony of the congregation rather than in the ascetic practices of the "angels' religion" that the author opposes.[10]

Colossians 3:17 gives another clue to the formative possibilities of ritual speech: "Everything you do, in word or in deed, let all be in the name of the Lord Jesus, giving thanks to God the Father through him." Here is a means for extending into everyday life something of the kinds of consciousness that are evoked in liturgical settings. In the *Apostolic Tradition* we see how the Roman church of the second century had evolved prescriptions for set times of daily prayer, beginning at dawn: "Let all the faithful, men and women, when they arise from sleep in the morning, before taking up any work, wash their hands and pray to God, and thus let them approach their work" (§41). Then at the third hour of the day, wherever one might be, one ought to "pray and bless God," for "in this hour Christ was fixed to the cross." Again in the sixth hour, recalling the "great darkness" that fell at the crucifixion. Also in the ninth hour, recalling the emission of blood and water from the side of Christ. One prayed again at bedtime. More striking is the directive to get up again at midnight, wash the hands, and pray again, together with one's wife, if she is a believer. "For the elders who transmitted the tradition to us taught that at this hour the whole creation rests for a moment to praise the Lord: stars, trees, waters stop for a moment and the whole host of ministering angels, to praise God together with the souls of the just" (§41). The reference to the ministering angels reminds us of the "Songs of the Sabbath Sacrifices" found among the Dead Sea Scrolls, which suggests similarly that the members of the Qumran community thought of their prayers as well as their daily behavior as being somehow conjoined with the angels' worship of God.[11] If the church was really able to persuade numbers of its ordinary members to get up every midnight to pray in this fashion, it would surely go a long way toward impressing on them an extraordinary context for the daily round of life.

Fasting is often mentioned together with prayer; limiting food on specific occasions was a widespread religious practice in antiquity. Other forms of abstinence were also thought appropriate preparation for approaching the deity; Paul suggests in 1 Cor. 7:5 that husband and wife may agree to abstain from sex during a period of prayer. Prescriptions for entry into pagan shrines often mention abstentions of various kinds.[12] The *Didache* sets Wednesdays and Fridays for Christian fasting, to distinguish their practice from "the hypocrites" (the Jews) (8:1). It also specifies that candidates for baptism and their baptizers should fast, along with "any others who are able" (7:4). Fasting is often preparation for receiving a revelation; for example, Hermas regularly mentions his fasting (6.1 [*Vis.* 2.2.1]; 9.2 [*Vis.* 3.1.2]; 54.1 [*Sim.* 5.1.2]). Modern interpreters often think of the physiological consequences, which perhaps would make entry into a trance state easier, but the "ancient lady" who appeared to Hermas identified fasting as an expression of humility: "Every request needs humility: fast therefore and you shall receive what you ask from the Lord" (18.6 [*Vis.* 3.10.6], trans. Lake). Moreover, the Shepherd suggests to Hermas an ethical reinterpretation of fasting, rejecting his previous practice as "a vain fast" and "nothing." "But fast to God in this way: do nothing evil in your life, but serve the Lord with a pure heart; keep his commandments and walk in his ordinances, and let no evil desire arise in your heart, but believe in God, that if you do these things and fear him, and refrain from every wicked act, you shall live to God; and if you do this you will fulfil a great fast and one acceptable to God" (54.4–5 [*Sim.* 5.1.4–5], trans. Lake).

After telling a parable about a servant who did far more than his master commanded, and then shared his reward with fellow slaves, the Shepherd gives Hermas some specific directives for his fasting: "After completing what has been written, in that day on which you fast you shall taste nothing except bread and water, and you shall reckon the price of the expense for that day which you are going to keep, of the foods which you would have eaten, and you shall give it to a widow or an orphan or to some one destitute, and you shall thus be humble-minded" (54.7 [*Sim.* 5.3.7], trans. Lake).

Fasting was of course only one of the forms of self-denial practiced by the early Christians. For some groups an ascetic regimen became the defining discipline of the Christian life. We have seen examples in chapter 4 from the Thomas literature, and in chapter 8 we shall have to consider in more detail the range of attitudes toward the body represented in Christian belief and behavior.

Gifts of the Spirit

We will fail to understand the symbolic web woven by the ritual life of the early Christian communities unless we keep in mind the culture of the miraculous to which the rituals belonged. Not only are the stories told by the Christians both about Jesus and about his apostles filled with miraculous events, but the actual practice of these groups at their meetings was fraught with expectation of extraordinary phenomena. Ecstatic speech—"speaking in tongues"—was so prized by some Christians in Corinth, for example, that Paul in one of his letters labors to curb its excesses and the divisiveness it produced (1 Cor. 14:1–33). In the course of his argument he mentions a number of other ecstatic phenomena: "When you come together, one has a psalm, another has a teaching, another has a revelation, another has a tongue, another has an interpretation" (v. 26). Meetings in the house-churches of Corinth will not have been somber. Earlier in the same letter, again in the context of urging unity on a fractious church, Paul mentions "miracles, gifts of healing," and "tongues" (12:28–30). The Letter of James gives these directives: "Are any among you suffering? They should pray. Are any cheerful? They should sing songs of praise. Are any among you sick? They should call for the elders of the church and have them pray over them, anointing them with oil in the name of the Lord. The prayer of faith will save the sick, and the Lord will raise them up; and anyone who has committed sins will be forgiven" (James 5:13–15, NRSV).

As James's prescription for curing the sick differs from practices recommended by empirical medicine, so also practices that expect the miraculous affect a community's moral calculus. In reckoning the consequences of one's actions, one must take account of divine intervention. The possibility of "sin," for example, enters into the discussion of illness and its therapy. It is not simply a case of certain beliefs being added to practice; the beliefs interpret the practices, while the practices reinforce the beliefs. Thinking theoretically, it is easy to set the formality of ritual against the spontaneity of charisma. However, if we examine the behavior of groups that are characterized by ecstatic phenomena—for example, modern Pentecostal Christian groups—we will see that there are pronounced regularities in their speech and actions. The "spontaneous" eruptions of charismata are triggered at predictable times, responding to specific cues of words, rhythm, music, bodily motion.[13] The experiences are powerful reinforcers of the behavior that brought them on, and of the beliefs that explain them. If one engages in ritualized occasions in which neighbors fall into trance and prophesy; if while the whole group joins in a rhythmic chant, others begin to speak in ecstasy but unintelligibly; if elders lay hands on sick persons and declare them healed; if stories of other miracles are recited; then unless one has the skeptical defenses of an ancient Lucian or a modern academic, one's moral world as well as one's imaginative world will very likely be affected.

Admonitions and Sanctions

Since the discovery of the Dead Sea Scrolls, many people have been struck by resemblances between the Essene sect of Judaism and the later sect that would become Christianity. The resemblances have sometimes been exaggerated, but they are quite real. Among them is the fact that, in both cases, each little community seems to have made itself responsible for monitoring the behavior of its members. Among the scrolls, the Community Rule and the so-called Damascus Rule both provide quite specific regulations for community life and for the way they were to be applied. We do not have any document quite comparable from the literature of early Christianity, but we do have ample evidence that the fundamental practices of early Christianity included mutual admonition and the sanctions that were applied to reduce deviance.

The practice of admonition is most visible to us in the letters that early Christians wrote. Christians were a movement of letter writers, as Stanley Stowers has pointed out, and the overwhelming majority of their letters were wholly or partly hortatory in function.[14] They urged groups and individuals to behave in ways appropriate to the writers' vision of Christianity. Not only so, they also urged the recipients to admonish one another or to submit to the instruction of their leaders.

As we saw in the previous chapter, the form and language of Christian exhortation and moral advice was often indistinguishable from those employed by philosophers and orators in the larger society. The Christian letter writers and, presumably, the local prophets and teachers freely adapted the topics and methods that characterized a long tradition in the Greek and Latin worlds of *psychagōgia*, the guidance of souls. Philosophy was widely construed as a kind of therapy by which the ills of the soul were cured, and Christian writers and speakers made that tradition their own, as had Greek-speaking Jewish writers before them.

In the philosophical schools, however, the therapy was applied to the individual pupils by their teacher. When moralizing orators took up similar language, perhaps addressing thousands in a public theater, the message was nevertheless still quite individualistic. The soul that is sick with self-concern, desire, passion, and confusion between what is essential and what is beyond one's rational control, must finally cure itself. With the important exception of the Epicureans (and perhaps, if we knew more about them, the neo-Pythagoreans), no "group therapy" was offered by philosophy. Nor was such cure of souls the business of ancient religion. One can almost agree with Edwin Judge that these Christian groups would not have looked like a *religious* movement at all to their contemporaries, for one did not go to cultic places and occasions to hear this kind of moral advice.[15] In the Christian groups, however, the topics that one would expect to hear from the educated elite—in the public orations of the professional speakers, in letters to clients and friends, in harangues by oddly dressed Cynics in marketplace or shop—were tossed about by the most ordinary people in the privacy of Christian houses. As Celsus would complain, Christians acted as if "the most stupid and uneducated yokels" could learn moral philosophy. Origen agreed—and argued that this redounded to Christianity's credit.[16]

Christian moralists drew not only upon the traditions of moral discourse practiced by rhetoricians and philosophers, but also upon the moral education of children in school and especially in the home. The fiction that baptism had made the converts into a new family is, after all, deeply embedded in their common language; they address one another as brothers and sisters, fathers and children. And the household, we have come to see, is the fundamental unit of urban Christianity. It was altogether appropriate that, just as in a natural family, moral training, advice, and admonition would take place in those household "meetings." However, in these households, it was not only the *pater familias* or a tutor hired by him who gave instruction and monitored the behavior of these grown-up "children." The householder found himself—or herself, for a substantial proportion of the early Christian patrons seem to have been women—competing for moral authority with a variety of charismatic teachers and leaders: prophets and prophetesses, seers and singers, itinerant apostles. The glimpses of Christian meetings that we get from the letters show us communities of mutual admonition. The *Epistle of Barnabas,* for example, urges the recipients to "be good lawgivers to each other, remain faithful counselors to each other, remove from yourselves all hypocrisy" (21:4, trans. Lake).

Not only did members of these meetings admonish one another, they also undertook to discipline one another by applying sanctions when admonitions were not heeded. Thus in the Gospel of Matthew, Jesus lays down rules for correcting the erring: "If your brother sins, go and confront him—between you and him alone. If he listens to you, you have won your brother. If he does not listen, take one or two [others] with you, that 'by the mouth of two or three witnesses every matter may be established.' If he ignores them, tell the Meeting. If he ignores even the Meeting, he must be to you like a gentile or a tax collector" (Matt. 18:15–18).

From an even earlier document, 1 Cor. 5, we have Paul's well-known demand that a fellow who was living with his father's wife be solemnly expelled and "handed over to Satan for the destruction of the flesh" (1 Cor. 5:5). As we saw above, Paul recalls an earlier letter in which he has directed the Corinthian Christians "not to mix" with immoral people "who go by the name of 'brother'" (6:9–11). Such shunning, which we also hear about in 2 Thess. 3:14, was a powerful sanction in the intimate communities that constituted the early Christian *ekklēsiai.* Even in modern times we know how effective a formal shunning of deviants can be in some of the sects that have descended from the left wing of the Reformation, like the Mennonites and Amish. The real power of the action may not even depend upon its success in bringing the accused person around. Even if that person simply abandons the sect altogether, the expulsion has been a vivid object lesson to those who remain.

Hospitality and Control

Hospitality was—and is—a virtue highly prized in the Middle East. In Greek tradition Odysseus was the paradigm of the wanderer, whose varying fates at the hands of his hosts exemplified the virtue of hospitality or the vice of ill-treatment of strangers. The Homeric hymn to Demeter celebrates that goddess's disguise as a wandering alien while she mourned the abduction of Persephone, and Zeus himself was often addressed as the protector of strangers. For Christians, a movement spread by itinerants, hospitality had special significance. In the great parable of the sheep and goats in Matthew, the Son of Man says to the ones on his right, "I was a stranger and you gathered me in," to the others, "I was a stranger and you did not gather me in." He explains then that his fate was that of the "least ones," who in Matthew are especially the itinerant preachers of the gospel, described in the persons of the Twelve in chapter 10, but perhaps also other marginalized members of the Christian movement (Matt. 25:34–46).

Hospitality (philoxenia) is prominent in Christian lists of virtues, for example, in the Shepherd of Hermas 38.10 (Mand. 8.10). In the rather tedious allegory of the twelve mountains that forms the ninth "parable" of Hermas's book, the exemplary believers from the tenth mountain are "bishops and hospitable persons." As the bishops "always, without ceasing, sheltered the needy and the widows, by their own ministry," so the hospitable "always gladly welcomed God's servants into their houses without making a show of it" (Hermas 104.2 [Sim. 9.27.2]). The concluding admonitions of the Letter to Hebrews begin, after urging brotherly love, with the command, "Do not neglect hospitality, for by this means some have unwittingly hosted angels" (Heb. 13:2). The allusion is doubtless to the stories of Abraham (Gen. 18) and Lot (Gen. 19). Abraham and Lot are the first two examples of "faith and hospitality" or "hospitality and religious devotion" cited in the Letter of Rome to Corinth; the third is "the hospitable Rahab," who, like the Patriarchs, "was saved on account of her faith and hospitality" (*1 Clem.* 10:37; 11:1; 12:1,3). The Corinthian Christians, too, are praised for the faith and hospitality they exhibited before their recent disputes: "Has anyone, indeed, stayed with you without attesting the excellence and firmness of your faith? without admiring your sensible and considerate Christian piety? without broadcasting your spirit of unbounded hospitality?" (1:2, trans. Richardson).[17]

This letter, as we noted before, opens by identifying both the sending and the receiving church as "resident aliens." The practice of showing hospitality to visitors reminds the Christians that, as Hebrews says, "we have here no enduring city, but we await the one that is coming" (Heb. 13:14). In his *Apology* Justin lists among the needy for whom a collection is taken on each Sunday "the aliens resident here" (*1 Apol.* 67.6). Care for those who were literally and legally aliens could remind the church of its symbolic status as "aliens" in the world.

The Pauline letters give specific instances of the importance of hospitality to the development of the Christian movement. In his letter to Philemon and the Meeting in the house of Philemon and Apphia about the slave Onesimus, Paul asks the host to "prepare a guest room for me" (Philem. 22). Among the Corinthians whom Paul singles out to mention in his letter to Rome is Gaius, "my host and host of the entire Meeting" (Rom. 16:23). Paul requests hospitality for the bearer of the letter, Phoebe, a minister of the Meeting in Cenchreae and "patroness of many, including myself" (16:1–2). Similar requests are made or implied when Paul sends other fellow workers to churches he has founded, such as Timothy (1 Cor. 4:17; 16:10–11; Phil. 2:19–23) and Titus (2 Cor. 8:16–24). The requests can also include "sending forth" *(propempein)* to the apostle's next destination, that is, making provision for travel (Rom. 15:24; 1 Cor. 16:6,11; 2 Cor. 1:16).[18] The Philippian groups provided financial support for Paul and his coworkers even when they were preaching in other provinces—a "partnership for the gospel" that was unique among the Pauline churches (2 Cor. 11:8–9; Phil. 1:5; 4:10–20 and passim).[19]

Hospitality thus served both symbolic and practical purposes for the early Christian movement. Housing and feeding visiting prophets and apostles not only made their ministry feasible, it also reminded the hosts both of the movement's self-proclaimed identity as "resident aliens" on earth and of its professed unity as a single "people of God" throughout the world.

Hospitality was exercised most often by householders who were able to take in traveling apostles in their own houses, but, as Justin attests, provisions began to be made early on for a communal treasury for such purposes. With the development in the second century of the monepiscopate, that is, a single bishop in each congregation and, later, in each city, the bishop gradually became the chief patron, exercising many of the functions that wealthier householders had performed in the early years.[20]

The exercise of hospitality was not always straightforward, however. The instructions for the Twelve sent out by Jesus, in the tradition of the Synoptic Gospels, include a word about dealing with the inhospitable: "Whenever you enter a house, stay there until you leave that place. And if any place does not receive you nor listen to you, when you depart from that place, shake off the dust under your feet as a testimony to [or against] them" (Mark 6:10–11; compare Matt. 10:11–15; Luke 10:5–12).

Inhospitality could be something more than common stinginess or xenophobia; withholding hospitality could be a weapon in disputes over right belief and proper behavior. We have a clear and somewhat ironic example in the two little letters from "the elder" attributed to John. Second John is addressed to a group of Christians ("the chosen lady and her children," either a patroness and the Meeting in her house or, more likely, a rhetorical flourish for "Lady Church," as in Hermas's visions). It warns against purveyors of doctrines not approved by the elder: "If anyone comes to you and does not bring this teaching, do not receive him into your house and do not even say 'Hello' to him" (2 John 10). In 3 John the elder complains to his friend Gaius that a certain Diotrephes has applied a similar rule, but with a twist: it is the elder's partisans who are now refused admission (3 John 10).[21] By the second century, rules begin to be formulated for dealing with the itinerants; for example, in the *Didache:* "Every apostle who comes to you should be received as the Lord. But he shall not stay more than one day— and a second, in case of need; if he stays three, he's a false prophet. When the apostle leaves he is to take nothing with him except bread until his next stay; if he asks for money, he is a false prophet" (11:4–6).

The Practice of Giving

Very early, doubtless following Jewish models, the Christians established the practice of giving to those of the community who were needy. Justin Martyr's description of the collection made at each Sunday Eucharist was mentioned above; it bears quoting in full at this point, in the translation by E. R. Hardy:

> And . . . when we have finished the prayer, bread is brought, and wine and water, and the president similarly sends up prayers and thanksgivings to the best of his ability, and the congregation assents, saying the Amen; the distribution, and reception of the consecrated [elements] by each one, takes place and they are sent to the absent by the deacons. Those who prosper, and who so wish, contribute, each one as much as he chooses to. What is collected is deposited with the president, and he takes care of orphans and widows, and those who are in want on account of sickness or any other cause, and those who are in bonds, and the strangers who are sojourners among [us], and, briefly, he is the protector of all those in need. (1 Apol. 67.5–6)[22]

This practice would have wide repercussions in the later institutionalization of the church and in its interaction with the larger society around it. Especially significant and familiar is the letter of Julian to the High Priest of Galatia, whom he had appointed in his attempt to restore "Hellenism," that is, the traditional worship of Greco-Roman gods. It would be necessary, wrote the apostate emperor (late in the fourth century), to create hostels for aliens and foundations to help the poor, for the Christians had by such means won their present dominance.[23]

In the earliest literature of the Christian movement, Paul's protracted efforts to raise money for the "poor among the saints in Jerusalem" furnish the clearest instance of how Christian giving began to be institutionalized. A vast number of articles and several monographs have been written on the subject of the collection, but most of them are concerned only with discovering Paul's motives, the theological ideas behind the effort, or the church politics involved in carrying it out. More to the point of our inquiry is the question, what must the collection have meant to those who participated in it?

The directive that Paul writes to the Corinthian Christians, at the end of his first extant letter to them, contains important hints: "On the first day of each week let each of you set something aside privately, storing up whatever each one can, if he has prospered" (16:2). Here is something novel, at least in the eyes of former gentiles: that ordinary people with no great wealth but out of each week's income should, not just in one grand gesture, but little by little, systematically gather what money could be spared, to send to a distant place, for people never seen called "brothers" and "saints." We could dwell on the images and ideas that Paul uses to motivate the effort, especially in 2 Cor. 8–9—his concern for "equity," *isotēs*, between the churches; his insistence upon the obligation owed Jews by gentile Christians; above all the model of Christ, who "for your sakes impoverished himself, being rich, that you through his poverty might become rich" (2 Cor. 8:9). Equally important, however, is the fact of the preparation itself. Would not the very act of dropping those hard-earned coins into a jar every Sunday have an effect on the way the participating members of the church would henceforth think about the morality of wealth and poverty?

The letter from the Roman congregations to the Corinthians, usually dated around 95, sets before them a more extreme example of self-sacrifice to aid the poor "We know many among ourselves," says Clement, "who have delivered themselves into slavery in order to ransom others" (1 *Clem.* 55:2).[24] Such heroic measures on the part of impecunious people to aid others still worse off were no doubt exceptional. They stand in vivid contrast to the need Hermas felt to cajole rich members of the Roman congregations into helping the poor.[25] Still, the practice of giving by no means disappeared in Rome, as Justin testifies in the passage quoted above. According to the letter of Dionysius of Corinth to Rome, quoted by Eusebius, the charitable efforts of the Roman Christians even extended to other places, "to many congregations in every city" (Eusebius, *EH* 4.23.10).

The *Apostolic Tradition* of Hippolytus, prescribing for the Roman churches at the end of the century, speaks of gifts for the sick and for widows and introduces the phrase "the bread of the poor" (§24). The common meal—now distinguished from the Eucharist: the prayer is *benedictio et non eucharistia*—provides a real occasion for feeding those in need, as Paul in his time wanted the Lord's Supper to do (25–28). For widows there were special meals, called *deipna chērōn*, provided by anyone able to do so (30). By the middle of the third century, Bishop Cornelius claims that the episcopal organization in Rome was supporting, among others, "above fifteen hundred widows and persons in distress" (*EH* 6.43.11, trans. Oulton). Giving had become a regular and central part of Christian practice. Indeed, Peter Lampe has speculated that it was the need to coordinate charitable efforts, along with the relations with churches in other cities, that first led to a central organization of the otherwise "fractionated" house-communities of Christians in Rome.[26] If that is true, then the practice of giving was actually one factor that propelled the institutionalization of the church, and the obligation for mutual support was built into the very fabric of the institution.

Practicing Ambivalence

There is one dimension of early Christian practice that we might easily forget because it is so obvious. While the movement's leaders would have liked the distinctive practices we have sampled to define the lives of all the converts, those practices were always competing for attention with the myriad of social practices that shaped the social fabric of the society around them. If, according to one interpretation of 1 Cor. 11:21,33, the poorer members of the congregation were arriving at the Lord's Supper too late to share the food, it was probably because they were slaves in other households, or hired workers or artisans who could not leave their shops. A traveling apostle must deal with shipping practices on the Mediterranean or Aegean, or with safe procedures on overland roads and in seedy hostels. Onesimus might become Philemon's "beloved brother" as well as his slave, but did that mean he would now be freed? All the peculiar practices of the Christians are embedded within a web of practices that connected them with the world whose form (Paul had said) was passing away.

One way of thinking about the great monastic movements that developed in the fourth century and later is as an attempt to resolve the tension between the practices of "the world" and the practices of the Christian community, by renouncing the former to the maximum extent possible. For most Christians, however, withdrawal from the world and ascetic warfare against it were not realistic options. For the vast majority, the Christian life was an amphibian life, life at the same time in the old world that was passing away and in the new world that was coming or, to use the language we have encountered in several places, life as resident aliens in the world. Note, however, that the practice of moving back and forth between two sets of social practices is itself a very special kind of practice. The amphibian life itself helps to mold moral sensibilities of the early Christians.

It may not always be true that, as the saying goes, practice makes perfect. It does seem to be the case that practice makes morals. Looking at the practices of the early Christians, we see two ways in which those practices nurtured moral sensibilities that the practitioners thought were distinctive to their faith. First, Christian practice was habituative. What we have seen confirms the ancient philosophical cliché, "Habit makes character," *ethos* makes *ēthos*. Earlier, when we considered conversion, I suggested that just as the development of moral dispositions is part of the same process of primary socialization by which people achieve their sense of identity as persons in community, so too resocialization into a countercultural or subcultural movement like early Christianity tries simultaneously to produce a new moral sense and a new identity. The repetition of distinctive practices drums into us the sense of who we are, because this is what *we* do. Often the practice is so constructed as to remind us that what we do is different from what *they* do: Christians' marriages, for instance, are to be "not like [the marriages of] the gentiles who do not know God" (1 Thess. 4:5). Stress on such distinctions is important in the shaping of identity, even if an objective outside observer will in some cases not be able to discover significant differences in fact. It is the practice as perceived by those within it that counts initially.

But that consideration shows immediately that we cannot separate acting from thinking or believing. The second reason practice is able to nurture Christian moral dispositions is that practice is communicative. That is why I have called this chapter "the grammar of Christian practice." The practices we have looked at are not just "doing things," they are also ways of saying things. Like a natural language, these practices "make sense" within a particular social setting. They all have a high degree of regularity, they imply some measure of organization, they press in the direction of institutionalization. They are essentially communal. Even those practices that are urged upon individuals in the privacy of their homes, like the regular hours of prayer legislated in Hippolytus's *Apostolic Tradition*, are extensions of the community's practice—indeed they are means of reminding individuals even when alone that they are not merely devotees of the Christians' God, they are members of Christ's body, the people of God. That was how the Christian movement differed most visibly from the other cults that fit more easily into the normal expectations of "religion" in the Roman world. The Christians' practices were not confined to sacred occasions and sacred locations—shrines, sacrifices, processions—but were integral to the formation of communities with a distinctive self-awareness.

CHAPTER 7

Knowing Evil

❖ ❖ ❖ ❖ ❖ ❖ ❖ ❖ ❖ ❖

The moral landscape—the picture of reality that, just beneath the level of conscious reflection, shapes our moral intuitions—requires dark colors as well as light. We need to know, at some level of awareness, what stands over against that which we take to be right and good. We require explanation for the retarding friction that sometimes inhibits our affirming the good, some myth to render graphic and plausible the conflicts that arise in our willing. We must, therefore, know about evil.

The way the early Christians pictured the causes and mechanisms of evil is an important part of their map of the moral world. The classic issue that arises when theologians discuss evil is the problem of theodicy: how evil could arise in a world governed by a God believed to be both all-powerful and good. The early Christians, like all theists, had to confront that issue, but we have no systematic discussion of it from the period we are describing, so it will not be central to our sketch. Nor do we need to solve the problem of the genealogy of the concepts employed by the early Christians—the sources and cultural lines of transmission of their images of evil. Whether a particular concept or mode of symbolization had its roots in the myths of ancient Babylon or in those of old Persian religion or perhaps in the Orphic movement in preclassical Greece is an interesting and important question, but it lies outside our immediate concerns. A definitive answer to that question, even if one were possible, is fortunately not essential and probably not even helpful for understanding the way the given concepts worked in the minds and lives of people in the cultural melting pot of the high Roman Empire. Our present task is simply to sketch a broad outline of the ways early Christians imagined the forces that stand against the good.

A Divided Universe

If we try to imagine ourselves into the position of some ordinary person in a Roman provincial city who is converting to Christianity in the first or second century, certain things about the Christians' talk will strike us at once. They talk about evil constantly; they name evil explicitly and variously; and they picture it more systematically than is common in the larger culture. In that more comprehensive picture, evil on the human plane is never the whole story or even the most important part of the story. From the beginning of their movement, it seems, the Christians live in a world with demons filled. Paul, explaining a change of travel plans, can say, "Satan prevented me" (1 Thess. 2:18) as casually as we might say, "My car had a flat tire."

Power and Magic

Talk about Satan and stories about demons abound in the lore and literature of early Christianity. Jesus confronts "demons" and "unclean spirits" on every hand and controls them. Often these stories are told in such a way that the central issue is power: the sinister force of the invisible demon against Jesus' superior might. The point can even be made with touches of humor, as in the tale of Jesus confronting the man possessed by a "legion" of demons in the land of the Gerasenes (Mark 5:1–17). A *legion* of demons begging "that he not send them out of the country" can hardly fail to have had a satiric political overtone at some point in the history of its telling. That these demons let themselves be tricked into entering a herd of hogs that then hurl themselves over a cliff into the sea will also have been both fitting and funny from a Jewish point of view. Neither of these overtones finds any resonance in Mark's use of the story, however. At the center of the story, in Mark's telling, is the direct confrontation between Jesus and the demon(s), who not only know Jesus' hidden identity and therefore might have power over him, but even try conjuring him (*horkizō*, v. 7) in God's name! Their ignominious defeat thus reveals how vast is Jesus' power—so awesome that the people of the vicinity beg him just to go away (v. 17).

Stories like this are told not only of Jesus, but also of his followers. In the Book of Acts and even more in the apocryphal Acts produced in the second century, both exorcisms and, as it were, competitive exorcisms and miraculous contests exhibit the superior power of genuine apostles in contrast to pretenders who are agents of an evil, opposing force. Think, for example, of the confrontation between Peter and Simon the Magician in Acts 8:14–24, or of the more elaborate contest between the same two later in Rome, according to the *Acts of Peter*, which climaxes in Simon's magical flight through the air, brought to a crashing end by a word from Peter.[1] The later lives of saints and monks also abound in confrontations of the holy persons with the devil or his agents. In his book *Christianizing the Roman Empire*, Ramsay MacMullen embarrassed and irritated many students of the early church by reminding them how pervasive are the stories that "explain" conversions by telling of exorcisms or contests between Christian miracle-workers and demons. Morton Smith's book *Jesus the Magician* had irritated even more people by showing how similar the world of the Gospel stories was to the world of magic.[2] The Gospels candidly report that opponents of Jesus thought him a magician—possessed by or possessing and controlling a powerful daimon: "Beelzebul, the prince of demons," or the spirit of the murdered John the Baptist (see Mark 3:22; 6:14–16). Such possession and control was the central mechanism of magic, as understood by its ancient practitioners and customers.

Our imagined convert to the Christian movement would hardly have found talk about demons novel. That exceptional skeptic Lucian of Samosata shows by his very parodies of such beliefs how common they were. In his skit *The Lover of Lies*, Lucian presents a tall-tale contest in which raconteurs top one another in stories about exorcisms, culminating in the report by one of personally witnessing an exorcism by "the Syrian from Palestine," otherwise unidentified. "Indeed, I actually saw one [a demon] coming out, black and smoky in colour."[3] Positive evidence is not hard to find, for a large number of magical recipes have survived from antiquity, mostly on scraps of papyrus recovered from the rubbish heaps of ancient Egypt.[4] The magical papyri are full of spells that promise immunity from attacks by demons—and others that explain how to employ demonic hit-men for one's own nefarious purposes. Indeed, one of the things that strikes us as we read these spells is how utterly amoral is this technical world of magic. Thus, alongside the benign mechanisms guaranteed to protect against dog bite, gout, headache, or fever, to counteract poison, catch a thief, remove a bone stuck in the throat, or get a stubborn donkey moving, we also find a series of spells to wreak vengeance by inducing coma or death or illness. This is followed by an antidote to the same, in case the enemy might have the means of turning the tables (*PDM* 14.675–94, 711–15; antidote: 706–10; a whole series of other "evil sleep" spells follow in the same papyrus). The lead tablets to be nailed up or buried and the cursing bowls to be deposited, all in order to do irreparable harm to rivals or enemies, are further examples of these somewhat less than charming charms.[5] One of the commonest types of magic spell is the love charm, and these regularly ask the conjured god to plunge the object of the user's affection into insanity or physical agony unless or until she or he runs to the charmer's bed.

Not only is the world of magical practice largely amoral, its theology, if one can call it that, is helter-skelter. The handbooks offer to their purchasers guarantees that they can command the needed powers for the designated purposes, and any and every god from highest to lowest, heaps of them in breathless incantations, are invoked, very often with the confident identification formula, "You are I and I you—whatever I say must happen" (*PGM* 13.795).

We must not imagine that to become a Christian meant automatically to remove oneself cleanly from the magical world view. While there is a strong tradition both in Judaism and in Christianity that tries to distinguish sharply between "magic" and "religion," in practice the distinction is often unclear at best. In antiquity, the monotheism of Israel had not kept some Jews from becoming adepts in magic. This fact is attested by the frequency of Jewish divine and angelic names in the papyrus spells, as well as by the specifically Jewish magic handbooks like the *Testament of Solomon* and the *Book of Mysteries*.[6] So also many Christians and near-Christians must have recognized that "Jesus" was a conjuring name that could readily be added to the standard repertoires. This was already a problem in the first century, as Mark 9:38–39 and Acts 19:13–16 demonstrate. In the former passage, John reports to Jesus that the disciples have stopped an exorcist who was using Jesus' name, "because he was not following us." Jesus, however, permits the practice. However, in the Acts story of the seven sons of Sceva, the attempt of these Jewish exorcists to use the name of "the Jesus whom Paul proclaims" has unfortunate (and humorous) results: the demon cries, " 'Jesus' I know and 'Paul' I understand, but who are you?" and the demoniac beats the would-be exorcists soundly. The magical papyri show traces of acquaintance with Christian tradition. We cannot be sure whether Christian influence is at work when "Evangelos" is invoked as a daemon, in a lesbian love-charm (*PGM* 32.1), but it is unmistakable in a spell for childbirth in which the foetus is addressed: "Come out of your tomb: Christ is calling you!" (*PGM* 123a.50).[7]

The Evil Empire

The leaders of the Christian movement from the very beginning struggled to impose upon the common, helter-skelter picture of a world filled with unseen powers a bipolar division that was fundamentally moral. On the one side are God and his "messengers" or "angels"; on the other are Satan and his "demons." The Christians, like other Jewish groups, gave a negative valence to the common Greek term *daimōn,* which ordinarily had a neutral sense, referring to any deity or, more and more in Hellenistic and Roman times, to the lesser divine powers who occupied the spaces and functions beneath the Olympians and their regional peers. By choice, trading on a trend in later Greek to use diminutives with a pejorative sense, they usually name a possessing force *daimonion,* "godlet."[8] Or they use the Jewish expression, "unclean spirit."

Whatever the ultimate impulse for this dualist conception of the spiritual world, it was already deeply rooted in certain circles of Judaism when the followers of Jesus began to emerge as a distinct sect, and those followers carried on this dualism wholeheartedly. In the Gospel story already mentioned, found in Mark 3:22–27, Jesus responds to the charge that he "possesses Beelzebul, and by the ruler of the demons he casts out demons. . . . How can Satan cast out Satan? If a kingdom is divided against itself, that kingdom cannot stand. And if Satan has risen up against himself and is divided, he cannot stand, but his end has come" (vv. 23–25, NRSV).

The other two Synoptics appropriately add here the saying from their other common source, "But if it is by the finger of God that I cast out the demons, then the kingdom of God has come to you" (Luke 11:20, NRSV). Satan now has a "kingdom." And it is set over against the kingdom of God.

The amorphous and amoral world thronging with gods and *daimones* thus becomes a neatly hierarchical world. The double hierarchy, the kingdom of Satan and the kingdom of God, is fundamentally different from the single hierarchical map that thinkers like Plutarch tried to impose on the swarm of unseen divinities.[9] The earliest Christians absorbed with their Jewish heritage the old prophetic scorn of "idolatry," which had been sharpened in the attack of some Greek Jewish authors on the polytheistic culture in which they lived. The attack could be expressed in a rational disdain for the stupidity of worshipping things made of stone or wood or in the shape of animals that "even as animals . . . are not so beautiful" (Wisd. 15:19, NRSV). People whose reasoning was so confused were bound to fall into moral perversity as well: so wrote the unknown Alexandrian author of the Wisdom of Solomon, chapters 13–15. Paul, one example among many, echoes similar sentiments in Rom. 1:18–32. In Gal. 4:8 he speaks of the former objects of worship by his converts as "things that by nature were not gods," and he approves the logic of the "knowing" Christians at Corinth who say, "We know that no idol is [really] in the world, and there is no God but one" (1 Cor. 8:4). He goes on, however, to suggest that there is some reality to these non-gods: in fact they are *daimonia* (10:19–22). This became a common belief among the early Christians. Robin Lane Fox describes well their mood: "Like pagans, Christians still sensed and saw the gods and their power, and as something, they had to assume, lay behind it, by an easy, traditional shift of opinion, they turned these pagan *daimones* into malevolent 'demons,' the troupe of Satan. They were most demonic when they were most plausible, lurking under the statues and working wonders and visions as if from the gods who were represented."[10]

In the dualist picture of the spiritual world—the apocalyptic picture, we may call it—opposition is the primary ordering factor. The realm of Satan and his host of *daimonia* or "unclean spirits" stands over against the realm of God and of the good, until at last the one will destroy the other. The conflict between these two realms becomes a structuring theme in the Synoptic Gospels, and thus the stories of Jesus' exorcisms take a much more determinative part in shaping the narrative than their mere number would suggest. It is instructive in this respect to compare the centrality of the exorcisms in the Gospel of Mark with the relatively incidental reporting of exorcisms in Philostratus's *Life of Apollonius* some two centuries later. In Mark, Jesus is depicted as God's champion, who secretly but decisively opens the conclusive battle of the realm of God against the realm of Satan.

The author of Luke-Acts extends the picture to characterize the apostolic mission of the post-Easter church as well. Satan's "fall" is revealed in the successive humiliation of his allies, the demons and the magicians. The cases of Simon Magus and the unfortunate sons of Sceva have already been mentioned. Paul's effective curse on Elymas the Magus, ending the latter's rivalry in the court of Sergius Paulus (Acts 13:4–12), is a further example, along with Paul's exorcism of the *pythōn*-spirit from the slave girl in Philippi (ruining her masters' fortune-telling business, 16:16–21), and the spontaneous burning of magical scrolls by converts (worth fifty thousand silver coins! 19:18–19).[11]

It was Luke, too, who added a significant element to the interpretation of the Beelzebul story by inserting at the end of the pericope the separate saying, "Whoever is not with me is against me, and whoever does not gather with me scatters" (Luke 11:23). To the two opposing camps of the unseen world corresponds a radical division in the human world. It is here that we begin to see the moral implications of the divided, apocalyptic universe. The choices people make, the things they do or leave undone, may place them on the wrong side of that great divide. They may find themselves allied with the crumbling kingdom of Satan rather than with the kingdom of God. In the encyclical letter we call Ephesians, we get a glimpse of the way, in the Pauline churches, the images of this cosmic warfare could be rather dramatically superimposed upon the routine admonitions about ordered life in a household: "Finally, find your strength in the Lord, in his mighty power. Put on the full armour provided by God, so that you may be able to stand firm against the stratagems of the devil. For our struggle is not against human foes, but against cosmic powers, against the authorities and potentates of this dark age, against the superhuman forces of evil in the heavenly realms" (Eph. 6:10–12, REB).

Choosing Sides

The struggle may not be "against human foes," in the eyes of Paul's disciple, but obviously once this dualist world view is firmly in mind, human foes will be seen as instruments of "the superhuman forces of evil in the heavenly realms." Indeed, demonic opposition becomes an all-purpose explanation for conflict—and a means for drawing boundaries between the insiders, the children of light, and the outsiders, the children of darkness. In similar language, the *Rule of the Community* at Qumran draws a sharp division between those who are governed by the Prince of Light (also known in other literature of the sect as Melchizedek, "King of Righteousness"), and those ruled by the Prince or Angel of Darkness (known elsewhere as the "King of Evil," *melki-resha'*). The initiate must vow to love the children of light and to hate the children of darkness. A scroll found in the same cave gives an elaborate scenario for "the War of the Sons of Light and the Sons of Darkness."[12]

In the Fourth Gospel those who do not "abide" among the believing disciples of Jesus are labeled as grandchildren of the devil, essentially "from below," incapable of understanding the one who is "from above" (John 8:31–47).[13] In the Apocalypse of John, the power and the economy of Rome are identified as instruments of the Great Serpent, the primeval enemy of God.

For the second-century apologist Justin, all opposition to the Christian movement—whether persecution, or failure of Jews to accept the Christians' reinterpretation of scripture, or resemblances between pagan cults, myths, or practices and Christian stories and sacraments, or the appearance of heretics like Marcion—all these stem from an elaborate plot by the demonic forces who are desperately trying to delay the destruction of their dominion.

Deviance within the group is likewise readily seen as a dangerous irruption of the evil power into the camp of the good. One who soils the purity of the community by an egregious violation of norms—the man in Corinth living with his father's wife, for example—must be "cleaned out" and "handed over to Satan" (1 Cor. 5). "Whoever sins is the devil's child" (1 John 3:8). "Firstborn of Satan" becomes a favorite epithet for a person deemed heretical (Polycarp 7:1; Irenaeus, *Adv. haer.* 3.3.4).[14]

Apocalyptic dualism thus provided for the early Christians a rich vocabulary of images with which to imagine a world divided between the few elect of God and the vast forces of evil arrayed against them. There were other sources as well, in their experience, in their milieu, and in the special traditions of the movement, for their varied and ominous sense of endangered existence. First there are the stories of conflict in Jesus' own life and, above all, of his shameful crucifixion, as remembered in the early Christian lore. These could serve as confirmation and comfort for Christians facing opposition: "If the world hates you, know that it has hated me before you. If you belonged to the world, the world would love its own, but because you do not belong to the world, but I have chosen you out of the world, for this reason the world hates you. Remember the word which I have told you: a slave is not greater than his master. If they persecuted me, they will also persecute you; if they kept my word, they will also keep yours" (John 15:18–20).

On the other hand, the corporate memory of Jesus' fate could serve as a warning for any who grew lax: "Now it is impossible, in regard to those who have once been enlightened, who have tasted of the heavenly gift and become partakers of holy spirit, and who have tasted the fair word of God and the powers of the age to come, once they have fallen away, to renew them unto repentance, as they crucify for themselves the Son of God and put him on ignominious display" (Heb. 6:4–6, trans. Attridge).[15]

Second, the opposition from relatives, former friends, and suspicious outsiders experienced by early converts sometimes made them feel that "the world" was opposed to all they believed: "You have spent time enough in the past doing what pagans like to do. You lived then in licence and debauchery, drunkenness, orgies and carousal, and the forbidden worship of idols. Now, when you no longer plunge with the pagans into all this reckless dissipation, they cannot understand it and start abusing you; but they will have to give account of themselves to him who is ready to pass judgement on the living and the dead" (1 Pet. 4:3–5, REB).

To express and to reinforce the sense of threat from human and super-human opponents, moreover, ancient rhetoric offered a rich treasury of invective. It was part of the arsenal of lawyers; Cicero's forensic speeches are full of delicious examples. It was regularly employed by the eloquent against any and all opponents, and doubtless the less literate population imitated the invective they heard in the agora or theater and added to it more homespun traditions of insult. It did not take long for Christians to develop their own vocabulary. Against outsiders: "Woe to you, scribes and Pharisees, hypo-crites! For you clean the outside of the cup and of the plate, but inside they are full of greed and self-indulgence. You blind Pharisee! first clean the inside of the cup, so that the outside may also become clean" (Matt. 13:25–26, NRSV). Or against other Christians—hear Paul against the more recent missionaries in Galatia: "The person disturbing you will bear the penalty, whoever it may be. . . . I wish those throwing you into confusion [about circumcision] would mutilate themselves" (Gal. 5:10,12). Or against the "superapostles" who followed him to Corinth: "Such people are fake apos-tles, underhanded workers, disguising themselves as apostles of Christ—and no wonder! For Satan himself puts on the disguise of an angel of light; it is no big thing if his ministers, too, disguise themselves as ministers of righteousness. Their end will fit their deeds!" (2 Cor. 11:13–15).[16]

The result was that Christians developed a fluent vocabulary for stig-matizing both outsiders and deviant members. The moral logic of a commu-nity that views the world under these images of dark and light, good and evil, brings pressure to withdraw, to separate, to guard the boundaries, to eye with suspicion the fellow within who is too different.

There were, however, some countervailing themes in the tradition. The spirit of the man turned over to Satan "for destruction of the flesh" is to be "saved in the day of the Lord" (1 Cor. 5:5). Paul argues for the reconciliation of another Corinthian who has insulted the apostle and has been censured by the church (2 Cor. 1–7). "Judge not, lest you be judged" is a maxim remembered (Matt. 7:1; Luke 6:37), as is Jesus' hyperbolic gnome about trying to remove the speck from the brother's eye while ignoring the timber in one's own (Matt. 7:3–5; Luke 6:41–42). The Letter of James elaborates the former: "Do not disparage one another, brothers. Whoever disparages his brother or judges his brother disparages the law and judges the law—but if you judge the law, you are not a doer of the law but its judge. There is One who is legislator and judge, who is able to save and to destroy. But you! Who are you to be judging your neighbor?" (James 4:11–12).

The apostrophe to the hypocritical judge is also used effectively in key places in the diatribal rhetoric of the Letter to Romans. Early on in the letter, after the long catalogue of the vices that characterize idolatrous society in typical Jewish and early Christian fashion (as we saw above), Paul abruptly shifts to the second person: "Therefore you, fellow, are without excuse, whoever you are, as you judge, for as you judge the other person you condemn yourself, since you the judge do the same things" (Rom. 2:1). At the end of the letter, when Paul recalls the dispute at Corinth over sacrificed meat (1 Cor. 8–10) and turns it into a generalized example for facing conflict within the Christian community, he uses the apostrophe again, to introduce the principal theme of this section: "You! Who are you to be judging someone else's house-slave? It is up to his own master whether he stands or falls—but he will stand, for the master is able to establish him" (14:4). A bit later, the apostrophe is repeated, with a significant modulation of the address and now explicit statement of the backing: "You! Why are you judging your brother? Or you, too! Why do you despise your brother? For we must all present ourselves before God's tribunal!" (14:10). Then the direct admonition: "Let us then no longer judge one another. Rather make this judgment: not to put an obstacle or stumbling block in the way of one's brother" (14:13).[17] Thus the notion of judgment could sometimes be used in Christian exhortation to curb divisiveness and excessive separatism.

Jesus' command to love one's enemies is remembered, wondered at, and commented on (Matt. 5:43–48; Luke 6:27–29). One of the ablest of the Christian apologists, Athenagoras, writing in 176 or 177, quotes the command as an epitome of the "God-taught" precepts "in which we are reared." To the effects of pagan philosophy, to which he applies a tradition of invective against sophists, Athenagoras contrasts the Christian life:

> And yet who of them have so purified their own hearts as to love their enemies instead of hating them; instead of upbraiding those who first insult them (which is certainly more usual), to bless them; and to pray for those who plot against them? On the contrary, they ever persist in delving into the evil mysteries of their sophistry, ever desirous of working some harm, making skill in oratory rather than proof by deeds their

business. With us, on the contrary, you will find unlettered people, tradesmen and old women, who, though unable to express in words the advantages of our teaching, demonstrate by acts the value of their principles. For they do not rehearse speeches; but evidence good deeds. When struck, they do not strike back; when robbed, they do not sue; to those who ask, they give, and they love their neighbors as themselves. (*Supplicatio* 11.2–3, trans. Richardson)[18]

Following the tradition of the cure of souls *(psychagōgia)* familiar in Greco-Roman philosophy, early Christian preachers urge their charges to examine themselves before accusing others. An eloquent example occurs in the second-century Valentinian *Gospel of Philip:* "As for us, let each of us dig down to the root of evil within us, and pull out the root from the heart. It will be plucked out if we recognize it. But if we do not recognize it, it takes root in our hearts and produces its fruits in our hearts. It masters us, and makes us its slaves. It takes us captive, so that we do what we do not want, and what we do not want to do, we do. It grows powerful because we have not recognized it" (83.18–29, trans. Pagels).[19]

Jesus' own example of accepting suffering without resistance is cited as a moral paradigm, for example in 1 Peter in the household rule addressed to slaves: "If you endure when you are beaten for doing wrong, what credit is that? But if you endure when you do right and suffer for it, you have God's approval. For to this you have been called, because Christ also suffered for you, leaving you an example, so that you should follow in his steps" (2:20–21, NRSV).

It is clear that the writer is not thinking only of slaves here, and further on he draws the general lesson for the whole community: "Beloved, do not be surprised at the fiery ordeal that is taking place among you to test you, as though something strange were happening to you. But rejoice insofar as you are sharing Christ's sufferings, so that you may also be glad and shout for joy when his glory is revealed. . . . Therefore, let those suffering in accordance with God's will entrust themselves to a faithful Creator, while continuing to do good" (4:12–13,19, NRSV).

Sin

There was no single Christian strategy for coping with the evil that they saw in the world and in themselves. There was, however, an overarching moral category for understanding the difficulties: the sense of sin. If the cosmic myths of unseen evil powers tend to place the source of moral wrong outside ourselves, the notion of sin locates the center of trouble squarely within the human story. At least that is true in the peculiarly Jewish understanding of sin that prevails in those circles of early Christianity which were destined to become dominant. The Christians and other Jews were not of course unique in supposing that among the faults one might commit, some were peculiarly religious. The notion that some kinds of offenses, accidents, or mistakes could render one religiously "dirty" and thus place oneself, one's family, and one's community at risk from the divine guardians of order was shared by Jews, Greeks, and Romans alike—and by most pre-industrial societies.[20] Such defilement might or might not have a moral dimension. Israel's monotheism, however, introduces a qualitative difference. Sin in Israel is rebellion against the one God who made all and to whom all are responsible. It is the violation of a relationship, a breach of contract, betrayal of a solemn treaty.

In the hymns of the Qumran community we see clearly how a dualist world view, with its ominous sense of dark powers controlling human lives, could be combined with a profound sense of sin, defined with respect to a closely bounded community and at the same time intensely personal.

> What is he that is born of woman
> in the midst of all Thy terrible [works]?
> He is but an edifice of dust,
> and a thing kneaded with water,
> whose beginning [is sinful iniquity],
> and shameful nakedness,
> [and a fount of uncleanness],
> and over whom a spirit of straying rules.
> If he is wicked he shall become [a sign for]ever,
> and a wonder to (every) generation,
> [and an object of horror to all] flesh.
> By thy goodness alone is man righteous
>
> . . . .
>
> [For Thou hast divided men] into good and evil
> in accordance with the spirits of their lot . . . .
> (1QH 13:14–17; 14:11–12)[21]

Here the ancient Deuteronomistic view of history, in which God straightforwardly rewards the nation when it keeps his rules but punishes it when it disobeys, is radicalized and personalized. Similar sentiments are expressed in the apocalypse that we call 4 *Ezra*, written around 100 C.E., reflecting on the horror of Jerusalem's destruction. The fictional seer and narrator complains that God has made the narrow way altogether too tight for any ordinary mortals to get through. The angelic interpreter replies:

> You are not a better judge than God, not wiser than the Most High. Better that many now living should perish, than that the law which God has set before them should be despised! God has given clear instructions to all when they come into this world, telling them how to attain life and how to avoid punishment. But the ungodly have refused to obey him; they have adopted their own futile devices and made deceit and wickedness their goal; they have even denied the existence of the Most High and ignored his ways. . . . Therefore, Ezra, it is emptiness for the empty, fullness for the full! (2 Esd. 7:19–25, REB)

"Emptiness for the empty, fullness for the full"—corollary and backing for the Jews' theocentric notion of sin was belief in a universal, final judgment. Again, "Ezra"'s angel speaks: "When the Most High was making the world and Adam and his descendants, he first of all planned *the judgement* and what goes with it" (7:70, REB, emphasis added).

It is remarkable how this belief in a universal judgment became standard among the earliest Christians, those who were previously gentiles as much as those who were Jews. It is present in the earliest Christian document we have, Paul's letter to the Thessalonians, and in his letter to the Roman groups Paul takes it to be axiomatic: "We shall all stand before God's tribunal" (Rom. 14:10, REB). Now there were certainly myths of postmortem judgment in other Mediterranean cultures besides the Jewish—the Orphic-Platonic stories and the classical Egyptian funerary ideology, for example—though it is hard to tell how widespread these were in popular belief of the Roman era. The Christian apologists recall the Platonic myths in trying to make their notions of the judgment intelligible. Justin, for example: "Plato similarly said that Rhadamanthus and Minos would punish the wicked who came before them. We say that this is what will happen, but at the hands of Christ—and to the same bodies, reunited with their souls, and destined for eternal punishment, not for a five-hundred-year period only, as he said (*1 Apol.* 8.4, trans. Richardson).[22]

Justin indicates important differences between the Christian expectation and the Platonic myth as it was popularly remembered; there were other significant differences as well. To some of those we shall return in chapter

10. For the present it suffices to see that the expectation of a universal judgment before the omnipotent deity powerfully supports a theocentric notion of sin and of both individual and communal responsibility. For that reason we often encounter the notion both in the context of moral exhortations addressed to Christians and in apologies concerned to exhibit the uprightness of Christian behavior.

The subjective corollary of the belief in a final judgment was the obligation laid on the individual to repent. The climax of the speech that the author of Acts places in Paul's mouth when he addresses the philosophers and leaders of Athens sums up the connection succinctly: "So, overlooking the times of ignorance, God now commands all people everywhere to repent, because he has set a day on which he will judge the human world in righteousness by a man he has designated, and he has given a pledge of that to everyone by raising him from the dead" (Acts 17:30–31).

"Repentance from dead works," according to the Letter to Hebrews, belonged to the "foundation" teachings, along with "faith in God, the doctrine of baptisms and laying on of hands, resurrection of the dead and eternal judgment" (Heb. 6:1–2). The passage that follows these verses, quoted above, declares that it is impossible "to renew . . . unto repentance" those who, once enlightened, fall away (vv. 4–6). On the basis of this passage, histories of Christian doctrine often assert as the standard teaching of the earliest churches that no repentance was possible for serious sins after baptism. The *Shepherd of Hermas,* according to this view, then makes the exception of a single repentance allowed the baptized. This, however, is far too schematic a picture of the development of Christian belief, shaped too much by the third-century controversies over restoration of the lapsed at the time of the Decian persecutions and, even more, by Reformation controversies over the medieval doctrine and practice of penance. Appeals for repentance are frequent in early Christian admonitions, and the threat of the judgment often hovers over them. Typical is the letter of Rome to Corinth, urging the rebellious younger members of the latter church to restore the elders they have supplanted: "Let us go through all the generations [of Israel recorded in the Bible] and learn that in generation after generation the Sovereign gave place for repentance to those who were willing to turn to him" (1 Clem. 7:5).

The *Shepherd of Hermas* is an important document for discovering other sides of Christian life at Rome, perhaps contemporary with 1 *Clement,* though some would put it later. Repentance is its central concern; the angel sent to deliver revelations to Hermas, whose disguise as a shepherd gives the work its title, declares, "I am in charge of repentance and to all who repent I give understanding" (30.2 [*Mand.* 4.2.2]). The book abounds with images of building (a great tower made of a variety of stones, each with its own metaphorical reference) and of purity (washing, hewing of stones, scenes of almost ribald sexual temptation and abstention). Although everything else we know of Christianity at Rome in the first two centuries suggests disparate groups, various small house-meetings, and several competing "schools" attached to individual teachers,[23] Hermas's images imply a remarkably unified and institutional conception of the church. The first heavenly figure introduced to Hermas, who at first he thinks is the Sibyl, is identified as the Church personified. Repentance here is seen as the means for purifying and uniting the church. There are hints that Hermas has previously held some position of leadership from which he has been removed, and that he may hope to be "restored to [his] office" (66.6 [*Sim.* 7.6]).[24] Hermas tells us a few tantalizing things about his personal life. He is a former slave; manumitted, he has become a tradesman, not always successfully. Curiously, he begins his narrative with the report of an encounter with his former owner, a woman named Rhoda. He sees her bathing in the Tiber and helps her out of the water. Although he insists that his thoughts were pure, doubt is cast on his innocence by two subsequent visions. In the first, Rhoda herself appears in heaven, "taken up to accuse you of your sins before the Lord" (1.5 [*Vis.* 1.1.5], trans. Lake). Then the "aged lady," who turns out to be the Church, confirms the charge: "but for all that the thought did enter your heart concerning her" (2.4 [*Vis.* 1.2.4]). The heavenly lady goes on to assure him, however, that it was not for this that God was angry, but "in order that you should convert your family, which has sinned against the Lord, and against you their parents" (3.1 [*Vis.* 1.3.1]).

Hermas is not the most adroit of writers, and the connections which ought to be made among the various themes of his work are not always apparent. Some things seem clear, however. Hermas presents his own anxiety (2.1 [*Vis.* 1.2.1]) and his failure to manage his household properly (3.1 [*Vis.* 1.3.1]) as paradigms of difficulties facing the Christian community in Rome, and especially its leadership. The affair of Rhoda does not reappear, though there are a few sexual allusions in the later visions. The most winsome of these is the account of the Shepherd leaving Hermas in the hands of twelve female virgins, who insist that Hermas "sleep with us as a brother, not as a man." They spend the night kissing, dancing, and praying

(88.1–9 [*Sim.* 9.11]); only later do Hermas and the reader learn that the maidens are really "holy spirits," and also virtues (90.2 [*Sim.* 9.13.2]; 92.1–2 [*Sim.* 9.15.1–2]). Sexual sins are thus not the issue for Hermas, but sex serves by synecdoche to represent the disturbances of household management and church unity that, in the visions of this fairly representative figure among the Roman Christians, beset the church.

Evil in the Commonplace

Much of the talk of sin and judgment must have seemed quite foreign and odd to the new convert. What was there in all this strange mythology that caught the interest and attracted the desire of the inquirer? Perhaps our imagined convert will have found some resonance between these images and the ways in which she or he confronted evil in the commonplaces of life. Multiple contingencies beset all human life, and people in antiquity were perhaps more constantly aware of them than we. Lifespans were, on average, short. A large proportion of children died before adolescence; a great many women died in childbirth. Famines occurred periodically, and epidemic diseases or great fires often swept through cities. Many parts of the Mediterranean basin were—and are—subject to earthquake. Travel was dangerous; violent crime was not infrequent on the highways or on city streets. The poor and the weak had few defenses against the powerful. When we read the dream manuals and astrological handbooks, we see at once in the questions people were anxious to ask the fortune-teller a pervasive awareness of life's vulnerability. No wonder Luck became a deity widely worshipped and appeased.

Martha Nussbaum has shown how the philosophical tradition, especially that of the Platonists and the Stoics, strove to secure the moral life against the accidents of fate—at too high a cost, she thinks, in terms of community and of wholeness. She finds Aristotle more realistic and more hopeful.[25] The philosophers belonged to an elite that had a number of resources for dealing with bad luck. Besides the austere philosophical therapy that undertook by mental training to transcend luck, there were more practical defenses, not always acknowledged. Having money and power helped. Belonging to a circle of friends with similar values and similar means helped, too. Friendship had to be constantly cultivated, however, for competition was a pervasive value, which had to be kept in check if mutual support was to survive.

But the elites were not well represented in the early Christian groups.

How did ordinary folk cope with the fragility of existence, with the evil that might fall on anyone any day? Among the common ways, two stand out: they could put themselves under the protection of strong patrons, and they could resort to magic. The magicians and the fortune-tellers were professionals who helped people ward off or negotiate with evil, sometimes to flirt with it. In their technical handbooks, we come closest to seeing the fears and the ambitions of those people who are silent in the literature and in the public affairs of antiquity.

A browse through the published collection of the magical papyri suggests that people resorted to magic with two chief ends in view.[26] The first was to acquire and then to protect scarce and fragile goods. The second was to get even with an enemy or a rival. Acquisitiveness and envy: perhaps these are universal human characteristics. Certainly they arise persistently in a limited-goods society, a zero-sum game in which if you win, I lose, and that is the way economic historians would characterize the typical perceptions of people in the Roman Empire. Small wonder that spells or amulets against the Evil Eye are ubiquitous in Mediterranean societies—in antiquity and even to the present day. A casual compliment from a stranger, in a Turkish village or in rural Italy—"What a beautiful child!" or the like—may bring a grimace of fear as readily as a smile, and the apotropaic "Mash' Allah," in the one region, or the gesture of the cross in the other. Mosaics from the dining rooms of wealthy families in such ancient towns as Antioch often included depictions of an eye attacked by sharp, pointed, or stinging things; one portrays a grotesque, ithyphallic dwarf with the motto *kai su*, "You, too!" perhaps implying "The same to you," another charm to ward off the envious eye.[27]

How did Christians cope with the anxieties of acquistion and envy? For the most part, they doubtless continued to use the same strategies they had used before their conversions; the magical papyri themselves offer considerable evidence for Christian magic. A new weapon in the arsenal of apotropaic gestures against the Evil Eye suggested itself in the sign of the cross; attested at least as early as the beginning of the third century to ward off demons— doubly effective if you blew into your fist before the gesture, the breath's moisture evoking the power of baptism.[28]

Christians had weapons not only against the Evil Eye, of course, but against the whole host of ghosts and demons and the wiles of sorcery to which ordinary life seemed so vulnerable. We have already considered the stories of Christian exorcisms, which fill our literature. Ignatius asserts that at the incarnation, specifically at the appearance of the miraculous star heralding Jesus' birth, "thence was destroyed all magic, and every bond [perhaps meaning "enchantment"] vanished; evil's ignorance was abolished, the old kingdom perished . . . " *(Eph.* 19:3, trans. Schoedel).[29] Other leaders, too, sought to identify magical practices with the realm of Satan, and to distinguish them from Christian miracles; we recall the confrontations in the Book of Acts and in the later apocryphal Acts.[30] Magic *(mageia, pharmakeia)* is among the vices that characterize the way of death or darkness in the *Didache* (5:1) and the *Epistle of Barnabas* (20:1), but perhaps not all Christians saw it that way; one person's magic is another's miracle. In the Roman rite of baptism by the end of the second century, an elaborate series of exorcisms and the renunciation of Satan and all his pomp fenced off the catechumen's entry into the Christian community.[31] In this way the church sought to establish itself as a demon-free zone, a realm of purity in an evil world. The sign of the cross, the breath's moisture of baptism could at any moment of peril remind the Christian of that zone of safety.

The central images of the Christian story, however, suggested more unusual responses. There was a strong tradition, anchored in words attributed to Jesus himself, of rejecting revenge. Rather, following the model of Jesus, one should love one's enemies. The paraenetic elaboration of this tradition, not yet attributed to Jesus, in Paul's letter to the Romans 12:14–21 rather pointedly expresses the sublimation of vengeance into nonretaliation: "Do not seek revenge, but leave a place for divine retribution; for there is a text which reads, 'Vengeance is mine, says the Lord, I will repay.' But there is another text: 'If your enemy is hungry, feed him; if he is thirsty, give him a drink; by doing this you will heap live coals on his head.' Do not let evil conquer you, but use good to conquer evil" (vv. 19–20).

Within the Christian groups, practical means for arbitration of disputes are sought: "If your brother sins," there are several steps to be taken, according to Matt. 18:15–18. It is disgraceful, Paul chides the Corinthian Christians, for disputes between Christians over material matters *(biōtika)* to be taken before pagan judges; to have a lawsuit at all was already a defeat (1 Cor. 6:1–11).

As for the acquisitiveness that we find so brazenly expressed in magical spells, Christian moral discourse tends to stigmatize it as *pleonexia,* greed. Money-lovers, the *philargyroi,* are opponents—the Pharisees in Luke, the rich who oppress in James; love of money is the root of evil for the Pastor (1 Tim. 6:10) and for Polycarp (*Philad.* 4:1), as for many non-Christian moralists.[32] Halvor Moxnes has argued that Luke adopts the perspective of "the moral economy of the peasant."[33] Yet, as William Countryman has shown, Christian views about the morality of wealth were marked from the beginning by "contradictions and accommodations."[34] Luke may elevate and idealize the moral economy of the peasant, but he knows well that the spread of Christianity was dependent from the beginning upon the protection and support of people with greater wealth and higher status than any peasant, and that its growth was not among peasants in the countryside but among the varied populations of the cities. The rejection of acquisition altogether, which would become a hallmark of some ascetic circles of Christianity, was possible only in very special circumstances.

At least potentially, however, the developing Christian movement had some very specific assistance to offer in the economy of the weak. To travelers in a dangerous world, it offered a network of hospitality among "brothers and sisters." To vulnerable people it offered the support of small, intensely connected groups, mutual care, mutual admonition, mutual assistance. With few exceptions it did not try to dismantle the common Greco-Roman structures of patronage, friendship, and affiliation, but worked out its own special variations on those patterns.

The experience of evil—harm or the dread of it, finitude, frustration—is shared by all people on earth. In the Greco-Roman world there were abundant manifestations of evil, and abundant, too, were the attempts to name, deflect, and control the multifarious bad things that might happen to one or that one might be tempted to *do*. Christianity, drawing upon the riches of Israel's scriptures, traditions, and imagination, named and systematized the sense of evil. Evil was, as it were, organized and regularized. Furthermore, at the center of their beliefs and symbolism, the Christians were given an immense sign of horror, of wrong and wickedness: the cross of Jesus Christ. This symbol they undertook to invest with a valence quite the opposite of its commonsense associations. It became for them the means of overcoming evil and the source of ineffable good. With such a paradoxical symbol at the generative center of their religious world view, the moral landscape of the Christians was never going to be simple.

CHAPTER 8

The Body as Sign and Problem

❖ ❖ ❖ ❖ ❖ ❖ ❖ ❖ ❖ ❖

For thoughtful moralists in antiquity, the root of many of our moral dilemmas seemed to lie in the fact that we inhabit bodies—or, as the Platonists used to say, we are imprisoned or buried in bodies. Philo, even though he is a Jew, is quite typical of such moralists when he represents the struggle for virtue, to which every good person is called, as a contest, in its simplest terms, between soul (or mind) and body. Philo finds this struggle inscribed on nearly every page of the Pentateuch, contrary to what most readers would think the text's plain sense. For example, the verse "But Er, Judah's firstborn, was wicked in the sight of the Lord, and the Lord put him to death" (Gen. 38:7, NRSV) evokes this explanation: "Even without a public indictment, God knows Er to be evil and puts him to death. For God is not ignorant of the fact that our leather burden (for 'Er' means 'leather'), the body, is evil, conspirator against the soul, a corpse, eternally dead" (*Allegorical Interpretation of the Laws* 3.69).

We may feel that Philo has drunk too deeply from the cup of Middle Platonism to be representative. Not everyone, even among the philosophers, viewed the body so negatively. The Stoic Musonius Rufus, for example, urges hard exercise for body as well as for mind, "since it so happens that the human being is not soul alone, nor body alone, but a kind of synthesis of the two." Still, he acknowledges that the soul, being the "better part," should receive first priority (fragment 6 in Lutz's translation). Some Stoics, less doctrinally consistent than Musonius perhaps, were almost as negative as Philo in their strictures against the body. It is hard to find among the philosophers of the Roman period the kind of matter-of-factness about the body that Aristotle had shown in an earlier era.

The major problems with the body were twofold. On the one hand, it was subject to contingencies of all sorts. It was forever getting sick or hurt; it needed constantly to be supplied with food, drink, and sleep; it could be tortured, imprisoned, or put to death. On the other hand, it seemed to have, as some said, a mind of its own: welling up out of it came drives and passions that could overwhelm the reason and sweep away prudent judgment.

We cannot really say to what extent ordinary people shared the asceticism that so many of the intellectuals affected. If they went to the synagogue, they might well hear homilies along the lines of Philo's expositions; if they joined the throngs in the theater to hear a popular orator, they might well get much of the same, with the allegories on Homer instead of Moses. For most people, however, life probably seemed stark enough without conscious asceticism, and the body sufficiently constrained by the struggle to survive, without engaging in high-minded attempts to transcend it, even if one had leisure for that. Certainly the manuals of the fortune-tellers and magicians give little hint that a philosophical dualism played much part in their clients' attempts to come to terms with the body's dangers and desires.

Christianity, at a time a little later than the period we are considering, democratized asceticism. The church's formal leaders and literary spokesmen more and more were drawn from those same educated elites who had espoused a philosophical dualism, but now they embodied it ostentatiously in their own renunciatory practice. And quite ordinary people could, with only their own bodies as their material and instruments, become heroes of the faith by martyrdom or extravagant renunciation of food, comfort, and sex. Asceticism became, as Peter Brown remarks, a career open to the talented.[1] These later developments Brown has catalogued with remarkable sympathy and attention to detail, often noting how difficult it is to determine exactly how overt enthusiasm for the ascetic life affected "the silent majority" of Christians who married, raised children, and preserved households, upon whom the survival and welfare of the church depended. The picture is already complicated and often unclear in the earliest documents we possess. Those documents offer nothing like the wealth of direct evidence that the later centuries provide, but they do show us some of the ways the Christians of the first two centuries thought with and about their bodies.

Paul

The letters of Paul are a good place to begin—not because we could imagine him to be typical of first-century Christian thinkers, and certainly not because anyone thinks his writings simple, clear, or consistent. He is, however, the earliest of the Christian writers whose works survive, and surely one of the most interesting. From the many texts that would give us some insight into Paul's thinking about the body, a few samples will indicate the main outlines. Only the first has to do with sex.

In 1 Cor. 6:12, as several times in this letter, Paul adopts the diatribal style used often in philosophical schools to portray mistaken inferences, opposing views, or students' typical failings and resistances.[2] He imagines an interlocutor responding to his previous remarks with the slogan *panta moi exestin*, "All things are permitted me." This is a phrase that is commonly applied in the political and moral rhetoric of the day to those who stand above ordinary constraints—either because they exercise real political and social power or because they have attained the inner freedom that especially Stoics and Cynics cherished. It was a commonplace of moral discourse that such freedom must accept self-limitation for the sake of the community. For example, Dio Chrysostom twice, in discussing ideal kingship, says, "Who must exercise self-control more rigorously than one to whom all things are permitted?" (*Or.* 3.10; 62.3). The Stoics taught that true wisdom conferred that kind of royal freedom on an individual, and Paul has sarcastically applied similar language to those in Corinth who boasted about the special wisdom they received from "their" apostles: "Without us you have begun to reign as kings" (1 Cor. 4:8). He will repeat the "All things are permitted" tag in chapter 10, where he responds to those who, knowing that "idols" are nothing, think eating sacrificial meat or accepting dinner invitations to pagan shrines or homes are matters of no consequence. All through this letter, in fact, Paul keeps returning to the question of how the freedom given to Christians is to be exercised without harming the purity and cohesion of the Christian community and the welfare of Christians who lack power and knowledge. Paul's answers to the slogan remain at first within the common usage: Not all things are beneficial; freedom that leads to being dominated by something defeats itself; not all things build up the community.

Then, however, he imagines his interlocutor saying something else: "Foods are for the stomach and the stomach for foods; God will after all destroy both" (v. 13a). Here is a specifically theological claim: our choices about bodily functions are matters of indifference because God brings them to an end. "Yes," says Paul, "but *the body* is not for *porneia* but for the Lord, and the Lord for the body; God raised the Lord and he will also raise us through his power" (vv. 13b–14). This is a quite remarkable claim. Paul wants his audience to understand that God, by raising Jesus bodily from the dead and promising thereby the resurrection at the end of all our bodies, albeit in a transformed, "spiritual" state (1 Cor. 15), lays claim on the body. Paul backs this claim with a direct, earthy example and two metaphors. One might entertain the notion that sin is essentially "outside the body" (v. 18), but at least in case of *porneia* in its strict sense, prostitution, that assertion is absurd. Union with the prostitute renders the body unfit, first, for its spiritual union with the Lord (v. 17) and, second, as a shrine of the Holy Spirit (v. 19). Finally Paul likens the Christian life, as he often does, to slavery, summing up: "You have been bought at a price; so glorify God in [or with] your bodies" (v. 20).

The concluding maxim makes a point very like the one that introduces the "gnomic anthology" epitomizing the moral implications of Paul's gospel for the Roman Christians:[3] "I urge you, then, brothers, through the mercies of God to offer up your bodies as a sacrifice, living, holy, pleasing to God, your rational service" (Rom. 12:1). The morality exemplified in what follows cannot then be based on a simple opposition between body and soul. Though Paul often sets "flesh" against "spirit," he usually avoids equating "flesh" with "body."[4] The human predicament is the result not of the limitations of physical existence, but of sin.

Paul is reasonably consistent on this point. For example, in the difficult passage 2 Cor. 5:1–10, it is clear from the context that Paul is relativizing empirical circumstances (4:7–15) and at the same time still holding to the belief that what is done "in the body" is morally significant. The "catalogue of circumstances" that Paul has so rhetorically constructed in the previous chapter would be worthy of a Seneca or a Musonius, and the sentiments are very similar to those the Stoics expressed. Like the heroic wise man, Paul is "afflicted in every way, but not crushed; perplexed, but not driven to despair; persecuted, but not forsaken; struck down, but not destroyed" (4:8–9, NRSV). Then, however, a unique antithesis: "At all times carrying about the death and decay [nekrōsis] of Jesus in the body, in order that the life of Jesus may also become visible in our body" (v. 10).[5] The model of Christ's crucifixion and resurrection entails for Paul a radical inversion of the values of everyday common sense. Yet the inversion is not simply an assertion of the superiority of the wise person's rational choice to the chance of circumstance, nor is it grounded in an anthropological dualism that sets mind or spirit against the body. In the saving act of Jesus and in the apostle's behavioral analogue to that act, the body is essential. "For we all must appear before the tribunal of Christ, in order that each may receive the reward appropriate to what we have done through the body, whether good or bad" (5:10).

Contemplating the end of his own life, as Paul does in his letter to the Philippians, a Philo or an Epictetus might have exalted the free choice exercised by the wise man's rational self, transcending whatever might happen to the body. Paul uses much the same kind of language, but the ultimate point is different. He expects that he will not be put to shame in the outcome of his trial but will exercise *parrhēsia*, boldness of speech, and thus "Christ will be magnified *in my body*, either by life or by death" (Phil. 1:20, emphasis added).

Before leaving Paul, we should quickly take note of one other example of the way a figure of the body commonly used by popular moral philosophy receives a different nuance when Paul colors it with reminders of Jesus' crucified and risen body. There is hardly a political metaphor more well worn than the representation of the commonwealth as a body in which the lowly peasant is as surely a "member" or "limb," though only as a foot or hand, as the nobility, who are more visible as "head" or "eyes." Socially and politically the figure is inherently conservative; any *stasis* in the community is as abhorrent, as unthinkable, as would be a rebellion of one's feet against the head.

In spite of the obfuscatory talk about Paul's "mystical realism" that fills the commentaries on 1 Cor. 12, his use of the figure is not materially different from the use by Cicero or Seneca or Plutarch. It is still a metaphor, it is still political, it is still conservative. However, what is to be conserved is not the status quo of an imperial regime, but the internal order of a cult community, in which leadership roles are thought to be "gifts" by the Spirit and consequently may come to people who do not belong to the levels of society that ordinarily are thought to be the heads and eyes. In fact, Paul warns the charismatics that they ought to give more recognition to people like Stephanas who are, at least for these groups, of the patronal class, and on whose benefactions the Christian meetings depend (1 Cor. 16:15–16). On the whole, however, he approves the "charismatic" governance of the community, but not the competition for new status within it made possible by the new talents raised up by the Spirit. The crucifixion and resurrection of Jesus' body now become a master metaphor infecting the commonplace political one. The effects of this new metaphor are implicit in 1 Cor. 12, in the form of the care for each other that is the duty of the individual "limbs" of the body. They become explicit elsewhere, for example in Paul's use of the

Christ-hymn in his paraenesis of Phil. 2 and in his discussion of the obligation of the more powerful and knowledgeable members of the community for those whom they regard as "weak" (1 Cor. 8–10; Rom. 14–15).[6]

The Thomas Tradition

For Paul, the moral sense of the body was sharply modified at certain key points by the tradition of Jesus' physical death and bodily resurrection. For some Christians, however, the triumph of Jesus was construed as a victory over the body, and the moral imperative for every Christian was to engage in a relentless warfare against the material and demonic world that confronted one most dangerously in one's own body. Some of the most vivid depictions of this struggle are to be found in the traditions that grew up around the name of the apostle Judas, known as Didymus or Thomas, regarded in this tradition as the twin of Jesus. We have already encountered these ascetic traditions in chapter 4, in our discussion of various early Christian attitudes toward the world. These traditions were first shaped, it seems, in eastern Syria, probably around Edessa, and we know them best from the *Gospel of Thomas*, the *Acts of Thomas*, and the *Book of Thomas the Contender*. The central elements of the tradition were apparently in place by the middle of the second century; some scholars think they can be traced well back into the first. Though these documents have often been described as "Gnostic" or else as "Encratite" in the sense used by ancient heresiologists, more recent studies suggest a more fluid situation in the earlier period. Bentley Layton writes, "Since there is nothing especially sectarian about the Thomas scripture, it must have been part of the normal canon of scripture read by Mesopotamian Christians in the second and early third centuries. It would have been read along with works such as the *Odes of Solomon* and Tatian's *Harmony* . . . ."[7]

As William Countryman has pointed out in his original discussion of early Christian sexual ethics, one of the ways in which religions traditionally use bodily symbols to create an orderly world of meaning and moral expectations is by rules about purity.[8] In the *Gospel of Thomas*, the disciples ask Jesus explicitly about purity rules, and receive at first an oblique reply: " 'Do you want us to fast? And how shall we pray? Shall we give alms? And what kind of diet shall we follow?' " Jesus said, " 'Do not lie, and do not do what you hate. For all things are disclosed before heaven' " (*GTh* 6 [33:15–21], trans. Layton).

In a parallel saying, the question is unexpressed, and the answer is sharper: " 'If you fast, you will acquire a sin, and if you pray, you will be condemned, and if you give alms, it is evil that you will do to your spirits. And when you go into any land and travel in the country places, when they receive you eat whatever they serve to you. Heal those among them who are sick. For nothing that enters your mouth will defile you. Rather, it is precisely what comes out of your mouth that will defile you' " (14 [34:14–26]; compare saying 104).

We know that Syrian Christianity sought to separate itself from Jewish communities, sometimes in very sharp polemics, and the antipurity sayings may represent an early stage of that separation. These sayings contrast concern for "religious" purity with moral action: "Do not lie, and do not do what you hate." "Heal the sick." And guard one's speech, for "what comes out of your mouth . . . will defile you." In fact, however, the Thomas tradition insists on a more thoroughgoing purity: "If you do not fast with respect to the world [Layton translates, "If you do not abstain from the world"], you will not find the kingdom of God" (27, following the Greek fragment in Oxyrhynchus papyrus 1.4–8).

How does one "abstain from the world"? In the Thomas tradition, as we saw in chapter 4, the goal is to disconnect oneself from the material world and its social structures in every possible way. "Jesus said, 'Whoever has become acquainted with the world has found the body [or, in another version of the same saying, "a corpse"], and the world is not worthy of the one who has found the body' " (80 [47:12]; compare saying 56). Again, "Wretched is the body that depends upon a body. And wretched is the soul that depends upon these two" (87 [48:4–6]; compare 112). Or: "Jesus said, 'It is amazing if it was for the spirit that flesh came into existence. And it is amazing indeed if spirit [came into existence] for the sake of the body. But as for me, I am amazed at how this great wealth has come to dwell in this poverty' " (29 [38:31–34]).

The last-quoted saying reveals the symbolic counterpart to the Thomas ethos of bodily renunciation: the true self has its origin in another world, a realm of light and truth. Several of the sayings of the *Gospel of Thomas* allude to the myth of the soul—for example, 49: "Blessed are those who are solitary and superior, for you will find the kingdom: for since you come from it you shall return to it." The myth is presented in allegorical form in the famous "Hymn of the Pearl" that is incorporated into the *Acts of Thomas*, and it echoes in Thomas's speech at the time of his martyrdom

(*Acts of Thomas* 159–69). Often regarded as "Gnostic," the Thomas version of the myth is only, as Layton says, "an uncomplicated Hellenistic myth of the divine origins of the self," familiar in the schools of Platonism and Pythagoreanism and in much popular thought. Philo, for example, finds the self's journey from its origin as the allegorical meaning of such biblical stories as Abraham's migration, the exodus, the crossing of the Red Sea, and Moses' ascent of Mt. Sinai, but he derives from it a far less ascetic ethic than does the school of Thomas.[9]

For the Thomas school, sex and its consequences, the entanglements of family life and household responsibilities, are the most dangerous snares of the world. "If you abandon this filthy intercourse," says Jesus to a royal couple on the eve of their wedding, "you become holy temples, pure and free from afflictions and pains both manifest and hidden, and you will not be girt about with cares for life and for children, the end of which is destruction" (*Acts of Thomas* 12, trans. Bornkamm and Wilson[10]). Here and elsewhere in the narrative, all "intercourse for production of children" (*koinōnia tēs paidopoiias*, Bonnet 203.19) is condemned, and that is clearly the ideal of the Thomas tradition, though in some of the homilies inserted into the narratives about baptism of converts, it is only adultery *(moicheia)* that counts as "the worst of all evils" (175.9; 181.15; 168.3,9; compare 160.13). The *Book of Thomas* declares that bodies are no different from "domestic animals," produced like animals by sexual intercourse and, like animals, mutable and perishing (138:39–139:11; compare 141:5–11). Salvation is escape from this flesh: "Indeed, if you leave the labors and passions of the body, you will receive repose from him who is good" (*Book of Thomas* 145:12–13, trans. Layton).[11]

The Valentinians

Although Valentinus seems to have known and used elements of the Thomas tradition, we do not find in the surviving representatives of Valentinian views the same animosity toward the body that is so typical of the Thomas documents. The ideal of Valentinus and his followers seems rather to have been a sublime indifference to the body, to be gained by acquiring the knowledge that it, like all the rest of the material world, is unreal. Valentinus whimsically imagined that Jesus' continence was so perfect that even though he ate and drank, he did not defecate.[12] The troubles of the body are like the terrors of a nightmare; those who have gained *gnōsis* "put them away like a dream in the night, and deem acquaintance [gnōsis] of the father to be the light" (Gospel of Truth 30:2, trans. Layton). Valentinus could almost agree with Prospero that "we are such stuff as dreams are made on," except that "we" the spiritual elect cannot be identified with those bodies that dissolve with the dawn of knowledge.

Death for the Valentinians cannot then be so much an enemy to be conquered as an illusion to be exposed. The Valentinian Treatise on Resurrection accordingly rejects the ordinary Christian arguments that the body itself must be raised to fulfill God's providence. Because the Valentinians have accepted the Gnostic inversion of the Genesis stories, in which the "forming" of Adam's body is the work of an ignorant and inferior creator of the illusory world, those arguments fail. Instead, the resurrection must be understood as the replacement of illusion by truth: "It [resurrection] is not an apparition; rather, it is something real. Instead, one ought to maintain that the world is an apparition, rather than resurrection, which became possible through our lord, the savior, Jesus the kind" (48:12–15).

So, too, the reality of Jesus' crucifixion, which is important in Valentinus's teachings, is to be found only in its figuring a higher truth: "Since the father of the entirety is invisible—and the entirety derives from him, from whom every way emanated—Jesus appeared, wrapped himself in that document ["the living book of the living, which is written in the father's thought and intellect," 19:34], was nailed to a piece of wood, and published the father's edict upon the cross" (Gospel of Truth 20:19–26).

The Valentinians proudly claimed to stand in the tradition of Paul, and this passage echoes an early disciple of Paul, the author in Paul's name of the Letter to Colossians (2:14). Paul did, as we have seen, boldly exploit the metaphorical potential of the crucifixion story, and Valentinus does indeed stand in that tradition. Yet at this point we see how a different metaphysics transforms the metaphor in quite another way, resulting in a moral emptying of the body's significance, an interpretation altogether foreign to Paul.

The Female Body: Power and Peril

The Valentinians may have thought the body an illusion, but that belief did not inhibit their exploiting its symbolic potential. Occasionally their allegories permit us to glimpse some of the underlying perceptions of the body that they shared with others of their time. That is especially true of certain notions of the female body and its processes that seem to most modern readers quite odd. For example, some of the Valentinians used sexual imagery to speak of the rebirth and liberation from fate that, they said, occurred when baptism was joined with *gnōsis:* "So long as the seed is still unformed, . . . it is a child of the female. But when it is formed, it is changed into a man and becomes a son of the bridegroom. No longer is it weak and subjected to the cosmic [powers], visible and invisible, but, having become a man, it becomes a male fruit."[13]

This curious argument evidently depends on one of the several views held by various people in antiquity on the subject of reproduction and the differentiation of the sexes. Some believed, with Aristotle, that the formation of the embryo was entirely the work of the male semen, the woman providing only "matter," that is, blood. Others thought both male and female produced "seed," which mingled to produce a foetus. Medical writers argued over the source of the seed, whether the blood alone, or a combination of blood and the breath or life-force *(pneuma)*, or substance from the brain and spinal marrow, or an essence drawn from all parts of the body.[14] The Valentinian allegory assumes the two-seed theory; it also shares the conviction of many (male) writers that the female semen was inferior to the male. The Latin Epicurean Lucretius (first century B.C.E.) presents a more neutral version of the two-seed theory: "In the intermingling of seed it may happen that the woman by a sudden effort overmasters the power of the man and takes control of it. Then children are conceived of the maternal seed and take after their mother. Correspondingly children may be conceived of the paternal seed and take after their father. The children in whom you see a two-sided likeness, combining features of both parents, are products alike of their father's body and their mother's blood. At their making the seeds that course through the limbs under the impulse of Venus were dashed together by the collusion of mutual passion in which neither party was master or mastered."[15]

One more quotation from a Valentinian source will make a little plainer that group's peculiar representations of "male" and "female" and thus help us to get behind their metaphors to the common, underlying perceptions of the female body:

> By the statement "In the image of God he created them, male and female he created them" (Gen. 1:27) the Valentinians say that the finest production of Sophia is meant, of which the male denotes the "election," and the female the "calling." And the male [beings] they call angelic, while the female are themselves, the superior seed. So also in the case of

Adam: the male remained in him, but the entire female seed was taken from him and became Eve, from whom the female beings [derive], as do the males from him [Adam]. The males were drawn together with the Logos, but the female, having become male, unites itself with the angels and enters into the Pleroma [the "fullness" of divine being]. Therefore it is said that the woman is changed into a man and the Church here below into angels."[16]

What is peculiarly Valentinian here is the representation of the inner self of the redeemable person as "female" and of its angelic alter ego or image as "male." Union of the two, restoring the primal, lost unity of the mythic beginnings, is the climactic step in the process of salvation as the Valentinians understand it. These special features of the Valentinian myth need not concern us further at this point. Two features of this symbolic picture, however, point to notions more widely held: the automatic identification of the "male" with the superior realm of being, and the startling assertion that the female not only unites with the male but may become male.

When the Valentinian writer identifies the higher part of the restored self with the male, he follows a philosophical commonplace. The only surprising thing about this particular passage is that the "female" after all is to be saved—by becoming "male." Ancient philosophical writers routinely equate maleness with ideas, reason, articulate speech, self-control, and the like, the female with emotion, physical drives, the senses, passion, and so on. A philosophical awakening could thus be represented as a person's ceasing to act and think in a "womanish" fashion, becoming "manly" in reason and virtue. That is the way Philo, the Jewish philosopher of Alexandria, explains "the deeper meaning" of the verse "The womanly matters ceased to be for Sarah" (Gen. 18:11, LXX). In his story of Abraham's marriage, Philo makes Sarah symbolize virtue and therefore, in a reversal of the roles in physical marriage, to impregnate Abraham with "good counsels and excellent words." Only after Abraham's encounter with God and his Powers at the oak of Mamre does Abraham become "wise" and thus able to act in a "masculine" (rational) way.[17]

It is hard to imagine that the philosophical clichés using femaleness in such pejorative senses could have arisen if there were not abroad in the society a tendency to regard women as weaker, less rational, and generally inferior to men. A great deal of evidence indicates such views were indeed widespread, at least among male authors. Unfortunately, so few of the writings of women survive from antiquity that we but rarely hear at first hand the sorts of things that women thought about themselves and their own bodies. (We will look at one of the rare instances in the next section.) The exposure of female infants provides perhaps the most chilling indicator of the lack of value placed on the female body. Hard evidence is scarce, but what there is, together with some cross-cultural comparisons, suggests that a typical father having to calculate whether the cost and risks of raising a newborn child could be balanced by its future benefits to the family would far more often choose to discard a girl than a boy.[18] On the other hand, it should not be assumed that such attitudes were universal. Examples abound of fathers who cherished their daughters and made provision for their welfare.[19]

That the "female," in the allegories, could nevertheless become "male" points to yet another surprising feature of ancient notions about the sexes. Despite the pervasive opposition of male to female in the clichés we have looked at, nevertheless there seems to be a certain fluidity between the two. Sarah can play a "male" role when needed for Philo's allegory of virtue. A man can be "womanish" in attitude, mind, or behavior. Some recent studies have suggested that, in the minds of people of the Greco-Roman world, male and female bodies were not so sharply distinguished as they are in our culture. Male and female stand rather at two ends of a continuum, a sliding scale. To put it another way, many people thought of the female as an incomplete or imperfect male, while a man was always in some danger of having his masculinity diminished or weakened.[20]

The wavering line between male and female may also help to explain another motif that sounds as a dark undertone through much of ancient literature, myth, and folklore: men's fear of the female. Doctors prescribed regimens for their patients designed to help prevent the loss of heat and vital spirit, which might occur in any relaxation of male discipline, but especially through excess of passion. Peter Brown summarizes the fears of the ruling elites with his customary eloquence:

> It was never enough to be male: a man had to strive to remain "virile." He had to learn to exclude from his character and from the poise and temper of his body all telltale traces of "softness" that might betray, in him, the half-formed state of a woman. The small-town notables of the second century watched each other with hard, clear eyes. They noted a man's walk. They reacted to the rhythms of his speech. They listened attentively to the telltale resonance of his voice. Any of these might betray the ominous loss of a hot, high-spirited momentum, a flagging of

the clear-cut self-restraint, and a relaxing of the taut elegance of voice and gesture that made a man a man.[21]

The irony of these anxieties is a familiar one: the other who is carefully confined to the margins of the public world and who is made to symbolize those qualities that are the negations of that world's cherished powers threatens, by that very defined weakness and inferiority, the stability of the dominant. The fear intrudes pervasively into the theory and practice of medicine. For example, Heinrich von Staden has shown how the writers of the rationalist Hippocratic tradition of medicine reject the use of excrement so common in folk medicine, with a single exception: it is regularly prescribed for gynecological ills. Faced with the mysteries of the female body— so little understood by even the most empiricist medical students of the time—the Hippocratics saw it as dangerously susceptible to impurity and fell back on a kind of counter-magic.[22] The womb itself, in popular belief, had almost demonic powers. Many thought that it could sometimes wander freely through the woman's body, producing "hysteria"—though the great anatomist of Alexandria, Herophilus, had demonstrated in the third century B.C.E. that it was in fact quite firmly anchored. The ominous power of the womb made it an important magical symbol: crude drawings of the womb, often transformed into a Medusa-like mask, appear on amulets and gems, presumably worn as protection against other dangers. Two similar figures appear in paintings on the walls of the third-century C.E. synagogue of Dura-Europos.[23]

In a society in which the woman's body was both indispensable and dangerous, object of desire and of fear, common moral intuitions shared by the ruling, male elites served two principal concerns, which we can call economic and therapeutic, respectively. I use "economic" in the ancient, not the modern, sense, referring to the need to maintain the good order of the household both within itself and with respect to the household's role in the larger community: for Greeks, the *polis*. Two dimensions of this order were uppermost in the minds of householders: assuring continuity of name and inheritance through legitimate offspring and assuring the honor of the family and its clan. By "therapeutic" I mean those measures that were felt to be needed to protect against the disordering, threatening powers of the female.

It is the economic concern, in the sense just explained, that is most clearly in play in the traditional rules of marriage of which Paul reminds the converts in Thessalonica: "For this is God's will, the way you are to be holy: you must abstain from illicit sex [porneia]. Each of you must know to acquire his own vessel in holiness and honor, not in the passion of desire like the gentiles who do not know God. And he must not in this matter transgress [the rights of] his brother and be greedy for what is his" (1 Thess. 4:3–6).

The pains taken in most modern translations to avoid the plain sense of the Greek testify to the discomfort the passage causes readers today. Nevertheless, its main points would have seemed quite commonplace in antiquity.[24] The wife is regarded as a mere receptacle; no hint of the "two-seed" theory here. The converts, like Jews, are to distinguish themselves from "gentiles" by avoiding passion, although in fact avoidance of passion was high on the agenda of pagan moralists, too, as we have seen. Paul's, or the tradition's, language is so full of economic terms that some commentators have wanted to translate the neutral term "matter" as "business." Instead, the language merely represents the central economic importance and danger of the woman's body in common moral reasoning. One may wonder what Prisca, or any of the other women leaders and "fellow workers" in Paul's entourage, may have thought about such language. Unfortunately, we have no word from them.

It is pleasant to fantasize that Prisca or one of the other "sisters" might have said a few things to Paul in private in the five years or so between his writing 1 Thessalonians and his next attested use of the same tradition. Be that as it may, he has changed the wording rather dramatically: "However, on account of illicit relations, let each man have his own wife and each woman have her own husband. Let the husband render what he owes to the wife, and in the same way the wife to the husband. The wife does not have authority over her own body, but the husband does; in the same way also the husband does not have authority over his own body but the wife does. Do not defraud each other, unless you agree [to refrain from sex] for a time in order to give your attention to prayer and then again to be together, lest Satan tempt you on account of your lack of control" (1 Cor. 7:2–6).

The "receptacle" notion of the woman's role in procreation has yielded here to a balance of mutual powers and obligations; indeed, procreation is not mentioned at all. There are still echoes of economic language, but now it aims not at the protection of the husband's goods in the community, but at limiting the dangers of passion in the private economy, so to speak, of sexual interchange between man and woman. Paul's own specific concern, in both letters, is the purity of the Christian group, to which "passion of desire" is a threat. In the Thessalonian passage, the threat is couched entirely in terms of the patriarchal economy, but in the letter to Corinth the therapeutic issue is foremost.

It was not Paul who raised the therapeutic question, however. The passage begins with a sentence I omitted in the quotation above: "Now about the things of which you wrote: 'It is good for a person not to touch a woman.'" In this slogan from the Corinthian group's letter, we hear the same high-minded disdain for "womanish" things of the body that thinks, "Foods are for the stomach and the stomach for foods; God will after all destroy both" (6:13), that is unconcerned that some fellow in the church is living with his stepmother (chap. 5), and that sees only "weakness" in scruples about meat offered to idols (chaps. 8–10). It is the voice of some of those who are the natural leaders and patrons of household communities, those who by status, training, and superior knowledge have the rational and rhetorical power to maintain decency and order. Their power was the sort that, as we have seen above, felt itself threatened by the draining effects of sex, by the contagious weakness of the female.

Paul's reply agrees with the premise that "it is good not to touch a woman"—for those who, like him, have the "gift" of celibacy. What is at stake for him, however, is not the preservation of the strength of the male leaders, but the protection of the purity of the Christian community—of the metaphorical body of Christ—against the polluting and distracting powers of desire. It is not sex but passion that threatens purity. Marriage itself serves Paul's therapeutic concern. Hence the unmarried and widows who are unable to exercise self-control (ouk enkrateuontai) are counseled to marry, "for it is better to marry than to be inflamed" (7:8–9), and the same advice is given to men engaged to virgins who have reached the stage of life at which the ancients thought girls tended to be obsessed by passion (7:36).[25]

Paul thus clearly thought that celibate men as well as celibate women were freed to direct their anxieties to "the things of the Lord" rather than "the things of the world," meaning here the world of household, sex, and children, and thus to be "holy in both body and spirit" (1 Cor. 7:32–34). The stories told in the Acts of Thomas and others of the apocryphal acts, not least the Acts of Thecla, often depict this liberation from the ties and dangers associated with the primary world of the female body.[26] In the fourth- and fifth-century church, egalitarian friendships between celibate male leaders and wealthy, ascetic women exemplify this transcendence of the ordinary roles assigned by gender. The form of this world, however, did not pass away, and the tensions between the free ascetics and the household-based church did not diminish as the institution grew more complex. The emerging bishops sought ways to channel and control the power of the monks and virgins; Athanasius's organization of the virgins of Alexandria against the study-circles of the Arians provides a vivid example. From the side of the ascetics, we have several poignant variations on the theme of the woman's becoming male, including the final saying of the *Gospel of Thomas:* "Simon Peter said to them, 'Let Mary leave us, for women are not worthy of life.' Jesus said, 'I myself shall lead her in order to make her male, so that she too may become a living spirit resembling you males. For every woman who will make herself male will enter the kingdom of heaven.' "[27]

The Bodies of the Martyrs

In the Thomas tradition and in much Christian asceticism, the body is alien to the self. The Christian is called to a contest or war against the world, and the primary battle is against one's own body. There is another kind of early Christian literature in which figures of athletic contest or combat are the controlling images: the accounts of martyrdom. In the martyr acts, however, the bodies of the martyrs are sacred, and the narratives often dwell on the physicality of their suffering and of their heroism.

One of the reasons, perhaps, for the positive value set on the body in the martyr stories is the popularity of the cult of the martyrs' relics. In what is usually regarded as the earliest extant martyr act, that of Polycarp, we already hear of the Christians' eagerness to obtain the saint's body, forestalled by Nicetes and the Jews. The disciples have to be satisfied with gathering the ashes for burial after Polycarp has been cremated (chap. 17). A similar motif appears in the account of the martyrs of Lyons (62–63); other martyr acts frequently report the successful gathering of the relics. The story of Bishop Fructuosus's martyrdom (A.D. 259) contains a curious variation of this theme. The bishop appears after his death to demand that those who have taken home separate bits of his ashes bring them back (6).[28]

The narrator of Polycarp's story, summing up his hero's sacrificial worship of God and Christ, calls Christ not only "savior of our souls" and "shepherd of the world-wide catholic church," but also "guide of our bodies" (*kybernētēs tōn sōmatōn hēmōn*, 19:2). The story, like many of the later ones, stresses physical details—the stamina of the aged bishop, his composure despite a scraped shin, his ability to stand unflinching in the flames without being nailed to the stake. Polycarp's prayer is "for the resurrection of life eternal, of both soul and body in the immortality of the Holy Spirit" (14:2). The body, which will be reverenced by the faithful in death and raised by God at the last day, is in the suffering itself the very instrument of obedient defiance of the devil and the Empire. The point is made most vividly in the martyrdom of Pionius, though it most likely comes from the Decian persecutions, a half-century later than our chosen terminus.[29] Stripped for execution, Pionius, "realizing the holiness and dignity of his own body, . . . was filled with great joy" (21, trans. Musurillo). The "holiness and dignity" are confirmed after he is burnt, when "his crown was signified even by means of his body" (22), for the corpse is found to be miraculously whole. Graphic details of the tortures may seem to us at times to verge on what Geoffrey Gorer has aptly called, in a modern context, the "pornography of death," a gruesome titillation of the reader.[30] But such details also convey the charismatic power with which the martyr's very body is invested.

Such power is nowhere more clearly manifested than in the stories of female martyrs. In the commonplace metaphors of ancient rhetoric and philosophy, the female always stands for the material, the physical, and the weak. The narrator of the Lyons martyrdoms stresses the reversal of this topos when describing the valor of Blandina, "through whom Christ proved that the things that men think cheap, ugly, and contemptuous are deemed worthy of glory before God" (17, trans. Musurillo). Doubly true in Blandina's case, for she is not only a woman but a slave—and her mistress, also among the martyrs, "was in agony lest because of her bodily weakness she would not be able to make a bold confession of her faith" (ibid.). Not so Blandina, who faced horrible tortures "like a noble athlete."

Most famous of the female martyrs are Perpetua and Felicitas of North Africa. Perpetua herself wrote part of the account that survives. On the eve of her scheduled appearance in the arena, she tells us that she had a vision in which she had to fight an Egyptian. When she stripped for this combat, she discovered that she had become a man. She defeated the Egyptian easily, treading on his head exactly as, in a previous vision, she had trod on a great serpent who guarded the foot of a ladder reaching to heaven—both opponents obviously representing the devil. The "manliness" with which Perpetua conducted herself is nevertheless not to be equated with the renunciation of everything associated with the feminine that we see sometimes in the ascetic literature—for example, in the final saying of the Gospel of Thomas, which suggests that only a woman who "makes herself male" can be saved.[31]

Both Perpetua and Felicitas were mothers, Perpetua weaning her baby in prison, Felicitas giving birth almost on the eve of her death and relinquishing her child to a "sister," that is, one of the Christian women, to raise. Some of the most poignant passages in the text relate to women's anxieties and the physical experiences of motherhood—Perpetua noting that she surprisingly experienced no pain in her breasts when she stopped nursing the baby; the bleeding of Felicitas in childbirth compared with the bloodbath of martyrdom; her dripping breasts a sight that evoked dismay even from the crowd. Here, quite exceptionally in ancient literature, we hear directly of a woman's physical experiences from her own point of view, as also in Perpetua's memoirs we see from her point of view the tensions and obligations of family, in which ordinarily the woman was expected to play a limited, private, and submissive role.[32] Here we see clearly signaled an enduring tension that would beset the Christian ethos. On one side is the traditional household, in which precisely the body of the woman—perceived simultaneously as essential to the continuation of family and community alike and as the vessel of passions and powers extremely dangerous to the health and honor of men and state—is the focus of her established roles. On the other side are the active, gender-transcending roles to which the Spirit might call a woman in the new faith.

The Bodies of Ordinary Christians

Martyrs and ascetic heroes and heroines were a very small minority of Christians. What conceptions of the body informed the life of the ordinary believers? We may receive some hints of these by looking at two documents that are rather less intense than those we have examined so far—indeed it may be said that they are so fashioned that they rarely capture or hold the attention of a modern reader. Nevertheless, both were exceedingly popular in the ancient church: the *Shepherd of Hermas* and the *Sentences of Sextus*. The *Sentences* are generally dated to the second century; some scholars would assign Hermas to roughly the same period, though others put him earlier. Hermas belongs clearly to Rome; the Sextus collection is thought to originate in the Egyptian church. Neither breaks new ground theologically or ethically; precisely for that reason they are of interest for our present purpose, and for this purpose we can ignore for the moment the puzzles that still surround both documents.[33]

As we saw in the previous chapter, the principal message that Hermas tells us he has received by a series of visions and other special revelations is that one great opportunity for repentance is now to be given to all Christians who have sinned since their baptism. Dire consequences are threatened against those who fail to repent, while those who do are warned that they must engage to live a strictly disciplined life thereafter—the rewards for which, however, will be marvelous.

One of the oddest features of Hermas's book is a kind of subtext of sexual allusions that runs throughout, but which is never developed. We looked at this theme briefly in the previous chapter; a few more details are now needed. The narrative begins with Hermas telling us how he fell in love with a woman named Rhoda, who had formerly owned him as a slave. He loved her only "as a sister," he insists. Nevertheless, when he saw her bathing in the Tiber and gave her his hand to help her from the water, he thought, "I should be happy if I had a wife of such beauty and character." He assures the reader that he had no other thought than that, presumably quite acceptable—yet we learn later that Hermas already had a wife of his own and children that were not behaving very well. Further, he soon sees a vision in which the woman appears in the sky to announce that she has been taken up to heaven to accuse Hermas "before the Lord." These curious scenes serve only to introduce Hermas's encounter with a different visionary woman, who turns out to be the Church personified. She affirms that Hermas's thoughts about Rhoda were indeed treading on dangerous ground, "For it is an evil and mad purpose against a revered spirit and one already approved, if a man desire an evil deed, and especially if it be Hermas the temperate, who abstains from every evil desire and is full of all simplicity and great innocence" (2.4 [*Vis.* 1.2.4], trans. Lake). Nevertheless, she assures him that God is angry with him for quite another reason, the dereliction of his family, and we never hear anything further of Rhoda.

It is striking that Lady Church calls Hermas *ho enkratēs*, blandly translated "the temperate" by Lake, but ordinarily connoting celibacy in early Christian literature. That was certainly the meaning of the word in the Thomas tradition that we looked at earlier, and it was the label assigned by the second- and third-century heresiologists to ascetics who resisted the discipline of the catholic bishops: "Encratites." *Enkrateia* and its cognates occur frequently in the Hermas book, and most of the passages, taken alone, would be quite at home in ascetic literature like the *Gospel* or *Acts of Thomas*. For example, when Hermas sees seven women who represent the virtues, the second of them, who is "belted and manly," is Enkrateia, the daughter of Faith (16.4 [*Vis.* 3.8.4]). Consequently, the first Mandate that Hermas receives from the Angel of Repentance commands that belief in the one God should lead directly to being continent. A kind of heroic continence in the face of temptation seems finally to be exemplified in the strange story of *Sim.* 9:11 (88), when Hermas is forced against his will to spend the night with twelve virgins. His expressed anxiety about this compromising situation contradicts the allegorical interpretation given the scene thereafter, in which the virgins are identified as virtues. The scene itself, as Dibelius says, is nothing other than a "Minnespiel," for the girls insist that Hermas must sleep with them, though "as a brother and not as a husband," and proceed to kiss and hug him, to play, dance, and at last lie down with him.[34]

The temptation is great to interpret these curiously dissonant erotic elements psychoanalytically, but it should be resisted. A dominant theme of the directives that the heavenly figures give to Hermas is that he must take proper charge of his household. Marriage is held holy, for example in Mandate 4; only remarriage after divorce is forbidden, and the reason for that is to allow a repentant spouse to return. It looks as though Hermas is trying to work out an ethic in which the values of Christian asceticism are adapted for the family life of a church that still consists of household-based groups, and he is doing this in an imaginative and allusive form, rather than in a systematic way. Still, it should be noted that the heavenly book that Hermas receives early on says of his wife that "in future she is your sister." The *via media* he is trying to work out may therefore include the possibility of some householders adopting a celibate life.[35]

The *Sentences of Sextus* seem to represent a similar adaptation of the ascetic impulse to practical life, drawing especially on Pythagorean sentiments, as Chadwick has shown. "Master pleasures," says one gnome (70), then "conquer the body in every way" (71a). The two appear to mean roughly the same, for self-control, *sophrosynē*, is high in Sextus's list of virtues, and a somewhat more modest demand is "Put aside the things of the body as much as you can" (78). Like Hermas, Sextus prizes *enkrateia*, but thinks it can be exercised by the married: "Let the marriage of believers be a struggle for *enkrateia*" (239). The body is grudgingly accepted; it is the "tent of the soul," it must above all be controlled. "It is arrogant to be vexed by the tent of your soul, but it is blessed to be able to put it aside gently when you must" (320).[36] Out of the wide diversity and experimentation that we find in the early Christian attitudes about the body, Hermas and Sextus represent the uneasy compromise that has beset the middle way of Christian practical ethics down to the present.

CHAPTER 9

A Life Worthy of God

❖ ❖ ❖ ❖ ❖ ❖ ❖ ❖ ❖ ❖

When the early Christians talked about human behavior, they also talked about God, usually in the same breath, as it were. Nothing could be less surprising than that. The same thing is true of all varieties of Jewish moral discourse in antiquity, as one can readily verify by sampling at random almost any surviving Jewish literature, from the Bible itself to the Dead Sea Scrolls to Philo to Josephus (the Book of Esther is an exception that proves the rule). Furthermore, it was by no means unusual for pagan moral philosophers in the Roman Empire to begin their discussions of ethics with theological statements. Plutarch, for example, insists that one of Plato's fundamental teachings is "that God . . . offers himself to all as a pattern of every excellence, thus rendering human virtue, which is in some sort an assimilation to himself, accessible to all who can 'follow God' " (*Mor.* 550D, trans. Babbitt).[1] The Stoic Musonius Rufus could use rather similar language—though his notion of what God was like was very different from that of Platonists like Plutarch. The human being, said Musonius, is the earthly image or copy of God, and only when a person becomes like God—for Musonius that meant living in accord with rational nature—could that person be virtuous and therefore happy (no. 17, Lutz[2]).

Now the ideal of godlike character, for a Plutarch or a Musonius, could only be achieved by the truly wise person—who was about as rare as the phoenix, the Stoics believed.[3] Progress in that direction could be achieved only by an austere process of reasoning and self-discipline. It was not, by any means, for everybody. The Christians, much as their leaders used the arguments and rhetoric of the philosophical schools, were trying to accomplish something rather different. By means of their rituals, their songs, their communal discipline and admonitions, they were trying to form people into a novel community. Among the philosophical schools, only the Pythagoreans and the Epicureans seem to have undertaken something similar. A moral life "worthy of God," as the Christians sometimes put it (1 Thess. 2:12; 3 John 6; *1 Clem.* 21:1; Polycarp, *Phil.* 5:1–2; compare Eph. 4:1; Phil. 1:27; Col. 1:10), was a life that the entire community was expected to embody.

"Theology and ethics" does not quite describe this process of community formation, and looking at the symbolic side of the process is not quite the same as what we usually call "New Testament theology." In keeping with our "ethnographic" project, we shall continue to interrogate our early Christian informants, via the texts they have left. Which are the most salient images of God's character and action among the things that early converts had to learn? What were the explicit or implicit links between these images and the kind of life expected of believers? It may be useful to divide these clusters of images into three categories, although the three often overlap. First, there are many passages in early Christian writings where God's intention is mentioned as an explicit warrant for desirable behavior: for short, God's will. Second, these imply or presuppose a much broader and more pervasive depiction of God's nature as the context within which all human action must be evaluated: God's character, so to speak. Finally, the early Christians regularly appeal to God's self-revealing actions, to which believers ought to respond.

God's Will

Nothing is more characteristic of that part of their ethics which early Christians absorbed from their Jewish roots than the notion that God, imaged as a person, wants people to behave in a certain way and takes measures to enable and encourage them to do so. Thus the statement "This is God's will" stands often as a warrant for admonitions addressed to the Christian communities, just as "Thy will be done, on earth as in heaven" was part of their prayer. The warrant has a prominent place in the hortatory letter of Paul to new converts, 1 Thessalonians, to which we have turned often in earlier chapters. The explicit admonitions of 1 Thess. 4 begin with this sentence: "This is the will of God: your holiness, that you should avoid fornication." God's will is holiness. The paradigmatic case here is sex, so that "holiness" is equated with "purity," that is, avoiding *porneia* or "lustful passion" or "impurity," and thus showing that the Christians are different from "the gentiles who do not know God." God is, moreover, the "avenger" when these rules are violated to the detriment of a "brother." This whole section of the letter is prefaced by the reminder that the apostles have taught the Thessalonian converts some specific "precepts" which showed them "how you ought to behave and to please God." The sexual rules of which they are here reminded are thus samples of those precepts which are already part of Christian tradition (having originated, no doubt, in Jewish communities).

The warrant is not specific to the Pauline circles of Christianity, but appears in various contexts. In 1 Peter 2:15 it supports the first rule of a household duty code, submission to imperial authority: "For [to do] thus is the will of God, by doing good to silence the ignorance of foolish people." The Matthean version of Jesus' parable of the lost sheep employs a negative formulation: "Thus it is not the will before your father in the heavens that one of these little ones should be lost" (Matt. 18:14). John 6:39–40 expresses a similar promise in distinctively Johannine language.

Doing God's Will

Most frequent of all is the phrase "to do the will of God," which imitates the language of the Septuagint. (See, for example, Heb. 10:5–10, where Ps. 40:7–9 is quoted and applied to Jesus.) In a saying preserved in Mark, Jesus defines his "brother and sister and mother" as "whoever does the will of God" (Mark 3:35; Matt. 12:50; quoted too in 2 Clem. 9:11). Again the Johannine groups develop their own variation: wanting to do God's will is prerequisite for understanding the truth of Jesus' teachings (John 7:17); the person "who does the will of God abides for ever," in contrast to "the world and its passion," which pass away (1 John 2:17). The little homily we know as "the Second Epistle of Clement," actually a sermon of an unknown author, provenance, and date but doubtless from the second century, frequently introduces its exhortations by the appeal to do God's will. For example: "Wherefore, my brethren, let us do the will of the father who called us, that we may live, and let us rather follow after virtue, but give up vice as the forerunner of our sins, and let us flee from ungodliness lest evil overtake us" (10:1, trans. Lake).[4]

Quite naturally the early traditions about Jesus depict him as the supreme example of the one who "came to do God's will" (Heb. 10:5–10). The Gethsemane tradition portrays Jesus' agonizing over the necessity of his death before submitting his own will to God's (Mark 14:36; Matt. 26:42; Luke 22:42).[5] The Fourth Gospel, while it discards the Gethsemane story

(John 12:27), uses a similar phrase to epitomize Jesus' entire mission: "I came down from heaven not to do my own will but the will of the one who sent me" (6:38; compare 4:34 and 5:30).

Order and Contingency

Paul had good reason to think of his conversion from persecutor to apostle as startling, contrary to his own will, and thus "through the will of God," and he uses this phrase regularly to characterize his apostleship (1 Cor. 1:1; 2 Cor. 1:1; Gal. 1:4). He can use the same formula to speak of other contingencies, such as travel plans (Rom. 1:10; 15:32) or generosity of groups of Christians (2 Cor. 8:5). It became a standard phrase in the epistolary language of those who read and imitated Paul's letters (Eph. 1:1,5; 2 Tim. 1:1; 1 Clem. inscription; Ignatius in the inscription of most of his letters).

The Letter of James castigates merchants who lay plans in disregard of their finitude and life's fragility; instead they ought to say, "If the Lord wills, I will live and do this or that" (4:15). In an uncertain world, God's will alone is firm, unchanging, and irresistible (Rom. 9:19; Heb. 6:17; 1 Clem. 27:5–6). In Luke-Acts, the irresistibility of God's will or plan (boulē) becomes a major theme, especially in the second volume, where the mission of the apostles and of Paul is pictured as the relentless "growth" of the "Word of God" despite internal dissension and external opposition and persecution. The truth of the claims made in the speeches of Acts and implied in the narrative of both volumes is backed by the assertion that all this happened "by the plan and foreknowledge of God" (2:23).[6]

The Letter of Rome to Corinth provides a particularly interesting example of the appeal to God's will in exhortation. As we saw earlier, this letter, written in the 90s, combines Greco-Roman commonplaces about political stability ("peace and concord") with a wealth of exempla from the Bible and from early Christian traditions and writing. All this is in the service of an attempt to persuade the Corinthian groups to restore leaders who have been supplanted by younger rivals. Though the letter is traditionally attributed to Clement and shows some rhetorical finesse, it is not merely an individual creation. However diverse the Roman household meetings of Christians may have been still, the letter pretends to represent them all, and the mode of argument would hardly have been idiosyncratic. Rather it is typical of much we have seen in a variety of Christian groups.[7]

The model Clement employs for God's will is imperial: it is *pantokratori-kos,* the will of an all-powerful sovereign (8:5). Clement insists, however, that God's will is characterized by stability rather than capriciousness. The regularity of nature derives from the accord of all things with his will, which is described as their obeying his decrees (chap. 20). God "founded the earth on the secure foundation of his own will" (33:3). The same peace and concord are therefore the intention of God for human communities, and above all for the people of God—for biblical Israel and now for the church. Drawing an analogy between biblical ordinances for the temple and priesthood and offices in the church, Clement insists that "where and by whom he wants [sacrifices and liturgies] to be conducted, he himself has appointed by his supreme will" (40:3). He warns that doing such things "contrary to what befits his will" *(para to kathēkon tēs boulēseōs autou)* received the death penalty in the biblical accounts (41:3). Good order in the churches was established, Clement teaches, through Christ and then the apostles (who in turn appointed the elders), and "both happened in good order from the will of God" (42:2). Any disturbance of that order, then, constitutes "desertion" from God's will (21:4), and the deserters must be admonished (56:2) and prayed for "to yield, not to us, but to the will of God" (56:1).

Discerning God's Will

Most of the admonitions we have looked at speak as if the will of God were perfectly obvious to the groups being exhorted or scolded. Yet it is surely reasonable to ask how the recipients of such chiding were expected to know what it was that God wanted of them. Returning to our first example, Paul's reminder to the Thessalonian converts, we learn in the same context that God *teaches* right behavior. Paul, like any Greek or Roman moral philosopher writing to a friend, assures his Christian audience that they do not need anyone to teach them about brotherly love. But not only does he mean something different by *philadelphia* from what Plutarch, for instance, would mean, he also gives a different reason for his audience already knowing this virtue: they are "God-taught," *theodidaktoi* (1 Thess. 4:9). As the ways by which the recent converts had been taught by God to love one another, Paul probably had in mind both scripture, in passages like Leviticus 19:18, and the precepts that he and his associates had communicated to them.[8] A century and a quarter later, the apologist Athenagoras applied the same adjective to all "the teachings that we follow," citing as primary example the saying of Jesus about love of enemies (*Supplicatio* 11.1; compare 32.2).

It does not follow that the early Christians thought it an easy or foolproof matter to discern God's will. The opening prayer of the Letter to the Colossians, for example, asks that the recipients be "filled with knowledge of his will in all wisdom and spiritual understanding, to walk worthily of the Lord to the end of pleasing [him] in every way" (Col. 1:9–10). In the midst of admonitions urging the addressees to "behave as children of light" rather than children of darkness, the author of Ephesians carries this thought further, freely using language of the Jewish wisdom tradition: "Watch rigorously, then, how you behave, not as unwise people but as wise, seizing the moment, because the days are evil. Do not therefore be fools, but understand what is the will of the Lord. Do not be drunk with wine, in which lies dissipation, but be filled instead with spirit, speaking to one another with psalms, hymns, and spiritual songs, singing and making music from your heart to the Lord, giving thanks always for all in the name of our Lord Jesus Christ to our God and Father" (Eph. 5:15–17).

As Paul said in Romans 12:2, it required a "transformation" by "renewal of the mind, for you to test what is the will of God, good, pleasing [to him], and perfect." One had to think differently, not in conformity with "this age," but one did have to think. And not infrequently, it seems, one had also to argue with other Christians who thought differently.

The difference of the Christian thinking, the nonconformity to this age, is often expressed, for example in the verses cited above from Colossians and Ephesians, by the notion that it is the Spirit that conveys the needed knowledge. There is plenty of evidence that the conviction held by most early Christians that God's or Christ's Spirit was active in their midst led to the offering of very lively and not always conventional advice in their meetings. It also led sometimes to conflict. In 1 Corinthians 14, Paul already cautioned against disruptive exhibitions of the Spirit's powers, and strongly urged that the more rational expressions of the Spirit's guidance be preferred to the more ecstatic, "for upbuilding." Eventually, church handbooks like the Didache would provide specific rules for weeding out false prophets (chaps. 11–13) or, as 1 John puts it, "testing the spirits" (4:1). Matthew's Jesus warned that in the last days he would not necessarily be pleased with miracle-working bearers of the Spirit; "doing the will of God" was what was required, and not everyone who seemed "spiritual" could be relied on to do that (Matt. 7:21–23).

The Will in Commandments

As a counterbalance to the uncertainties of charismatic power, the Gospel of Matthew connects discipleship rather closely with following "commandments." This is not surprising, for in the biblical and Jewish tradition the most assured way of discerning God's will was obviously by referring to what he had specifically ordered, either through the great codes of the priestly and legal traditions, or through his living representatives, priests and prophets. Thus Jesus' "Great Commission" in Matthew, which directs the apostles to "make disciples of all the gentiles," adds that they are to teach them "to observe everything I have commanded you" (28:19–20). We are accustomed to contrast that with the convictions of the Pauline circles, who saw in "the Law" a barrier to the unity of Jewish and gentile converts in the body of Christ. Nevertheless, we have seen that Paul did not hesitate to talk about "precepts" backed by God's authority or the Lord's (Jesus'), and occasionally he even spoke of "commandments" (1 Cor. 7:19; 14:37). Presumably, later Christian moralists had fewer qualms about this kind of language, for it becomes the commonest way of pointing out how Christians ought to behave, for example in the *Didache*, in *Barnabas*, in the *Shepherd of Hermas*, and in most of the so-called "church order literature."

Even if one construes explicit commandments as the primary way of knowing what God wants us to do, however, that does not necessarily put an end to debate, as anyone who has read the Mishnah or the Talmuds knows. Commandments have to be interpreted; different commandments sometimes seem to contradict each other; new situations show things in a different light. The Gospel of Matthew, again, illustrates the problem. Jesus in Matthew not only gives commandments, he also alters the force of old commandments, even contradicting them, even commandments of Moses found in the Bible (most emphatically in Matt. 5:21–48). Further, in his controversies with the scribes and Pharisees, Matthew's Jesus uses scribal kinds of argument, including midrashic reinterpretations of scripture. It is not hard to guess that leaders of Matthew's own community, including the author, engaged in similar kinds of interpretive moves. This is true of all the main circles of the early Christian movement.

When the early Christians made "the will of God" their ultimate norm, they thus implied that there is an absolute ground for their ethics. Yet the qualifications we have observed show that the absolute norm was not absolutely clear. The phrase "the will of God" is a relentlessly personal metaphor. If the will of a human is complex, never completely fathomed by another, how much more the will of the all-knowing God?[9] This fringe of personal indeterminacy is, of course, frequently suppressed by those who insist on knowing God's will, but very often it is quite explicit. The personal quality of God's directing human behavior is especially emphasized by those who use the alternate, equally biblical forms of expression "to please God," to "do what is well-pleasing in his sight," and the like (for example, 1 John 3:23; 1 Thess. 4:1; Col. 1:9–11; 1 Pet. 3:4). Add to this observation the fact that these same authors can often speak of the believer as God's or Christ's slave, so that "to serve God" entails the unlimited obligation of a slave to his owner, and we see that the notion of "pleasing God" contains a hint of potential arbitrariness on God's part. This whole complex of metaphors, so fundamental to early Christian paraenetic language, can be redeemed for a coherent ethics only insofar as God's own self-consistency can be asserted and maintained. "The will of God" is at best a brittle concept when isolated from a depiction of what, for lack of a better word, we may call God's *character*.

God's Character

Not only in the Bible and in Jewish tradition, but also in Greco-Roman moral literature and rhetoric, moral endeavor can take the form of striving to be like God (see the introductory paragraphs to this chapter). Sometimes this endeavor can be expressed by naming specific attributes of God that his followers ought to imitate. To be sure, Aristotle thought it inappropriate to use the word *virtue* of a god (*EN* 7.1.2). Nevertheless, in discourse that makes of God a moral example, we are clearly dealing with an anthropomorphic metaphor, so we may perhaps defy Aristotle and speak of "God's virtues," as the early Christians did without compunction. There are many examples.[10]

God's Virtues

The recurrent refrain of the Levitical Holiness Code, "You shall be holy as I am holy," echoes frequently in Christian writings, whether or not we are justified in talking with Bishop Carrington and others of "a Christian Holiness Code" (see, for example, 1 Pet. 1:15–26; compare 1 Thess. 4:3–8).[11] Changes can be rung on this: for example, the saying of Jesus that has come down to us in two forms, in Luke 6:36, "Be merciful as our Father is merciful," and in Matthew 5:48, "Be perfect as your heavenly Father is perfect." Perhaps 1 John 3:3, which takes Jesus rather than God as the model, is also a paraphrase of this refrain: "And everyone who thus hopes in him purifies himself, as he is pure."

Examples can be multiplied easily. Several of the New Testament writers take up the axiom that partiality is alien to God. The word they use is that peculiar Greek translation of a Hebrew phrase, "taking the face, the mask, the persona" (prosōpolēmpsia). That is, God does not pay attention to human definitions of status, but accords to all perfect equity. Paul uses this axiom to introduce the central theme of his letter to Romans, that in the new age begun in the crucifixion and resurrection of Jesus Christ God treats Jews and gentiles impartially (Rom. 2:11).[12] The Lukan schematization of the same point is similarly stated in the speech of Peter to Cornelius in Acts 10:34: "In truth I now grasp the fact that God is not a prosōpolēmptēs," that is, a judge blinded by status. Paul's disciples employ the notion in direct paraenetic contexts. In Col. 3:25, slaves are warned that no favoritism will be shown them in punishing any wrongdoing of which they may be guilty. In Eph. 6:9, the warning is rather to the owners: "And masters, you behave the same way toward them [the slaves], forgoing bluster, knowing that both they and you have a master in heaven and that there is no favoritism with him." The Colossians passage makes a similar point to the owners, but using an alternative expression of the virtue involved, "justice [to dikaion] and equity [isotēs]."

In a short diatribe, the Epistle of James dramatizes the inconsistency of social favoritism with "the faith of our glorious Lord Jesus." Suppose a man enters the Christian meeting wearing the gold rings and splendid clothing that instantly signal his wealth and power (in former times the perquisites of Roman knights and local senators, now sported more generally by people on the rise),[13] and at the same time a poor man in shabby clothes comes in. James imagines that the leaders will act as every social convention would have taught them, showing honor to the rich man while discriminating against the poor. All wrong! says James. Rather, "Has not God chosen the poor?" So also ought the leaders of the Christian synagogue (2:5–7). James depicts God as an ungrudging "giver" (1:5; compare Rom. 12:6; 1 Pet. 4:10–11; and so on), as compassionate and merciful (5:11), as "untempted by evil" (1:13)—all as models of the ways Christians ought to treat one another.

The great variety of the virtues attributed to God and of the ways in which they could be connected with the behavior wanted from members of the Christian groups is richly exhibited in the letters of Paul. The oneness of God entails unity in his people: between Jews and gentiles (Rom. 3:29–30), among people with diverse spiritual "gifts" (1 Cor. 12:5–6). Because "God is not a God of disorder but of peace," confusion sowed by charismatics in the meetings is not to be tolerated (1 Cor. 14:33).

The opening blessing of 2 Corinthians describes God as "the father of mercies and God of all consolation, who consoles us in our every affliction to the end of empowering us in turn to console those in every affliction through the consolation by which we ourselves are consoled by God" (1:3–4). That deliberately plerophoric statement sets the theme for the first seven or eight chapters of this letter (or of the perhaps originally separate letter which these chapters may preserve), which is trying to heal a breech between the Corinthians and Paul. Paul uses this theme to try to set into a theological interpretive framework the altercation between him and the Corinthians and the internal dissension at Corinth connected with that altercation. In this way he is attempting to cement the tenuous reconciliation that has been patched together by Titus (7:5–16). In a hermeneutical tour de force, Paul wants to persuade the Corinthians to see the grief *(lupē)* he has caused them by his previous visit and letter (2:1–4; 7:8–12) and the grief they, especially one of them, have caused him (2:5–11) within the category of "the sufferings of Christ" (1:5) and the "afflictions" in which God provides "consolation." The conflict between them can thus be managed and, he hopes, reconciliation made possible.

If, as seems likely, chapters 10–13 are (part of) a later letter, the attempt was not altogether successful, for the outsiders that Paul calls "superapostles" have in the meantime been fishing in the troubled waters of Corinth and have turned many of the Christians more decidedly against Paul. Yet it is probable that Paul ultimately won out, the evidence being both the preservation of these letters and the fact that some time later, writing from Corinth, Paul gives no hint of trouble there and says that the long-planned collection for Jerusalem is going forward (Rom. 15:26). The Roman church four decades later assumed a similar outcome, for *1 Clement* both recognizes that the Corinthian Christians had been a fractious lot already in Paul's time and takes for granted that they acknowledge the authority of Paul's letters.

The same letters exhibit the importance for early Christian moral discourse of one of God's most fundamental characteristics in the covenant traditions of Israel: God's fidelity. In the Corinthian correspondence, Paul frequently emphasizes his own faithfulness and stability—not surprising in the tense situation to which those letters were written. It is characteristic of Paul's mode of moral argument that even as he is asserting those qualities in himself in a defensive stance, he simultaneously presents them as qualities to be imitated in the community he addresses, and he grounds them in the faithfulness of God and of Christ. The connection is vivid in 2 Cor. 1:18–19, where Paul defends himself against a charge of inconsistency or vacillation: "But faithful is God, that our speech to you is not Yes and No, for God's son Jesus Christ who was proclaimed by us among you . . . was not Yes and No, but in him was Yes." The formula "Faithful is God" occurs with special frequency in the Pauline letters, but also widely in other early Christian literature (for example, in 1 Cor. 1:9 and 10:13; 1 Thess. 5:24; 2 Thess. 3:3; 1 John 1:9). It is especially often connected with the reliability of God's promises, as for example in Heb. 10:23, "Faithful is the one who has promised." Here the formula backs the preceding admonition, "Let us hold fast the confession of hope without wavering" (v. 23a) and, less directly, the following exhortation, "Let us give thought to one another to produce an incitement to love and good works" (v. 24). The stability of God's promises provides the necessary context for moral action, particularly when the action is itself defined as *faithful,* that is, action befitting the pattern of God's action, which may defy the customary and commonsensical. Among the chain of examples of such faith that the following chapter of Hebrews compiles from scripture, Sarah's case makes the connection most explicit: "By faith also Sarah herself, though sterile, received the power to conceive, though she was beyond the age of childbearing, for she deemed faithful the one who had made the promise" (11:11).

The fundamental exemplar of God's fidelity, however, for the author of Hebrews, for the Pauline groups, the Johannine groups, and many other circles of early Christianity, was the story of Jesus Christ, particularly of his death and resurrection. Thus "the faith of Christ Jesus" is a foundational element of Paul's theologizing in the letters to Galatia and Rome; Jesus' faith or faithfulness is identical with his obedience and his self-sacrifice. God's faithfulness, in turn, is most fully exemplified in raising Jesus from the dead.

"Love" and "peace" are attributes of God that figure frequently in the Pauline letters, as elsewhere in early Christian admonitions. The closing admonition of 2 Cor. 10–13—a letter that is very severe and sarcastic—now appeals to the addressees, "Put things in order, listen to my appeal, agree with one another, live in peace; and the God of love and peace will be with you" (13:11, NRSV). Shortly after dealing with the Corinthian crisis, Paul wrote his letter to the Romans, in which the "God of peace" (15:33; 16:20) becomes a central motif: God is the one who makes peace, who reconciles enemies to himself and to each other, warranting the explicit and implicit admonitions of the letter.[14]

Throughout the Johannine literature, God's love and Christ's love stand as models:

> Beloved, let us love one another,
>   for love is of God,
> and everyone who loves is born of God
>   and knows God.
> Whoever does not love does not know God,
>   for God is love.
> This is the way God's love was displayed among us:
>   that God sent his unique Son into the world,
>   that through him we might live.
> In this is love:
>   not that we have loved God,
>   but that he loved us
>   and sent his son,
>   an expiation for our sins.
> Brothers, if God thus loved us, we are also obliged to
>   love one another.
>   (1 John 4:7–11)

It is also in the Johannine letters that we find the statement "The doer of good is of God; the evildoer has not seen God" (3 John 11). Variously expressed, this is the common assumption of all early Christian moral discourse. As Jesus says in Mark 10:18, "No one is good [agathos] but the one God." God is thus the transcendent definer of virtue not only by his self-revealed will but by what he is in himself. No room here for the cynicism of Archibald MacLeish's jaded Satan, Mr. Nickles: "If God is God He is not good; / If God is good He is not God."[15] No early Christian or Jew could have thought that jingle anything but silly, nor for that matter could a Plutarch or a Musonius. If one knows God, one knows the good.

In their apologetic works, however, the Christians were quick to attribute vices to the pagan deities and to contrast with them the virtues of the one true God. They could draw upon centuries of Jewish polemics against the polytheism that surrounded the diaspora communities, and which the Jewish authors often equated with laxness of morals. Justin, who like Paul before him identified the pagan deities as "evil demons," draws the contrast starkly, refuting the common accusation against the Christians that they were atheists: "We certainly confess that we are godless with reference to beings like these who are commonly thought of as gods, but not with reference to the most true God, the Father of righteousness and temperance and the other virtues, who is untouched by evil" (1 Apol. 6.1, trans. Hardy). Moreover, Justin explicitly claims that a virtuous God polices the virtue of his believers: "We have been taught and firmly believe that he accepts only those who imitate the good things which are his—temperance and righteousness and love of mankind and whatever else truly belongs to the God who is called by no given name" (10.1).[16]

The argument becomes part of the standard repertoire of Christian apologetics. For example, Athenagoras, writing a few years later than Justin, quotes liberally from Homer to illustrate what poor moral examples the Olympians constitute. He sums up:

> It does not belong to God to prompt acts contrary to nature. Rather,
>
> > When the demon plots against a man,
> > He first impairs the mind.
>
> God, on the other hand, is perfect goodness and is always doing good. (Supplicatio 26.2, trans. Richardson)[17]

However, it is not so easy after all to say just how the virtue of the utterly transcendent God could be accessible to us. When we talk about knowing God's character, it is easy to fall into mystification. To try to avoid that, we need to keep in mind the social process in which the language we have been studying was embedded. The leaders, advisers, and exhorters to good behavior among the early Christians were able to use the virtues and, more generally, the character of God as warrants for their advice, because they could assume their audience knew who God was. They knew who God was because they had been taught, directly and indirectly, as part of the resocialization or "conversion" process by which they became members of the Christian communities. That does not mean that they were all "lay theologians," nor that their conceptions of God were rigorous or clear, nor that they were all in agreement. It does mean that they shared some root metaphors or images, which were shaped by the interaction between notions they already held before their conversion and the specific things they were taught as Christians, the stories they were told, the scriptures read to them, the hymns they sang and the confessions they recited, their rituals and daily practice. As Carol Newsom remarks about the function of hymns in the Qumran community, "Praise constructs the object of praise."[18]

Further, while trying to avoid mystification, we should not fall into the illusion that the whole process was entirely rational and controlled, like some early twentieth-century plan for religious education. Knowledge of God certainly had its experiential elements, including what we could quite legitimately call "mystical"—trance experiences or possession phenomena, the various workings of the Spirit already mentioned. It is the case, however, that the shape of mystical experience or the materials which the mystical intuition recasts into novel shapes are always supplied by the premystical, mundane experiences of the mystic. The God who speaks to the Christian mystic is, in short, the Christian God, and that must mean the God whose features the mystic has learned.

Other Voices

Our outline of the early Christian portrayal of God's character has so far been drawn almost exclusively from those circles of the movement that were to become the dominant voices in that process of self-definition which eventually constructed "orthodoxy" over against "heresy." It is more difficult, because of the nature of the surviving sources and more especially because of the length and power of the tradition that has shaped our reading of them, to reconstruct exactly what each of the contending groups believed before the lines between them hardened, even now that new manuscript discoveries over the past forty years have vastly improved our hindsight.

At least we have learned enough to know that we must avoid rigid categories. In the first two centuries divergent schools often shared more than the polemics between them acknowledge, and many notions that later would be deemed unorthodox were widely accepted. On the other hand, the diversity was real. The golden age of original unity of the faith is a fantasy created by the heresiologists of the second century; what was to be "Christian" had to be discovered by trial and error. Some sharply profiled differences in beliefs about the nature of God emerged in the second century, and we must take account of them in order to understand more adequately the moral landscape of the diverse Christian groups then, or even to understand accurately the beliefs that were to become catholic. The whole story is obviously much too long to tell here; an all too brief sketch of two representative viewpoints will have to suffice. The Valentinians and the Marcionites were probably the strongest and most durable of the groups that were moved or pushed to form distinct movements or sects; they also posed the sharpest alternatives to the characterization of deity that we have observed so far.

The God of Valentinus is the transcendent Absolute of Middle Platonism with human features painted in from the loving savior of Paul and the Fourth Gospel. From the Gnostic sect Valentinus learned how to transform the biblical myths of creation in such a way that the supreme God was removed altogether from the act of creation and from all engagement with the material world. The utter transcendence of the highest reality, as pure intelligent being, undivided and uncontaminated mind, was immensely appealing in the small study circle of which Valentinus was the "spiritual guide," to use Peter Brown's term, and which was so characteristic of the Valentinian movement.[19] The delight of "knowing" was at the same time the passion of teacher and pupil on which such circles thrived and the very means of connection with the supreme object of knowing, itself the ground and essence of knowing. The *gnōsis* was not, of course, merely intellectual; it contained a strong emotional and mystical component. Its chief vehicle was myth.[20]

Myth was necessary, because the human mind is befogged by the mist of ignorance that besets the entire generated world of matter from its very origins in error and deception, the result of the error, fall, and seduction of "Wisdom" from her proper place.[21] For Valentinus, human language affords no trustworthy representation of reality: "Names given to worldly things are very deceptive, since they turn the heart aside from the real to the unreal. And whoever hears the word 'god' thinks not of the reality, but has been thinking of what is not real: so also, with the words 'father,' 'son,' 'holy spirit,' 'life,' 'light,' 'resurrection,' 'church,' etc., it is not the real that one thinks of but the unreal, although the words have referred to the real. The names [that one has] heard exist in the world [. . .] deceive. If the names were situated in the eternal realm, they would not be uttered on any occasion in the world, nor would they have been assigned to worldly things: their goal would be in the eternal realm" (*Gospel of Philip* 53:23–54:4, trans. Layton).[22]

On the other hand, the only access to the spiritual reality is through the "types" and "images" of language and matter. Hence the Valentinian groups had a sacramental practice and theology, though its nature and extent remain matters of debate. They also had at least an ambivalent relationship with the "psychical" Christians who lived solely by faith, having not yet attained knowledge.[23]

Given the ambivalence of the Valentinian understanding of the world, it is perhaps not surprising that it is so difficult to know just what constituted typical Valentinian behavior or whether there was a characteristic Valentinian ethic. Even Irenaeus, who regularly portrays heretics as morally depraved, presents no consistent picture of Valentinian morals. Sometimes they are depicted by their opponents as ascetics, sometimes as sexual libertines, sometimes as ordinary married folk. Similar divergences exist in reports about their responses to persecution. Perhaps they regarded the affairs of the body in a quasi-Stoic way, as *adiaphora*, matters of indifference, to be chosen or rejected as might be most expedient.[24] The essential practice of the Valentinians was the "healing seance" (Brown) of the study circle itself; it was "becoming acquainted" with the truth. Anything in the physical and ordinary human world, so distant from true divinity, could be at best no more than an imperfect learning aid for that quest.

Marcion, if we can rely on a picture of his teaching and personality necessarily based on reports by his enemies, was in many ways Valentinus's opposite. Impatient with ambiguities, he had little taste for allegory, myth, or philosophical subtleties. Characteristically, his first major writing was a collection of "Antitheses," contrasting the morals (to put it bluntly) of the Old Testament God and his prophets with those of the God of love who appeared out of nowhere in Jesus Christ. There could be no unity or even any compromise between them: things had to be either the one way or the other; no God of both mercy and justice, of creation and redemption. Marcion was a biblicist, in a strange sort of way even a literalist, more than a theologian. The image of God that possessed him with the fervor of a zealot, the image that he painstakingly demonstrated from the letters of Paul and the Gospel of Luke (once he had cleared away all the references to the Old Testament deity, which he thought the other apostles had smuggled in), was an exquisite distillation of the God concept into pure love. Marcion's God redeemed misbegotten humanity for absolutely no reason extrinsic to his own grace. Marcion was also a doer, with huge energy, an immensely effective church organizer. The practice of the Marcionites was rigorously ascetic, communal, focused, intensely sectarian. Its point was to snatch people away from the Creator by detaching them from the household that was the formative institution of the mainstream church and thus from the ties that chained them to the Creator's failed world.[25]

God's Roles

The metaphorical descriptions of God that are expressed or presupposed by early Christian writers include particular attributes like the ones I have called "virtues," and other human attributes, such as emotional states: God is angry, pleased, jealous, loving, patient, forgiving, and so on. In addition, God is described under clusters of characteristics that together imply something like a social role. God is said to act as a father or a mother, as a judge, as a friend, as a warrior, as a ruler, as a householder, as a long-range planner, as a teacher, and so on and on. Many of these "roles" are no more than occasional metaphors; others, however, are so frequently and consistently used as to establish pervasive ways of thinking about who God is and how he can be expected to act. We have space for only a few examples.

God as Monarch

In the nineteenth and the first part of this century, the concept of the kingdom of God was central to much discussion of Christian ethics—especially among liberal Protestants. The discovery that this notion belonged to the repertory of ancient apocalyptic visions and thus could not mean what people like Harnack and Ritschl and Rauschenbusch wanted it to mean has led to an embarrassed silence about the kingdom of God in more recent ethical discussion. (The kingdom metaphor has reappeared of late, for example, in titles of books by Stanley Hauerwas and John Howard Yoder.[26]) We can avoid some of the problems we inherit along with the term by focusing, as the early Christian texts mostly do, not on the kingdom but on the depiction of God as king. Of all the constellations of metaphors for God that we find throughout the Hebrew Bible and Jewish tradition and then in specifically early Christian discourse, this is the most pervasive.

Not only God but also Christ are depicted commonly as a king. Jesus was, after all, crucified as "King of the Jews." The old Israelite conception of the Davidic king as God's vice regent, as his "anointed," was ready at hand, in a form modified by Israel's long history of frustrated political expectations and growing eschatological hopes. The "enthronement psalms" which preserved the old court ideology of Israel were pressed by Christians into their liturgical poetry about Jesus' enthronement in heaven, his receiving the throne-name "Lord," and so on. The mysterious figure "like a son of man," whom Daniel saw enthroned with God at the final judgment, was in Christian eyes, of course, Jesus.

Both the theological and the christological uses of royal imagery are far too complex and ubiquitous in Christian language and, later, art to be catalogued here. We can consider only two or three features of the royal imagery in the New Testament, ignoring for the moment the differences in their application to God and to Christ. These are all rooted in the variegated depiction of God in the Hebrew Bible, and that in turn drew upon not only Israel's own royal pomp, but also the grander trappings of the great ancient Near Eastern empires, human and divine. In the eastern provinces of the Roman Empire, however, these old Semitic royal images were, with some changes, readily understandable. Sometimes the Christian interpreters could combine them with images drawn from the court ceremonial of Rome's emperors.

The image of a king is first of all an image of power; if he is absolute monarch, rather than vassal of an emperor, then the power is absolute. The law of the king, his commandments, his will, therefore brook no contradiction. We have noticed a number of examples of this sense of royal power when we discussed the concept of God's sovereign will. The heavenly King, in the biblical tradition, is the vindicator of justice. Very often that notion employs military imagery, and such imagery is not altogether absent from the early Christian depictions of God and Christ, especially in eschatological settings (a vivid example is the warrior of Armageddon in Rev. 19:11–21; see also 16:12–16).

More frequent than the military images are the judicial ones. At the time Christianity began, the notion of a *final* judgment not only of nations but also of individuals was just beginning to be widely accepted in Jewish thought. The first Christians were among those Jews who took it for granted. In the earliest Christian document we have, we learn that Paul had managed to teach it to the gentile converts in Thessalonica: God's son who had been raised from the dead would save them from "the wrath that is coming" (1 Thess. 1:10).

That the king was the court of last appeal was of course universally understood. To be a citizen of Rome meant, among other things, that when indicted anywhere in the Empire, with a few exceptions, one could appeal to

Caesar. Christians sometimes talked this way about their "citizenship in heaven," expecting vindication from the heavenly King when earthly courts failed them. Thus the author of 1 Peter promises that, in the judgment about to begin with the household of God, those who suffer according to the will of God can, "by their good actions, trust their souls to the faithful creator" (1 Peter 4:19). This expectation of a just judgment from the highest court could sometimes be expressed in a way we may find a bit ugly, as in some of the early martyrologies. In one, for example, the Christians being led into the arena to be killed signify by gestures to the procurator, "You [have condemned] us, but God [will condemn] you."[27]

The tension depicted in such scenes reminds us that God's metaphorical role as king also entails construing ethics as loyalty to the monarch. Thus Polycarp is reported to have replied, when the proconsul urged him to gain his release by cursing Christ, "Eighty-six years I have served him, and he never did me any wrong. How can I blaspheme my King who saved me?" (*Mart. Polyc.* 9:3, trans. Shepherd).[28] As the author of Acts recalled, Christians were sometimes accused of "acting contrary to the decrees of Caesar and saying that there is another king, Jesus" (17:7). However, that author is at pains to show that the accusation was really false; the Christians were not subversive at all. In the writings of the New Testament itself and in a good many other Christian writings of the first two centuries, the relationship between God's ultimate kingship and the temporal reign of Caesar is depicted as benign—for example, in Romans 13:1–7; 1 Peter 2:13–17; Titus 3:1. In other places, the two realms are seen as unalterably antagonistic, and one must choose between God or Christ and Caesar. The conflict is depicted in particularly stark terms, of course, in the apocalypses and martyrologies. Even in the more delicately drawn scene of Jesus' trial in the Fourth Gospel, though the kingship of Jesus is "not of this world," it requires a decision in this world, and the most poignant irony in this Gospel comes when the Jews who refuse Jesus as their king are made to say (perhaps parodying the refrain of a Passover hymn), "We have no king but Caesar" (John 19:15).

In less dramatic ways, at a very simple and individual level, daily behavior can be taken as a moral test of loyalty. Such a notion is expressed in a sentence that apparently belonged to the catechism of the earliest Christians, at least in the Pauline area: "Those who do x, y, and z [lists of various vices] cannot inherit the kingdom of God" (1 Cor. 6:9–10; compare 15:20; Gal. 5:21; Eph. 5:5). Alternatively, as Paul puts it in another place, converts were instructed "to behave worthily of the God who called you into his own kingdom and glory" (1 Thess. 2:12).

God as Owner

Alongside the political metaphor of God's kingship, and often crossing or mingling with it, is the more domestic metaphor of God as lord of a household, as master and owner. Paul can twice punctuate his admonitions to the Corinthians, for example, with the statement "You have been bought at a price" (1 Cor. 6:20; 7:23). From that it follows that, as God's slaves, they must so act that their master is honored (6:20), and they must not become slaves of others (7:23). So also in the Letter to Romans, chapter 6, Paul depicts the conversion of Christians as a change from being slaves to sin to being slaves of God and of righteousness. The familiar saying of Jesus "No one can serve two masters" makes the same point in proverbial fashion, with "Mammon" rather than "Sin" as the alternative owner (Matt. 6:24; Luke 16:13).

It appears curious to us, no doubt, that in a society where slavery was ubiquitous, metaphors of slavery should be used so frequently in a positive sense to speak of salvation and the moral life. Commentators routinely point out, of course, that such metaphors were common in the Hebrew scriptures to describe the relationship of Israel and especially of certain chosen leaders, above all prophets, to God. Still, the metaphor had to make sense in the quite different culture of the Greco-Roman cities. In the language of Hellenism, talk of being slaves of the gods was rare, specialized, and usually positive. Two things must be noted about the ways such a metaphor would be heard by ordinary people in those cities. First, to speak of being God's slave was a particularly effective way of communicating the obligation of absolute obedience to God's will. Second, slavery in the Roman Empire was a complex and diversified institution. The expressions "slave of God" or "slave of Jesus Christ" might sound odd at first, but people were quite accustomed to thinking of "slaves of Caesar" as sometimes exercising enormous power and even enjoying extraordinary, though reflected, honor. One's attitude toward slavery also obviously varied according to one's own status in the society. The disdain expressed by a Petronius or a Pliny for former slaves who have risen in the world was presumably not necessarily shared by other slaves or freedmen who might hope to rise themselves.[29]

God as Parent

The representation of God as "Father" is too familiar and too pervasive in the early Christian texts to require demonstration. It was a natural and quite ancient metaphor. Zeus is regularly called "father of the gods and men" from the time of Hesiod on; his Latin name "Jupiter" (Iuppiter) derives from the epithet *iovis pater*, "Father Jove."[30] That Yahweh was the father of Israel was a firm element in Israel's covenant traditions, and the relationship occasionally could be expressed by parental images of unsurpassed tenderness, as in these lines from the prophet Hosea:

> When Israel was a child, I loved him,
>   and out of Egypt I called my son.
> The more I called them,
>   the more they went from me;
> they kept sacrificing to the Baals,
>   and offering incense to idols.
> Yet it was I who taught Ephraim to walk.
>   I took them up in my arms;
>   but they did not know that I healed them.
> I led them with cords of human kindness,
>   with bands of love.
> I was to them like those
>   who lift infants to their cheeks,
>   I bent down to them and fed them.
> (Hos. 11:1–4, NRSV)

No wonder, then, that the epithet "Father" and images of household management and childrearing by the father or, more rarely, the mother came easily to the lips of early Christian preachers and teachers. It was, of course, the patriarchal household of the Greco-Roman cities, rather too stern in its discipline and rather too male-hierarchical in its allocation of power for modern tastes, that provided the common models. For example, in Paul's extended metaphor on the functions of the law in God's plan for Israel and the nations (Gal. 3:23–4:7), God acts as a proper, well-to-do *paterfamilias*. He assigns the oversight of his children's education to a slave chosen for that purpose, a *paidagōgos*, fixing a date on which they will come of age. Until then, they are so closely watched and so firmly disciplined that their life is no different from that of the household's slaves.[31]

Also from Paul's argument (Gal. 4:6) and from a parallel in Rom. 8:15, we are able to deduce that the early ritual of baptism included a moment when the initiate cried out, using the Aramaic of the movement's earliest days, "Abba! Father!" thus signifying adoption into God's own family. The prayer Jesus was said to have taught his disciples began with the same simple address (preserved only in Greek): "Father" (Luke 11:1–4), elaborated in Matthew to that Gospel's characteristic name for God, "Father in heaven" (6:9; this phrase or its equivalent, "heavenly Father," occurs nineteen times in Matthew, of its forty-four total uses of "father" for God). The usage spread, naturally, to other prayers as well—for example, the eucharistic prayers in *Didache* 9:2,3 and 10:2. The Johannine literature, including the Apocalypse, calls God father almost exclusively as father of Jesus. By way of contrast, the particularly severe polemic of John 8:41–42 denies to "the Jews" who reject Jesus' claims the right to call God their father.

Paul coined a style of letter opening that spoke of "God the Father and our Lord Jesus Christ," a style that would be widely copied in later Christian letter writing. Paul's unknown disciple, the author of Ephesians, in a rhetorical passage fancies the word *patria*, "clan, family," applied to any kinship group "in heaven and on earth" to derive from God's name *patēr*, "Father" (Eph. 3:14–15). Paul and other writers could amplify the paternal epithet by adding attributes in a genitive construction: "Father of mercies and of consolation" (2 Cor. 1:3); "Father of lights" (Jas. 1:17); or equivalent constructions, like *1 Clem.* 23:1, "the all-merciful and beneficent Father."

What dominant values did the wide and habitual use of such language infuse into Christian imagination? For one thing, relatedness itself is valued; to become a Christian was to be adopted into a new family or even to be "born anew" with a divine parent and new siblings. This is not quite so simple, however, as the "affirmation of family values" so dear to modern politicians and, with a rather different notion of family, to many ancient apologists. To join the new family meant to reject the old, and to what extent that might mean rejection of the whole order implied by "family" was, as we have seen earlier, a matter of some controversy among different wings of the Christian movement. For Johannine Christians, faith in God as Jesus' father meant separation from the Jewish communities to which they had belonged and denial of the Jews' claims upon God as Father. For the *Gospel of Thomas*, to acknowledge the true Father and Mother would bring abuse from the world, from which the true believer, becoming a "passerby" and "solitary," must sever all connections, especially those of sex and family. For those Christians whom Peter Brown calls "the silent majority," on the other hand, the household remained, as it had been in the beginning of Christian expansion, the core of the church's structure, its order affirmed "in the Lord."

For all who called God "Father," power was doubtless one central connotation, for power and ownership belonged to the father in ancient households, and order, peace, and concord flowed from that power according to ancient ideals. Nevertheless, we can hardly fail to notice how often the epithet "Father" is accompanied in our texts by language suggesting affection, patience, mercy, pleading, consolation, and kindness. By and large, the first Christians (like other sects of Jews) were taught to conduct their moral life under the all-seeing eye of a God who was simultaneously a stern patriarch and a forgiving and caring parent.

God's Actions

The third major way in which early Christian discourse represents the theological context of ethics is by describing God's actions. The "Two Ways" that was so popular as an elementary statement of Christian morals (as we saw in chapter 5) begins with the commandment "You shall love the God who made you" (*Did.* 1:2; *Barn.* 19:2). That God had made both the physical world and the human world was a firm part of the belief of most Christians, even though the more educated writers adopted the negative theology beloved of middle Platonists, which seemed to contradict a positive action by God in material things. Athenagoras, for example, affirms that Christians confess "the one uncreated, unending, invisible, impassible, incomprehensible, uncontainable" God, "by whom," nevertheless, "the universe came into being, through his *logos* [word, reason], was ordered and is sustained" (*Supplicatio* 10.1).

Some Christians, like some philosophers, saw a contradiction here. Perhaps Athenagoras, like Philo before him, thought "through his *logos*" a sufficient solution to the problem of an "impassible" God actively creating a material world. The same apparent contradiction, after all, could be found in Plato's *Timaeus*, and some middle Platonists solved it by distinguishing the Demiurge or creator from the supreme God. The Valentinians, as we have seen, followed in that line, but exploited the myths of the Gnostic sect to increase the distance and difference between the Fullness of the spiritual world and the Rulers who had cobbled together the physical world. Marcion employed a much simpler myth and theology. There were two gods, one just, the other good; the one made the world, though not very well, and the other saved people out of it. For Marcionites, however, as for most Christians of the emerging mainstream, it was self-evident that the supreme God *acted*.

The actions most Christians attributed to God were of two sorts. There are the continuing activities that are characteristic of the divine nature; they are intrinsic, as it were, to those "roles" that believers assign to God. For example, God governs, and his governance entails that he rewards virtue and punishes vice. So also he may patiently overlook some wrongdoing or forgive it altogether, or act decisively to reconcile enemies (for example, 2 Cor. 5:18–21; Rom. 5:6–11). He legislates, commands, chastises, appeals, predicts, reveals. As parent, he loves, cares for, reproves, disciplines.

The other sort of activity attributed to God comprises unique "historical" acts. The first Christians, being Jews, inherited in their Bibles certain ways of talking about God acting in, through, and behind human events. The fact that the Bible of the Greek-speaking synagogues, the Septuagint, was also the Bible of the Christians meant that the stories of creation and fall, of the calling of Israel, of Israel's covenant, disobedience, punishment, and restoration—all became the Christians' stories, too.

To those stories of God's paradigmatic acts in the past, the Christians added their new stories. Central, of course, was the identification of God as the one "who raised Jesus our Lord from the dead" (Rom 4:24; 2 Cor. 4:14; Gal. 1:1; Col. 2:12; 1 Pet. 1:21; Acts 5:30; and so on). That claim, too, had extraordinary implications for the ways in which all God's actions could henceforth be construed, and those construals had very broad ethical implications—for instance, for the ways power and authority were to be understood. For both Jews and Christians, the actions of God in the past encouraged the belief that God would act also in the future: to redeem his people, to punish the wicked, to manifest his Messiah in glory, to create a new heaven and a new earth.

To speak of God as acting is to tell, or to imply, a story. Hence, rather than continuing our somewhat abstract discussion of the patterns of God's action, we will do better to break off here and turn to the characteristics of early Christian narrative. For the future of Christian and more generally of Western moral sensibilities, the most prolific consequence of belief in an active God is the generation of moral narrative. How the early Christians came to tell a unique set of stories embracing the moral history and destiny of humankind is a tale in itself, which will occupy us for our final two chapters.

CHAPTER 10

Senses of an Ending

❖　❖　❖　❖　❖　❖　❖　❖　❖　❖

I t requires no particular philosophy to discover
that time passes and, once past, cannot be brought back, though the puzzle of
time is one that captivates philosophers. The aging Seneca states more
elegantly than most the feel of time gone by: "omnia in idem profundum
cadunt," "all things fall into the same abyss" (*Epistle* 49.3) or, in another
place, "Quicquid aetatis retro est, mors tenet," "Whatever years lie behind
us are in death's hands" (*Ep.* 1.2, trans. Richard M. Gummere).

For Christians, however, even the dead are raised, and those deeds fallen
into the abyss have not fallen from God's memory. To the ordinary sense of
the directionality and irreversibility of an individual's times, the Christians
add a new and ominous dimension: the conviction not merely that each
person's life has its terminus, but that the entire human story and the world
itself run toward a point that is not merely end but also goal, summing up,
and absolute correction of the fallen *omnia*.

In many kinds of contexts of early Christian rhetoric, the terminal
phrases come tumbling out: "And then comes the end . . . ," "In the last
days . . . ," "But the end is not yet . . . ," and the like. What John Gager has
called "End-time language" is quite characteristic of the speech of the first
Christians.[1] There can be little question about the source from which they
drew such talk; it is the special idiom of those apocalyptic circles of Judaism
from which the first followers of Jesus had absorbed so much of their
language and their perception of the world. Its deeper roots, in the prophetic
tradition of the "Day of YHWH," in the metaphorical power of individual
prophets who could picture a political crisis in images of the world's creation
reversed and undone, in Israel's experience of exile and chaos and its confrontation with the myths and mathematical astrology of other ancient Near
Eastern cultures—these things need not concern us here. The point is how

natural thought of "the end" was to the first Christians, and how strange to most of their neighbors. Such thoughts were quite foreign to ordinary Greek and Roman sensibilities, however many antecedents and parallels one might legitimately point out to this or that aspect of the eschatological scenarios. As Robin Lane Fox observes, "Thinking pagans had worried more about the beginning of the world than about its possible end."[2]

The effects of Christian imaginings of the end upon Western thought and art can scarcely be exaggerated. In his brilliant Mary Flexner Lectures, *The Sense of an Ending* (from which I have gratefully borrowed the title of this chapter, with a modification made necessary by early Christianity's diversity), Frank Kermode shows how the modern novel depends for its inmost form—even in those versions that rebel against form—upon the paradigm of the end that was created by the Christian Bible. The Bible, he says, "is a familiar model of history. It begins at the beginning ('In the beginning . . .') and ends with a vision of the end ('Even so, come, Lord Jesus'); the first book is Genesis, the last Apocalypse. Ideally, it is a wholly concordant structure, the end is in harmony with the beginning, the middle with beginning and end. The end, Apocalypse, is traditionally held to resume the whole structure, which it can only do by figures predictive of that part of it which has not been historically revealed."[3]

The power of the sense of an ending to generate narrative will concern us in the next chapter. For the present, we limit our inquiry to the more direct ways in which the varieties of eschatological consciousness among the early Christians affected their moral dispositions.

Final Judgment

The end toward which we are all hastening is to stand before the judgment seat of God and there receive just reward or punishment for the lives we have lived. Contemplation of that end will make good persons better and will restrain those inclined toward evil. These sentiments are expressed in early Christian writings more often than many modern readers would like, and they are implied even more frequently. Among the apologists of the second century, Justin provides a clear example. Good rulers ought to welcome Christians, he insists, because

> more than all other people we are your supporters and allies in maintaining public order. We believe, you see, that it is impossible for a wrong-

doer or a greedy person or a conspirator—or a virtuous person—to hide from God, and everyone is headed for either eternal punishment or eternal salvation, depending on the merit of one's deeds. If all people knew this, not one would choose wickedness for a moment, knowing that the wicked goes straight to eternal punishment by fire, but in every way each would exercise self-restraint and adorn himself with virtue, in order to obtain the good things that come from God and to be spared the punishments. (1 Apol. 12.1–2)

These notions very early become part of the repertory of Christian moral admonition. Writing to the Galatians, Paul can back up rather mundane advice to converts, that they ought to help support their instructors, by a saying, probably traditional, about rewards (Gal. 6:6). He then expands his exhortation to include general care for the community's life: "Make no mistake about this: God is not to be fooled; everyone reaps what he sows. If he sows in the field of his unspiritual nature, he will reap from it a harvest of corruption; but if he sows in the field of the Spirit, he will reap from it a harvest of eternal life. Let us never tire of doing good, for if we do not slacken our efforts we shall in due time reap our harvest" (Gal 6:7–9, NRSV).

A traditional formula quoted several times in letters of Paul's school warns that "no one who [is characterized by a variable list of vices: prostitution, impurity, licentiousness, idolatry, sorcery, and so on] will inherit the kingdom of God" (1 Cor. 6:9–10; Gal. 5:21; Eph. 5:5). And of course, most dramatically of all, the two eschatological chapters that close Jesus' teachings in the Gospel according to Matthew reach their climax in the scene of "all nations" gathered before the Son of Man, who, like a shepherd separating sheep from goats, sorts out those who have helped "my smallest brothers" from those who have neglected them. "The latter go away to eternal punishment, but the just to eternal life" (Matt. 25:46).

The Christian imagination could not long leave the fates of the sheep and the goats—particularly the goats—unelaborated. The second-century Apocalypse of Peter describes in obscene detail how punishments in hell are made to fit earthly crimes: blasphemers hang by their tongues; women who adorned themselves for adulterous liaisons, by their hair; murderers writhe in a pit full of venomous snakes and worms, while their victims watch with satisfaction; and so on. Here, of course, we see one variant in the long tradition of depictions of the underworld that stretches from the Nekyia of Homer (Od. 11) to Dante's Inferno. Albrecht Dieterich's classic monograph

Nekyia has gathered the early examples in abundance, comparing the *Apocalypse of Peter*.[4]

Not to everyone's taste, now or in antiquity. Tertullian complains, early in the third century, "We are laughed at for proclaiming that God will be judge" (*Apol.* 47.12, trans. Glover). Sophisticated Romans had long been deriding popular beliefs of punishments awaiting the soul after death. Best known of the skeptics, of course, are the Epicureans, for whom such beliefs were the very antithesis of the serenity at which their philosophy aimed. Stoics, too, had little use for such notions. Seneca's famous letter of consolation addressed to Marcia, though the first part of it sounds rather more Platonic than Stoic, rejects all notions of judgment and punishment in the next world as "mere tales" (*fabulae*, 19.4). The satirists Juvenal and Lucian have great fun lampooning the afterlife beliefs of "the common herd" as well as their funeral practices (Juvenal, *Satires* 2.149–52; Lucian, *On Funerals, Dialogues of the Dead, The Downward Journey, Zeus Catechized, Menippus*).

Nevertheless, despite their tendency to hyperbole, the satires may serve as evidence that such beliefs were in fact widely held—though the dearth of any epigraphic evidence for belief in afterlife judgment and the extreme rarity of inscriptions even implying belief in survival of any sort after death must make us skeptical.[5] Not all educated people, on the other hand, rejected beliefs in postmortem judgment. The always credulous Aelius Aristides (second century) praises Serapis as both psychopomp and judge of the dead, "assigning places to every person according to the merit of their life on earth" (*Or.* 45.25). Certainly it is true as well that some Jewish circles had developed elaborate notions of postmortem judgment by this time. The Jewish beliefs seem to have been no more uniform than those of other people in the Greco-Roman world, however, and the more detailed pictures of judgment and punishment after death are found in rather late sources, such as the *Testament of Abraham*.[6]

One tendency in the emerging Jewish beliefs in postmortem judgment, while it is by no means universally held, is in one sense characteristic, because it follows logically from monotheistic belief. This is the notion that judgment is universal and punctiliar. This understanding of judgment arises especially in the context of apocalypticism. It is, of course, also the picture of judgment that dominates early Christian beliefs: the notion that, as the author of Acts has Paul say, God "has fixed a day on which he will have the world judged in righteousness by a man whom he has appointed" (Acts 17:31, NRSV). This belief in a single, universal, *final* judgment was destined to have an extraordinary generative power in shaping the moral narrative of human life that was beginning to emerge in Christian sensibilities—more about that in chapter 11.

Two documents from the Christian groups in the city of Rome, both from the last decade of the first century, illustrate the diversity of views, or at least of emphasis, about the final judgment. The letter of the Roman church to the Corinthian church (1 Clement) and the Shepherd of Hermas are both preoccupied with repentance, the former urging irregularly installed presbyters at Corinth to step down in favor of those they supplanted, the latter exhorting Roman Christians, especially their leaders, to proper discipline. The letter, though it constantly pounds the theme of God's disciplining his people, illustrated by countless quotations from scripture, speaks of future judgment only in the most sparing terms, and then in a way that could imply mundane chastisements more readily than *final* judgment.[7] The ideals upheld by Clement are concord and peace, the social and political ideals of the Greek and Roman urban elites, and to back them up he looks mostly to the past, to biblical examples as well as those of Greek and Roman tradition and literature. Hermas, on the other hand, models his discourse on the apocalyptic style—though comparison with the roughly contemporary Apocalypse of John shows how far the Roman writer is from the distinctive temperament and intensity of the apocalypticist. Indeed, one can argue whether the *Shepherd* is most usefully called an apocalypse. The part traditionally called "Mandates" is gnomic in character and reminds one of the Greek-Jewish sapiential writings. The conversations between the angel and Hermas in the "Visions" and "Similitudes," while broadly conforming to the apocalyptic convention of visions interpreted by a heavenly figure, in style and content resemble more a moralizing exposition (based on a typical kind of art criticism) like the *Tablet of Cebes* (discussed in chapter 2).[8] Nevertheless, the *Shepherd* does share with apocalyptic writings an intense expectation of future judgment, wearisomely reinforced by one after another of the "revelations" related by the author. And these multiple visions of God's ineluctable final decision stand squarely behind Hermas's moral exhortation. The Shepherd's final admonition sums it up: "Therefore do good deeds, all you who have learnt of the Lord, lest the building of the tower be finished while you delay to do them. For the work of the building has been broken off for your sake. Unless therefore you hasten to do right the tower will be finished and you will be shut out" (114.4 [*Sim.* 10.4.4], trans. Lake).

The notion of final judgment that emerges in catholic Christianity holds that it is not only universal but also corporate in its moral implications. What we have been talking about so far is the use of the belief in a final judgment as a sanction for individual behavior. That is the implication of the belief that Justin emphasized in his *First Apology*—quite naturally, for it was obvious, and it resonated with popular beliefs held by at least some ordinary people. What is more distinctive about the eschatology of the early Christians, as of other apocalyptic groups, is that expectation of a final judgment is at the same time expectation of the final definition and vindication of the community. When initiates into the Christian group are taught that those who do x, y, and z "will not inherit the kingdom of God," they are not merely being warned that if they revert to such vices they will someday be punished. They are being told something about the community to which they are now joined, something about the character of the people over whom God reigns in the new age. The images in which the coming judgment are figured in the *Shepherd of Hermas* are explicitly corporate, even institutional; the metaphor of building predominates, and it is the health of the Christian house-churches of Rome that is the object of Hermas's prophetic concern.

The social boundaries of the new community significantly frame its moral sensibilities. The converts perceive their moral norms as different from those of the outsiders, and the outsiders are only too ready to believe that they are different indeed, in pernicious ways. Even in cases where an unbiased observer might find very small differences in fact, the perceptions of difference produce hostility and conflict. The question of moral obligation becomes a question of loyalty to a community that sees itself as righteous and under attack. Apocalyptic imagery is perfectly suited to reinforce such loyalty: God's judgment will vindicate his own. Making the punishment metonymically fit the crime, God will render to the oppressors oppression, to the oppressed relief (2 Thess. 1:6; compare Phil. 1:28). Stories of the solidity of the martyrs' faith are told and retold to cement the solidarity of the communities they represented—against the evil empire that destroyed them.

There is more to the eschatological temperament, however, than support for the embattled group, more even than theodicy. Christian belief in resurrection and vindication extends without limit the boundaries of moral responsibility. Not only does the expectation of final judgment provide for a final weighing up of the behavior of every individual, the resurrection entails an infinite extension of the community and therefore of the mutual relationships and responsibilities entailed by community. This is quite clear in the consolation section of 1 Thess. 4:13–18, followed as it is directly by the moralizing and apocalyptic pericope of 5:1–11. The two units are closely linked by the repetition in 5:11 of the words of 4:18 (a rhetorical *inclusio*): "Console one another, then, with these words" (4:18, REB). The speech of consolation in the face of bereavement is here dramatically different from, though recognizably parallel to, the consolation of ordinary Greco-Roman rhetoric. The apocalyptic language of separation, of the moral opposition between the children of light and the children of darkness, is here pressed into an assurance of the ultimate unity of those who are "in Christ." The living are consoled by being challenged so to live that they and those in Christ who are dead will be reunited, "and thus we shall always be with the Lord" (4:16–17).[9]

Disestablishing the World

The sense of an ending does more than provide a myth to justify the separation between the righteous community and the larger culture around them. It disestablishes the world. By declaring that all that is taken for granted will end, eschatological scenarios undermine the cultural system that masquerades as common sense. In chapter 4 we considered the negative images of the world held by some groups of early Christians. Those world-images are closely linked with the ways those groups imagined the world's end. Some idea of the variety of their thinking may be gained by considering four quite different examples from early Christian thinking about the end of things and the implications of each for one's moral relationship to the world. The first example is Paul's remarkably varied use of End-time language, for purposes that sometimes seem contradictory. The second is the radical counterculture advocated by the author of the Apocalypse. The third is the internalized eschatology—eschatology without an ending—of the *Gospel of Thomas*. The fourth is the eschatology of Valentinus, at once cosmic and internalized.

Paul

In his epistolary rebuke and appeal to the Galatian Christians, Paul accuses the missionaries who have come after him there of introducing "another gospel," which he insists is false, for there can be no other gospel than the one he preached before. From the point of view of the rival apostles, on the contrary, it is Paul who is the innovator. Paul has radically violated the standards of Judaism by permitting gentiles to join the community without being circumcised and without being required to keep the Sabbath and festivals. Paul writes to defend those innovations, and he does so by the strategies of apocalypticism. We find analogous strategies in the foundation of cults by millenarians in modern times, and particularly close analogies in the interpretive work of the Teacher of Righteousness of Qumran and his successors in that community. In Galatians, Paul insists that with the coming of the Messiah, a new age has begun in which old promises are fulfilled in novel ways. He engages in an imaginative and radical reinterpretation of scripture and tradition to explain and justify the novelties.

The situation to which Paul's first surviving letter to Corinth is addressed is quite different. Here one or more groups of the Corinthian Christians are fully prepared to celebrate the novelty of the Christian proclamation, and to draw from it implications of radical freedom in their moral lives. "All things are allowed," they say. "We all have knowledge," and therefore all are free from scruples about such things as eating sacrificial meat, or even matters of sexuality. Some of their slogans have an eschatological ring: "Food's for the belly and the belly for food—and God will destroy both the one and the other" (1 Cor. 6:12–13a; 8:1). The moral implication could as well be ascetic as libertine: "It is good for a man not to touch a woman" (7:1). Scholars remain divided over the ideology of these Christians whom Paul writes to correct: Are they some kind of proto-Gnostics? Are they on the contrary people who have taken Paul's apocalyptic eschatology only too seriously? Are they merely the better-educated minority of the converts, who have assimilated Paul's gospel to some of the ideals of popular moral philosophy, celebrating the autonomy of the truly wise man? Or are they several things at once, perhaps divided among themselves? The last alternative seems most probable; fortunately, we do not have to determine all the details of the Corinthians' beliefs in order to understand the main outlines of Paul's response.[10]

Paul responds by using, as those free spirits of Corinth apparently had done, a combination of the peculiar language of apocalyptic eschatology with commonplaces from the moral rhetoric of Greco-Roman popular philosophy, especially the Cynic tradition.[11] What is astonishing is that Paul uses the combination here, not to justify innovation, as he did in writing to the

Galatians, but to insist upon the real though limited claims on the moral agent of things as they are. "It *is* good for a man not to touch a woman, but—because of fornications—let each man have his own wife and let each woman have her own husband" (1 Cor. 7:1–3). "*We* all have knowledge," but there are those in the community who do not. For the sake of these "weak" Christians, watch out lest "this knowledge of yours" result in the destruction of "a brother for whom Christ died" (8:1–11). It is true that "the time is compressed" and that "the form of the world is passing away." Therefore the dealings the Christian has with the world are "as if they were not." Nevertheless—or rather, just for that reason—"as the Lord has allotted to each, as God has called each, so let each person behave"—slave or free, circumcised or uncircumcised, married or unmarried (7:17–40). Here the sense of an ending, precisely by relativizing the demands of the common-sense world, makes room for the Christian to live in it, Paul claims, without anxiety. The end-time language does not work by an abstract logic of its own, in Paul's moralizing discourse, but always within the context of a particular community's situation.[12]

The Apocalypse

John, the author of the Revelation, would not have approved much of Paul's advice about living in the world in the short time before the end. "Everything that is sold in the meat market you may eat without making a judgment of conscience" (1 Cor. 10:25) was the kind of advice John would expect to hear from the female prophet he labels "Jezebel" (Rev. 2:20). We would not be surprised if her real name had been "Prisca" or "Lydia" or one of the other women prophets in the Pauline circle. To John, in the light of the things that "must soon take place," things visible only through the visionary experience from the vantage point of heaven, the present world is unrelievedly evil and frightening. Not only meat markets, but all markets, it seems, are infected by the evil of the great whore who sits at the center of all trade and all power. Not only the kings of the earth, but all the merchants and traders of all kinds of goods, all the sailors and captains "who work the sea," will be plunged into mourning at her destruction—she who is Babylon and Rome (chap. 18). Those who participate in the culture dominated by Rome are those castigated for being "lukewarm" or "asleep" (3:2–3,15–16). Withdrawal and opposition are called for from those who will be "faithful witnesses." Rome is the embodiment of the "ancient dragon" who opposes

God and is ultimately to be destroyed (chaps. 12; 13; 20:2). The Jewish communities in the Asian cities receive scarcely better marks: they say they are Jews but are not, but are the synagogue of Satan (2:9; 3:9). The sense of an ending that John strives to communicate to the churches of Asia breaks all ties to the present world; its moral message is of separation and "holding fast."[13]

The Gospel of Thomas

The judgment of the world in the *Gospel of Thomas* is, if anything, even more negative than that in the Apocalypse, as we saw in chapter 4. Yet both its images of the world and its use of language about the end are quite different. When we come to the *Gospel of Thomas* from having read the Apocalypse, we are immediately struck by the almost total absence from Thomas of allusions to what we would call the political world. It does contain a version of Jesus' saying about Caesar's coinage, but the point seems to lie in an addition to the version we know from the Synoptics: "Give unto Caesar the things that are Caesar's, give unto God the things that are God's, *and give unto me that which is mine*" (100; 49:29–31, trans. Layton, emphasis added). What is wrong with the world, for Thomas, is not that it is dominated by the satanic adversary of God and, through Satan, by Rome. Rather, the world is evil because it, like the body in all its relationships, traps the self and hinders its flight to its true "repose." It may be significant that the Thomas tradition took shape on the far eastern fringes of the Roman Empire, in the area around Edessa, ruled at that time by native kings under Roman hegemony. Rome did not seem in those parts quite the constant presence that so oppressed the seer John.

The sense of the end conveyed by Jesus' "secret words" in this Gospel is fundamentally different from the traditional apocalyptic sense of a universal climax and conclusion of the age-old struggle between evil and good, between the powers of God and the powers of the Adversary. Here, instead, the end must be discovered by each individual: "The disciples said to Jesus, 'Tell us how our end will come to pass.' Jesus said, 'Then have you laid bare the beginning, so that you are seeking the end? For the end will be where the beginning is. Blessed is the person who stands at rest in the beginning. And that person will be acquainted with the end and will not taste death'" (18; 36:9–16, trans. Layton).

Again: "His disciples said to him, 'When will the repose of the dead come to pass, and when will the new world come?' He said to them, 'That [repose] which you are waiting for has come, but for your part you do not recognize it' " (51; 42:7–11). The kingdom is not to be waited for; it is "spread out over the earth, and people do not see it" (113); it is "inside of you; and it is outside of you" (3; see also sayings 111 and 57).

Here is a sense of an ending without a temporal moment, or at least quite independent of any thought of a "time" when the end "comes." This interior sense of the end, which is born at the instant one comes to know oneself truly, yields quite a different set of moral dispositions from those that John urged upon the Christians of Asia. For Thomas as for John, the economic order is dangerous, but not because it involves compromise with the order dominated by the whore Rome-Babylon. Rather, trade entangles us with the world as such—but so does family life, so does sexuality, a settled living, indeed everything that connects "a body to a body." The repose promised by the Apocalypse is given to the holy ones who have come through the great persecution, who hold fast until the end. In the face of that struggle and that end, a fiercely disciplined and separated community must be forged. In contrast, the repose sought by Christians of the Thomas tradition is to be found deep within the self that has become a solitary, a *monachos*, a passerby, severing all ties, detached from all sense of place, waging a holy war not against Babylon but against the body.

Valentinus

Valentinus seems to have drawn upon the Thomas tradition, for the myth of the soul that is at the heart of his interpretation of Christian salvation is the same, in its essential outlines, as that in the Thomas literature. That myth of the soul's origin in another world, its being cast into materiality and forgetfulness, and the possibility of its rescue by acquiring true self-knowledge also resonated effectively with the beliefs of the more mystical wing of middle Platonism, which seems to have shaped much of Valentinus's thought. With this Christian-Platonist myth and with his penetrating but eccentric readings of much of the emerging New Testament, Valentinus combined a great cosmogonic myth, which he adapted, Irenaeus tells us, from a sect who called themselves "the knowing ones," the Gnostics. This myth explains how, out of the primeval unity and light, by a series of emanations, there devolved multiplicity, darkness, and ultimately our material world. The result was that (Platonic) forgetting which is the source of all evil. As Valentinus's own *Gospel of Truth* puts it: "Inasmuch as the entirety *[plērōma]* had searched for the one from whom they had emanated, and the entirety was inside of him—the inconceivable uncontained, who is superior to all thought—ignorance of the father caused agitation and fear. And the agitation grew dense like fog, so that no one could see. Thus error found strength and labored at her matter in emptiness. Without having learned to know the truth, she took up residence in a modeled form [the human body], preparing by means of the power, in beauty, a substitute for truth" (16:4–20, trans. Layton).

Now Valentinus conveys a very keen sense of an ending. "Inasmuch as the completion of the entirety is in the father, the entirety must go to him. Then upon gaining acquaintance *[gnōsis]*, all individually receive what belongs to them, and draw it to themselves" (*Gosp. Truth* 21:8–13). Gnosis, by reversing error, reverses the process of devolution by which the illusory world came into being. When the elect all learn who they are, they are rejoined to their "angels" or "images," and as unity supplants the disorder of illusion, the material world at last vanishes.

Thus, ironically, by adapting the Gnostic myth of the world's origins, Valentinus restores that apocalyptic sense of a universal, final resolution that we found lacking in Thomas. This seems ironic, because temporality itself is part of the illusion that arises in the befogged state of our present existence.

Now what manner of morality arises from such a sense of the end? The catholic opponents of the Valentinians accused them of many wicked things, but we have to take those polemical assertions with more than a grain of salt. We really know hardly anything about the practical moral teachings of Valentinus, much less about the actual behavior of his followers. One exception is a paragraph in the *Gospel of Truth*: "Make steady the feet of those who have stumbled, and stretch out your hands to those who are sick. Feed those who are hungry, and unto those who are weary give repose; and awaken those who wish to arise, and get up from your sleep. For it is you who are unsheathed intelligence. If strengthening is thus, it is truly strong" (33:1–10).

The first part of this sounds like very conventional Christian or Jewish exhortation, though like almost everything in Valentinus's rhetoric, it is perhaps subject to double entendre. The specifically Gnostic exhortation is the appeal to quicken one's own understanding and to use it to "awaken" others who belong to the elect and are capable of Gnosis. Then the exhortation continues: "Focus your attention upon yourselves. Do not focus your attention upon others [or other things], that is, ones whom you have expelled. Do not return to eat what you have vomited forth" (33:11–15).

How much responsibility a Valentinian Christian felt toward people who were not responsive to the call to the "higher" understanding is a question that modern scholars continue to debate. Probably the Valentinian practice varied widely from one individual, or from one cell of Valentinians, to another.

Relativizing Our Own Certainties

One further use of language about the end of things played a minor but potentially important role in the formation of Christian sensibilities. In the admonitions from several different sectors of the early Christian movement, we occasionally hear a warning against confusing things that seem ultimate in human timetables with the end that God will bring. In a time of deep affliction, we are told, some may say, "Look, here is the Christ!" or, "Look, there! Do not believe them" (Mark 13:19). "When you see Jerusalem surrounded by armed camps, then know that—its desolation has come near" (Luke 21:20). Only that: the mundane event, not the end. This war does not bring the kingdom. "It is not for you to know times and seasons that the father has set by his own authority" (Acts 1:7).

To a community divided by a novel kind of competition for status through possession of spiritual knowledge and wisdom and ecstatic "gifts," Paul, in the digression of his famous "hymn to love," contrasts these temporary powers with the virtue that endures: "For it is in part that we know and in part that we prophesy, but when the perfect comes, the partial is done with. When I was a child, I spoke as a child, I thought as a child, I reasoned as a child; but when I became a man, I had done with childishness. For we see now by means of a mirror, in enigmas, but then face to face. Now I know in part, then I shall know just as I have been known [by God]" (1 Cor. 13:9–12). The "then" which is not yet, the consummation still beyond human reach, which Ernst Käsemann taught us to call the "eschatological reservation," has wide moral implications.[14]

These implications become especially clear when the belief in a final judgment is invoked precisely to suspend excesses of human judgment now: "Judge not, that you be not judged" (Matt. 7:1; Luke 6:37; 1 Clem. 13:2; Polycarp, Phil. 2:3). From theological positions as far apart as those of Paul and the Epistle of James, we hear attempts to restrain in this way the natural tendency in close-knit sects to impose upon the group the moral or theological perceptions of the more powerful or the more vocal. Thus James: "Be patient. Establish your hearts, for the coming of the Lord is at hand. Do not grumble, brethren, against one another, that you may not be judged; behold, the Judge is standing at the doors" (5:8–9). And Paul, to the Romans, urging "the strong" not to hold "the weak" in contempt for their naïve scrupulosity, and the weak not to condemn the strong for their apparently heedless freedom: "Who are you who are judging . . . ?" (14:4; compare 2:1). "Why do you pass judgment on your brother? Or you, why do you despise your brother? For we shall all stand before the judgment seat of God" (14:10).[15]

With sophisticated rhetoric, Paul especially exploits the power of the belief in God's final judgment to chasten and embarrass the all-too-human eagerness of his converts to judge one another. Judgment language is particularly thick in the first four chapters of 1 Corinthians, where Paul seeks to disarm a factionalism that is emerging around claims of several circles to have received superior spiritual wisdom from their preferred apostles: Cephas or Apollos or Paul (1 Cor. 1:12; 4:6–7). With not a little sarcasm, Paul contrasts the Christians' pretensions with their meager worldly status and God's values with the world's values (1:18–31) and ridicules the childishness of their religious competition (3:1–4). Using himself and Apollos as primary examples, he depicts the judgment in traditional prophetic images of fiery testing: the work of each will be revealed only by the fire of God's judgment. Until then, differences between them are of no consequence; they are mere "servants through whom you came to faith, and each has only what the Lord gave" (3:5). Even "if someone's work is burned up, the person himself, though suffering loss, will be saved, as one escapes through a fire" (3:15). In stark contrast, the community itself is "the temple of God"; "If anyone ruins the temple of God [by the kind of factionalism Paul sees emerging], God will ruin that person, for the temple of God is holy, the temple that you together are" (v. 17).

Concluding this part of his admonition, Paul takes up judgment language again, using the first person, as before, to provide an example, but generalizing to the situation of all believers: "It is a trivial matter to me that I should be judged by you or by a human 'day.' Indeed, I do not even judge myself. I have nothing on my conscience, yet that fact does not acquit me: the one who judges me is the Lord. The upshot is this: do not judge before the time, until the Lord comes, who will illuminate the secret matters that are in the dark and bring into the open the intentions of hearts—then the due praise will come to each person from God" (4:3–5).

In two other places in the same letter Paul actually insists on an immediate judgment by the community, but there, too, the expectation of God's final judgment restrains and relativizes the human, though in rather different ways. In the case of the incestuous man, in chapter 5, Paul declares: "Though absent in body yet present in spirit, I have already made the judicial decision as if present about the one who has acted in this way: with you gathered in the name of our Lord Jesus and my spirit with the power of our Lord Jesus, to deliver the man in question to the satan for destruction of the flesh, in order for the spirit to be saved in the day of the Lord" (5:3–5).

Though much remains unclear about the exact picture Paul is constructing, the last clause again sets the "day of the Lord" in contrast to the community's judgment, even though the latter is here demanded. Still different is the demand in 11:27–32 that all those eating the Lord's Supper "test" and "judge" themselves, to escape being "judged" and "disciplined" by God in the sickness and death already experienced among them, not to mention the yet worse alternative of being "condemned with the world." Here what is urged is an individual self-examination in order to avoid God's judgment on the discrimination against poorer members of the congregations practiced by the better-off, thus "discerning the body" and upholding the unity of the church. What is common to the Pauline rhetoric in all these cases is the attempt to use belief in the ultimate judgment by God in order to relativize or to restrain judgments made by individual believers or factions.[16]

The "eschatological reservation" is a minor theme in the moral discourse of the early Christians. Yet, looking back over the history of the church, we may perhaps wish that it had been heard somewhat more often. What is perhaps most evident from our sampling of the eschatological language of the writings that have come down to us from the first two centuries of the Christian movement is its variety, both in formulation and in application. Through all the variable images, nevertheless, we discern a controlling conviction that the defining point for the responsible and flourishing life lies in the divinely appointed future moment. For the vast majority, it was literally future; for some, like the ascetics of the Thomas tradition and the Platonizing Gnostics, it was metaphorical. For the latter, time's end could best serve as image of the timeless repose beyond or above the line of time. How one construed the end had a great deal to do with the story one imagined of the life to be lived now.

CHAPTER 11

The Moral Story

❖ ❖ ❖ ❖ ❖ ❖ ❖ ❖ ❖ ❖

The ancients knew that stories helped to inculcate morals—or to corrupt them. Young men, Plutarch said, could hardly be kept away from the fables and myths of the poets altogether, and besides, there was much good to be learned there. Only, he warned his friend Marcus, they ought to be careful to teach their sons *how* to listen to poetry, for "they require oversight in their reading even more than in the streets."[1] One of the ways Moses showed himself a superior legislator, Philo claimed, was that he set the laws within a narrative—a narrative, moreover, that begins with the origin of the world.[2]

Alasdair MacIntyre, among philosophers, and Stanley Hauerwas, among theological ethicists, have argued that narrative is not merely a help for moral teaching—a relish to make the main dish go down easier, as Plutarch put it—but it is essential to proper moral reasoning. Moral discourse need not always be in the form of narrative, but MacIntyre and Hauerwas argue that to be coherent and successful it must be connected with narrative. To speak of virtue entails that we tell stories.[3]

MacIntyre claims that virtue cannot exist without moral narrative, because of "the narrative character of human life." "Man is," he says, "essentially a story-telling animal."[4] Such claims may be rather too sweeping,[5] but we may surely accept at least the observation that narrative has played a central role in the formation of Western moral sensibilities. Moreover, a particular narrative, consistent in its broad outline though wondrously variable in detail, has been at the heart of the Christian moral vision.

Moral Biography and Moral History

It may be useful to distinguish two different types or levels of moral narrative. The first is the individual biography. The shape of a particular life, usually a *great* person—and in antiquity that generally, though not always, meant a great *man*[6]—is portrayed as typifying virtue or a particular set of virtues. It is this typifying biographical narrative that MacIntyre has principally in mind, for it is ideally suited for representing his neo-Aristotelian conception of virtue. The story of a life unfolds toward its *telos,* and each age of each society has its own finite list of ideal characters who enact the virtues of that culture in their stories.

In antiquity, Plutarch's *Parallel Lives* afford an obvious example. As C. P. Jones has observed, "Plutarch insists frequently on a double purpose: he wishes to demonstrate the character of his subjects, and to bring himself and his readers to imitate them."[7] Certain Jewish writers were quick to adopt this Greek genre of moralizing biography. One thinks at once, of course, of Ben Sira's "Let us now praise famous men and the fathers of our race" (44:1), though the sketches that follow are not yet "biographies." For full-blown biographies, we must wait for Philo, who introduces his stories of the Patriarchs by propounding the notion of persons who are "living laws," the "archetypes" of which particular laws and customs are but "copies." "These are such men as lived good and blameless lives, whose virtues stand permanently recorded in the most holy scriptures, not merely to sound their praises but for the instruction of the reader and as an inducement to him to aspire to the same."[8]

The other kind of narrative with which we are concerned is history. While Hellenistic historians and rhetoricians debated the extent to which history ought to appeal to the emotions of its audience, they generally agreed that all history ought to be useful. Its usefulness generally included the teaching of moral lessons as well as of political and strategic ones. For the most part in Hellenistic histories, these moral lessons are either quite general—illustrating the unpredictable turns of fortune—or they focus, like biography, on individual examples of virtue or vice. In the great historical compositions of the Hebrew Bible, on the other hand, especially in the Deuteronomistic History, the notion of the covenant between God and Israel, which frames and interprets the action, places the behavior of the nation as such at the center of moral attention. The difference should not be exaggerated, for the Deuteronomist historians regularly single out the behavior of the kings as decisive. Neither should we allow ourselves to fall into the error of an earlier generation of theologians in imagining that "the Hebrew mind" possessed some peculiar qualities of temporal and historical consciousness unlike the "mythic" or "cyclical" time of other ancient Near

Eastern peoples, including the Greeks. James Barr's acid critique has dissolved those romantic notions. Nevertheless, it is in this great composition, extending from Deuteronomy through the Books of Kings, that we meet most clearly in ancient history the notion of the moral responsibility of a people as a whole, governed by its obedience to one law of the one God.[9]

When Josephus came to write his *Antiquities of the Jews,* following the model of Dionysius of Halicarnasus's *Roman Antiquities,* he set out the work's moral quite explicitly: "The main lesson to be learnt from this history by any who care to peruse it is that men who conform to the will of God, and do not venture to transgress laws that have been excellently laid down, prosper in all things beyond belief, and for their reward are offered by God felicity; whereas, in proportion as they depart from the strict observance of these laws, things [else] practicable become impracticable, and whatever imaginary good thing they strive to do ends in irretrievable disasters" (*Ant.* 1.14, trans. Thackeray).[10]

Here the Jewish author has embedded into a thoroughly Greek style of historiography the moral schema of the Deuteronomists. Both history and the writing of it have a moral end.[11]

Out of these varieties of moralizing narratives, there emerges in early Christianity a peculiar variation. At latest by the time of Irenaeus, toward the end of the second century, some Christians had come to think of a genuinely *universal* history. It encompassed the story of the world, for it began "in the beginning," and the history of humanity, from its creation and its fatal, primeval error, through the subsequent dialectic of God's saving or punishing actions and human responses and derelictions, to the climactic act of redemption and the ultimate judgment of all.

We may also call this universal history a *canonical* history, in two senses. First, it provides the governing paradigm of human life for catholic Christianity. Second, it is coextensive with the canon of scripture. Indeed, the telling and retelling of the history and the emerging canon of scripture were dialectically related, each reinforcing the other as each grew in comprehensiveness and definition. If we think of the story as canonical, however, a couple of cautions are in order. Neither the canon of scripture nor the plot of scripture's story, as read by Christians, was invented by a committee, nor did they appear one day full-blown, like Jonah's *qiqayon* plant.

By the end of the early period to which I have limited this investigation, the Christian groups are getting used to the idea of a distinctively Christian set of writings larger than the Jewish scriptures. They have also discovered the practical advantages of the *codex*, or book, in place of the scroll, and that discovery would soon make it possible for them to gather all their sacred writings between two covers. But they have only begun to sort out such questions as which of their writings to include and in what order. By the time official lists are laid down, more than a century later, documents like the *Shepherd of Hermas* and the *Epistle of Barnabas* have ceased to be approved for reading in worship and so are no longer included in the great biblical manuscripts. The rival Gospels written by Valentinus and anonymous others are banned by the councils and bishops, and all the Acts of Apostles but one are made "apocryphal."

Nevertheless, even then, many of those excluded works continue to exercise their influence, some, to be sure, only within particular sects driven to the periphery, but others more or less overtly in the life of the Great Church, as a kind of penumbra around the canon. Anyone who examines the themes of narrative art in the Middle Ages and the early Renaissance will be aware how long and how pervasively these other stories continued to shape the popular Christian mentality. To call our central story "canonical" thus does not at all imply absolute closure or invariability. Nevertheless, it has been central, not merely in theological and liturgical traditions, but in wide reaches of Western culture.

Beginning, Middle, and End

A good story needs a beginning, a middle, and an end: an old-fashioned sentiment, but one still shared by all but the most avant-garde readers. Not only does the canonical history satisfy that requirement, it may have helped to shape our prejudice about what a real story ought to look like. For Kermode, it is "a familiar model of history"; for Frye, the quintessential romance, archetype of the pattern on which the classical novel depends. Gabriel Josipovici, quoting Frye, admirably sums up the power this narrative once had, and its loss:

> It's a magnificent conception, spread over thousands of pages and encompassing the entire history of the universe. There is both perfect correspondence between Old and New Testaments and a continuous forward drive from Creation to the end of time: 'It begins where time begins, with the creation of the world; it ends where time ends, with the Apocalypse, and it surveys human history in between, or the aspect of history it is interested in, under the symbolic names of Adam and Israel.' Earlier ages

had no difficulty in grasping this design, though our own, more bookish age, obsessed with both history and immediacy, has tended to lose sight of it. Neither theologians nor biblical scholars have stood back enough to see it as a whole. Yet it *is* a whole and quite unlike any other book.[12]

A perfectly wonderful beginning was provided by the first Book of Moses, and that first act of the divine drama was freighted with morally consequential themes. I have already noted how Philo and other Hellenistic Jewish writers underscored the appropriateness of this cosmic starting point for the ethical story that they found in the Torah. For Christian apologists of the second and third centuries, these reflections on Moses' account of the beginning of things furnished fitting material for their own schemes of the history of culture. Convinced that Moses was prior to Homer, let alone Plato, they claimed the "barbarian" philosophy of the Jews as their own, the original and true philosophy of which the Greek schools were only feeble and imperfect imitations.[13]

That cosmic beginning was for many Christians quite enough to get the story going, and all that was needed from the Jewish scriptures. Such was the attitude of the Gnostic sect, of Valentinus and his followers, and of others of like persuasion. We will come back to their alternative story of cosmic failure and human redemption. The pioneers of Christian narrative, however, either born Jews or deeply learned in the Jewish scriptures and traditions, knew that the beginning told in the Torah's first chapters was prologue for other beginnings, that the cosmic beginning was prelude for the human story, and that the human story quickly focused in, by a kind of narrative zoom lens, on the tumultuous history of a single people. Those readers and listeners knew that the Bible they claimed as their own was centrally a story of Israel. They knew, moreover, that there was not only the cosmic Beginning and the equally abrupt beginning of Israel, in each case summoned into being by the voice of the same God, by his "Let there be" addressed to the *tohu webohu* of nothingness and by his "Go you!" addressed to Abraham.

Beyond these, there were also false starts, reversals, and new beginnings. There was God's sorrow that he had made humankind and his decision to blot out all that he had created—and yet his decision to begin again, with Noah. There was the arrogance of the tower builders and the Lord's interdiction by confusing their language: the beginning of human inability to understand the speech of the other. Yet the speaking Lord continued to call into being out of unlikely material. He called forth a child for the centenarian Abraham and the barren Sarah, who laughed at the promise; he made a wrestler with God, Israel, from the wily deceiver, heel-grabbing Jacob. He called into existence a confederacy bound by treaty to the Lord out of a terrified band of escaped slaves gathered at Sinai, who did not want to be there. They became a confederation of tribes constantly threatened by dissolution or extinction at the hands of "the nations round about" and even more by their own jealousies, blood feuds, and violent passions, in the years when "there was no king in Israel, and every person did what was right in his own eyes," yet again and again rescued from oblivion by the same Lord who "raised up" a savior for them and at last gave them a king. Sin and destruction, repentance and rescue continue to be the themes of the (Deuteronomistic) history of the monarchy. Throughout the narrative the sordid vies with the sublime, the pathetic with the miraculous. This story has neither the fated concentration of tragedy nor the comfortable closure of comedy, nor is it, like epic, grounded in the presumed constancy of aristocratic mores. Here all things change, yet the beginning and the multiple new beginnings echo again and again.

The ending, on the other hand, is quite a different matter. While many episodes come to dramatic ends in the scriptures of the Jews, and occasionally a prophet like Jeremiah could metaphorically describe a coming political and social disruption as an undoing of creation itself, there is in those canonical scriptures nothing like that end that some Jews of the Hellenistic and Roman periods, including the first Christians, began to anticipate. That profound "sense of an ending" which, as we saw in the previous chapter, possessed so many of the early Christians was born out of their own experience and their own new stories, which led them to read the old stories of Israel in novel ways.[14]

One impetus for the Christian rereading of Israel's story from the point of view of a unifying end is so obvious that we may easily overlook it. The followers of Jesus had first of all to cope with the devastation of their hopes by the end of Jesus' own life. It may fairly be said that Christianity began when that end was transformed, in the beliefs and celebrations of those followers, into a new beginning, into the beginning of the end. That, in part at least, is what theologians mean when they say that for the early Christians the crucifixion of Jesus became an "eschatological event." By believing that God raised Jesus from the dead, the faithful discovered in God's story a colossal *peripeteia*. This marvelous reversal of human expectations, on the one hand, must exert a tremendous pull on all the former reversals, the partial ends and new beginnings, the falterings and restorations of the rhythm in Israel's story, like a giant magnet dragging them into new polarities. On the other hand, like the peripeteia of a classical drama, this reversal must signal the onset of the dénouement; it anticipates the end.

By calling Christ "the last Adam" and echoing the story of Adam's creation and disobedience in his description of Christ's work (1 Cor. 15:44–49; Rom. 5:12–21), Paul had already established a strong link between the story of the beginning and the heart of the Christian story. He was not the first to do so; he alludes in several places to language that was already traditional in the ritual of baptism. At baptism, it was said, the believer took off "the old human" laden with vices and broken by social divisions, and put on Christ, "the new human," in whom "there is neither Jew nor Greek, there is neither slave nor free, there is no 'male and female' " (Gal. 3:28; compare Col. 3:11; 1 Cor. 12:13)—in short, in whom is restored the paradisal unity before Adam's sin, even before the separation of Woman from Man.[15] The link suggested the inevitability of the closing of a circle, a grand plan by which God had contrived to knit up the raveled ends of human character that had come undone in the Garden. It was that grand plan that the second-century apologists undertook to color in, with their talk of the Logos continually sowing seeds of truth which were however badly nourished in the soil of sinful humanity, constantly blighted by demonic opposition or twisted imitations. They thus began to fill in the outline of the middle.

There were in fact now two middles, and it was out of the dialectic between them that the central plot of our narrative emerged. One was a story already given in the great biblical histories of Israel, together with their poetic and prophetic summaries and their supplements produced in the Hellenistic and Roman eras. It was the story, of more than epic dimensions, of the calling, covenant, sin, and redemption of Israel. The other center, of course, was the story of Jesus Christ: of incarnation, life, sacrifice, and resurrection.

We need now to look at a few examples of how these central paradigms took shape, and how they in turn formed a narrative matrix that could bring forth new senses of a moral life's context and direction.

Stories of Jesus

The first Christians were enthusiastic storytellers. Before any of them were yet called "Christians," they were telling stories about Jesus and repeating stories that he told. Thanks to their memory and imagination, we remember Jesus as a master storyteller, whose parables seem to many the very epitome of his mission and message. His followers told stories about him and about their own experiences. In the words that one of their most elegant narrators of the second generation put into the mouths of the apostles, "We cannot but speak of what we have seen and heard" (Acts 4:20, RSV).

Paul's Story

We have not thought of Paul as a storyteller, for the Jesus stories of the Gospels are absent from his letters. Yet his use of narrative is very important for our particular interest, because Paul's central concern was to use the narrative to form a moral community. The pivotal story for Paul was simple and astounding: God's son and anointed one was the very Jesus who was most shamefully crucified, dead, and buried, but whom God then raised from the dead, exalted to share his own throne and very name in heaven, to sit at God's right hand as Lord until all things would be subjected to him and God alone would reign in righteousness over all his people and creation. The drama of Paul's career turns on his recognition that that story shattered and recreated his own conception of a life lived in obedience of God's will. In other words, that story imperiously rewrote the story that his own life must follow (though Paul never tells his own story beyond a few episodic hints). For him it equally shattered and recreated—but preserved!—Israel's fundamental reason for existing in the world as God's people.[16] When Paul writes to the various communities he founded, it is invariably to suggest, cajole, argue, threaten, shame, and encourage those communities into behaving, in their specific situations, in ways somehow homologous to that fundamental story. In the process, Paul uses older stories and older rules, maxims, customs, and moral commonplaces to interpret the Christ-story—but simultaneously uses the Christ-story to transform those older stories, rules, maxims, customs, and commonplaces. That led to a certain polyphony in Paul's discourse.[17]

Paul's most profound bequest to subsequent Christian discourse was his transformation of the reported crucifixion and resurrection of Jesus Christ into a multipurpose metaphor with vast generative and transformative power—not least for moral perceptions. In that gospel story Paul sees revolutionary import for the relationships of power that control human transactions. He works out this import not in a social theory but in his response to specific crises of leadership and dangers of schism within the Christian house-communities, especially at Corinth. If God's power is manifested in the weakness of the cross and God's wisdom in the foolish claim that the crucified was the Messiah, then it is no longer obvious that the high-born, wealthy, well-educated, rhetorically sophisticated should always have their way, while those who are socially "nothing," those who are "weak"—the women, the slaves, the poor, the uneducated—are simply to obey.

To underscore the point, Paul hints at the story of his own life since his conversion, which God has made to conform to the story of the cross, forcing him to live by hope of the resurrection. "For I think," he says, "God has publicly displayed us apostles as the last, as people under death sentences, as a theatrical spectacle to the world of both angels and humans. We are fools for Christ's sake; you are clever in Christ. We are weak; you are strong. You are glorious; we are dishonored" (1 Cor. 4:9–10). Yet he makes it plain that he is not talking about a simple inversion of values. Those who have no status or prestige in the households and assemblies of Corinth but only the ecstatic power given by the spirit of God may nevertheless also be guilty of being "inflated" by their own pseudo-knowledge and windy, tongue-speaking power. Thus Paul's use of the metaphor of the cross resists its translation into simple slogans. Instead he introduces into the moral language of the new movement a way of seeking after resonances in the basic story for all kinds of relationships of disciples with the world and with one another, so that the event-become-metaphor could become the generative center of almost endless new narratives, yet remain a check and control over those narratives.

Inventing the Gospel

When Mark sat down to write "The beginning of the Gospel of Jesus Christ, Son of God," he set in motion another decisive movement in the retelling of that central story.[18] As in Paul, the controlling moment in the story is the crucifixion. Also as in Paul, the story is defined as "gospel," and the gospel is reinforced by the words—the first words in Mark's account, after the title—"as it was written." But now the story is not only an eventful and expansible metaphor, it is approaching a biography, in the Hellenistic pattern.

Didactic and moralizing biographies were common, as I noted earlier. Mark's, by comparison with, say, Plutarch, is in style and language much cruder, closer to vulgar speech. Yet the Gospel's moralizing is much less overt, its art more subtle and surprising. Above all we are drawn into the story by the interaction between Jesus and his disciples—who ought to be our heroes and models, as they surely were for the communities for which Mark wrote. Yet they are astonishingly dim-witted, cowardly, and wrong-headed heroes. Their very failure to understand what Jesus was about underscores the mystery of Jesus' person and his way to the cross, while his true identity as God's son is recognized only by the demons he conquers and, at the center of the story's ironic climax, by the Roman officer in charge of the squad that crucifies him. The Christian reader knows that the story has a miraculous happy ending. Yet Mark leaves that ending untold; the reader must supply it, left standing with the women seized by fear and ecstasy at the empty tomb, sent with the disciples back to Galilee and the beginnings. No easy answers here, no simple slogans to sum up discipleship: to follow Jesus is to follow his story, from Galilee to the cross and back again, from bafflement to astonishing discovery.

The plot of Mark unfolds with an air of mysterious and divinely determined inevitability, and that mood may be one of its most important contributions to the sense of a moral universe growing in a devoted listener to its tale. The very first episode occurs *kathōs gegraptai*, "as it was written": the Baptist appears as has been prophesied; his dress and demeanor (1:6) echo the scriptural description of the prophet who "must first come . . . and restore all things" (9:11–13). What he prophesies, besides "repentance for forgiveness of sins," is the coming of another, more powerful than himself (1:7–8), who is then immediately introduced to the story's auditors. (They are, in fact, in all probability already quite well acquainted with him and the story; it is the kind of story that works well only when it is *re*told and its basic plot is familiar.)

God in Mark is a hidden but active sovereign, a mysterious director, a manipulator, who brings about what he has planned from of old. What he brings about is not straightforward, not a simple morality tale, but shocking in its reversal of expectations. Yet the competent hearer knows the strangeness of the tale itself, has made some kind of peace with it, else he would not be here listening. The listener is thus in on the secret—just as the disciples in the story are—but in that case the resistance of those very disciples, which becomes such a dominant motif in the story itself, must sound a discordant note. The insider does not fare well in the story. To know the secret of the kingdom of God does not automatically put one in the right, and if we are alert we become uncomfortable even as we read with our knowing superiority to the disciple characters, a superiority that the story encourages.

The God of Mark is benevolently ruthless, at the same time rigorous in the accomplishment of his purpose (what "must" take place) and inscrutable, unpredictable from the human perspective. What moral stance is appropriate in the face of such a God? Blind submission? But "blindness" is something to be overcome in this story, metaphor for an obtuseness that must be cleared away. The narrative and the selected sayings are constructed in such a way as to invite, to demand thinking and rethinking and making choices. Submission must be absolute, but not blind. What process of moral reasoning is required, then? The story is imperious; it subverts other ways of thinking, other stories, it demands to become itself the dominant former of the convert's moral reasoning. In comparison with other ancient biography, what is unique about the Christian Gospels is not their genre or this or that element in the story, but this imperious and subversive assault on moral sensibilities.

Matthew

The author of the Gospel that stands first in the canon's order, whom tradition calls Matthew, keeps Mark's story, but takes out some of the mystery. He draws more of the morals for the reader, too, depicting Jesus as the legislator of his community, in some passages making him look rather like a new Moses. Even more than in Mark, the community's own history has been worked into Matthew's story of Jesus. The rivals of the Christian groups in the large Jewish communities in and around Antioch, probably led by the forerunners of the rabbinic academies and courts, become Jesus' enemies: "Scribes and Pharisees."[19]

Readers have often noticed that the idiom of Jesus' teachings and controversies in Matthew resembles rabbinic forms found in the later compilations of Mishna, Tosefta, and the early midrashim.[20] One of Matthew's strategies is to depict Jesus as a teacher of wisdom, a "sage" like Ben Sira or like the rabbis' own prototypes in the great chain of tradition in the Mishnah tractate *Abot*. He thus resembles the ideal that the rabbis have for themselves—yet committed disciples do not call Jesus "teacher" and "rabbi" in Matthew; only outsiders, opponents, and his betrayer use these titles.[21] Matthew's Jesus draws the distinction sharply, in a direct polemic against those "who love . . . to be called 'Rabbi' by people," as an instruction to his disciples:

"But *you* are not to be called 'Rabbi,' for you have one teacher and you are all brothers. And you are not to be called 'father' on earth, for you have one heavenly Father. Nor may you be called 'instructor,' because you have one Instructor, the Messiah" (Matt. 23:7-10).

The portrait of Jesus as sage had already taken shape, to a certain extent, among those who collected and compiled Jesus' aphorisms, parables, and other wise sayings, and Matthew expanded on that portrait, even as he wove one such collection into his Gospel. He has gathered many of the sayings into speeches set on five different occasions in Jesus' career; the first of these is the familiar Sermon on the Mount (Matt. 5-7).

The Sermon on the Mount serves as an epitome of Jesus' teaching.[22] In similar fashion, both in Jewish and in Greco-Roman tradition, the philosopher sets before his hearers a way of ethical living that leads to "happiness." The "beatitudes" or "makarisms," a form familiar in Jewish wisdom literature, are thus a fitting introduction. A reader familiar with popular philosophies of the day would find much here in common with Cynic teaching: simplicity of life and speech, boldness and defenselessness, readiness to defy public conventions. The terms of discourse, however, are explicitly Jewish. The Law and the Prophets must be fulfilled, exceeding the righteousness of scribes and Pharisees (5:17-20). One must imitate the perfection of God (5:8) and expect his reward.

Not only is the ethic epitomized here Jewish, it is sectarian; that is, it requires a deliberate choice to follow the authority of Jesus and not that of other Jewish leaders and teachers. The opposition to other traditions is most explicit in six antithetical statements in chapter 5, which take the form "You have heard that *X* was said, but I say to you, *Y.*" The peculiar way that Matthew has employed this form in reworking certain statements from the tradition implies the specifically sectarian demand that prudential and publicly enforceable rules be tested by a transcendental norm: the only valid standard is "the will of the Father in heaven."

Yet the "will of the Father" is not an abstract perfection, for the rules laid down here belong to the realm of everyday: marriage, truth-telling, facing foreign soldiers and other enemies, giving alms, praying, forgiving people, fasting. There is no clear line between sacred and secular. On the other hand, Matthew provides no code of behavior. Although the risen Jesus in Matthew directs that new disciples must be taught "to observe all that I have commanded you" (28:20), we have here no system of commandments. The rules are exemplary, not comprehensive, pointers to the kind of life expected in the community, but not a map of acceptable behavior. Still less does Matthew's Jesus state philosophical principles from which guidelines for behavior could rationally be derived. We are left with the puzzle that while Jesus plays the role of a conventional sage in Matthew, his teachings recorded here do not add up to an ethical system.

In order to achieve the "righteousness" that Matthew demands, members of his community need to know much more than Jesus' collected teachings. From this Gospel we can deduce some of the things they did know: the story of Jesus' career, told with pathos and mystery in Mark's Gospel; the presence of ascetic, Spirit-possessed prophets who wandered into their town, imitating Jesus' poverty, homelessness, and detachment and guided only by his image and his Spirit that spoke within them; the ordered assembly with its elders, its powers to "bind and loose," its "scribe[s] trained for the kingdom of heaven" who by their careful study of scripture knew how to draw from the Jewish treasure "what is new and what is old." The writer has brought all these together, but in the composite it is the narrative that dominates.

The first words of Matthew's Gospel make evident the author's purpose to awaken some special memories in knowledgeable readers: *biblos geneseōs*, "scroll of generation" or "Book of Genesis." That, of course, was the name by which Greek readers knew the first book of Jewish scripture, in which this and similar phrases appear (for example, Gen. 5:1; see also 2:4). The genealogy of Jesus, which follows in Matthew, connects him by a carefully arranged pattern with the great epochs of the biblical history: Abraham, David, the Babylonian exile. Succeeding elements in the birth story reinforce this impression. Events occur "in order that what was spoken through the prophet might be fulfilled." The repetition of details familiar from the biblical stories or their elaboration in popular lore link this one "born king of the Jews" with Abraham, Moses, Israel in Egypt, the exodus, and Sinai. Some of the motifs—dreams, astrological portents, conflict with tyrants— were common in Hellenistic biographies of extraordinary individuals and are therefore appropriate stylistic devices to emphasize that Jesus is "the one called 'Anointed' " (1:16). However, their principal function here is to suggest a predestined plan that all participants in these events were obliged to follow, a plan continuous with the sacral history of Israel.

Continuity is not the only note sounded here, however. The massacre of children by Herod, in his vain attempt to eliminate the young rival, not only recalls the story of Moses, it also foreshadows the crucifixion of "the King of the Jews." Thus Matthew invests his narrative with the same pathos he found in his model, the Gospel of Mark, but he does so in a very different way. In this Gospel the rising conflict will ultimately set Jesus not only against the leaders of Israel but against "all the people," who are made to answer Pilate, "His blood be on us and on our children" (27:25, NRSV). Matthew's picture of history has evidently been shaped both by the common Christian memory of Jesus' crucifixion and also by this particular community's conflicts with the reorganized Jewish communities in postwar Palestine and Syria.

We get another hint of Matthew's sense of history in Jesus' instruction of the Twelve in chapter 10. One might think that the manner of life prescribed here—poverty, mendicancy, homelessness—is being set forth as an ideal for discipleship in Matthew's church. Such an ascetic life later became the norm in eastern parts of Syria, as we have seen in our discussion of the Thomas tradition in earlier chapters. Perhaps the itinerant prophets mentioned several times in Matthew already represented that life in Matthew's city.[23] Nevertheless, not all the instructions given by Jesus to the Twelve are binding on Matthew's community. The restriction of the mission to Israel alone (10:5–6) is explicitly removed in 28:19. Further, Matthew has lifted 10:17–22 from Jesus' apocalyptic prediction of future disturbances in Mark 13:9–13. The changed context has the effect of removing the predicted difficulties from the reader's future, placing them in the community's past experience. Verses 40–42, moreover, emphasize the reward for those who receive the wanderers, not for the wanderers themselves. Discipleship in Matthew is not identical with imitation of the ascetic life of Jesus or his twelve special missionaries. Thus, for all the church's inevitable retrojection of its own experiences into the time of Jesus, this author does find ways to accord to the past an integrity of its own. It is not only a model for the present but also a basis that is different from the present and which therefore required different responses.

The narrative of Matthew is thus something more than setting and backing for Jesus' teachings. The Teacher is also the Messiah, who cares for, heals, calls, and transforms his people. He is also the Judge, the Son of Man who as God's agent exercises the final judgment on all humankind. The relationship of the Christian groups to this Messiah/Son of Man/Son of God is modeled by the course of discipleship described in the narrative, but there is also an awareness that new occasions teach new duties. Discipleship is "following" the person identified in the story, who, raised from the dead, goes on leading the community. It is therefore possible to ask not only What *did* Jesus say? but What *does* he now wish his people to do?—a sort of inquiry that obviously produced considerable dissension among the prophets and other leaders of the Matthean community.

There is indeed an uneasy tension in this Gospel, as there must have been in the Christian communities of its time and place. The rigorist imitators of Jesus' ascetic life have their say, but it is countered by the parables that warn against premature attempts to purify the church. The tension is not resolved, but suspended. All must face judgment by the Son of Man, and all will be surprised, for neither a literalist imitation of his lifestyle, nor a rigorist obedience to his words as law, nor a charismatic appropriation of his miraculous power is any guarantee of faithfulness. Yet it is those whose actions are in accord with the character of that same Son of Man as rendered by this narrative and with the plan of God in which he is the protagonist, who find themselves among the sheep on the right hand.

Continuing the Story

The author we know traditionally as Luke puts the story onto a broader stage and extends it. This author knows and uses the conventions of Hellenistic history writing and also of the Hellenistic novel. To the story of Jesus he adds a second volume, the Acts of the Apostles: the first history of the church. The two volumes together constitute a new stage of self-reflection, by a member of the movement, on the movement's own identity and the meaning of its own beginnings and early history. How the movement is connected with the sacred story of Israel and how it engages the institutions and customs of the Greeks and the Romans are questions that Luke-Acts develops thematically.

The history is in some ways also the beginning of the literary tradition of Christian self-defense, the "apologies" of the second and third centuries. Like those later apologies, it is at the same time a mirror for the Christian communities themselves, presenting a model of their appropriate interaction with that larger world and of their life within their communities. So the early disciples in Jerusalem are depicted as realizing simultaneously the ideal of Greek friendship—friends are "of one heart and one soul" and "have all things in common"—and the Deuteronomistic picture of Israel's sacral beginnings in the wilderness, when "there was no needy person among them" (Acts 5:32–37). The Christian protagonists in this story exhibit constant piety toward Jewish tradition and practice and harmlessness toward the institutions and authority of Rome and the provincial cities. Yet when challenged by Jew, Greek, or Roman, always in Luke's account because of unjust accusations, they speak out with unflinching courage and "boldness of speech" (*parrhēsia,* one of the author's favorite words). Thus they are models of civic virtue, by no means "advocating customs that are not lawful for . . . Romans to observe," as their accusers say (16:21).

Those standard virtues are exercised, however, within a larger narrative with quite particular accents. One of these is the supernatural conflict that this narrative posits as the underlying rationale of the overt conflicts experienced by its characters. With the advent of Jesus, there begins the story of "the demise of the Devil," as Susan Garrett calls it.[24] The "miracles" of the protagonists are set against the "magic" of opponents and the wiles of demons in scenes that depict the outbreakings of this underlying and controlling warfare of God and his Messiah against Satan and his agents. This Lucan theme foreshadows Justin's more lapidary elaboration, sixty or more years later, of the demons' devious, age-old opposition to the truth that finally emerges in Christianity. Within such a plot, the exercise of virtue is more than progress toward the individual's goal of the well-crafted life, rewarded with honor and ultimate happiness: it is enlistment on the side of God against the forces of darkness.

The outcome of the struggle, of course, is foreordained: another of the special accents of the story in Luke-Acts. As we saw in an earlier chapter, "the plan and foreknowledge of God" control all that happens in this narrative. The divine inevitability of the plot, which moves so mysteriously in Mark, here comes to the surface. The little impersonal Greek verb *dei,* "it must," which in Mark declares the necessity for the Son of Man's suffering, Elijah's coming, and the events of the end, becomes in Luke-Acts a leitmotif. The author's summaries, which punctuate the action, and the speeches of the leading characters, which in the standard style of Hellenistic history writing interpret the action's meaning to the readers, make the point quite clearly that what must take place is the "growth" of the "word of God." The heroic and civic virtues of the positive characters are all subordinated to that end, the success of which is guaranteed by God and his Spirit against all opposition.

And what exactly does this author mean by "the word of God"? He uses a number of shorthand synonyms: "the kingdom of God," "repentance," "Jesus and the resurrection." The referent is in fact deliberately multiple.

Most directly, what is meant is the missionary proclamation and its reception, whose irresistible spread "in Jerusalem and in all Judea and Samaria and as far as the end of the earth" (1:8)—or at least to its center, Rome—is the central thread of the second volume. It is at the same time the whole of "the word sent to Israel," which is nothing less than the story of volume one, that is, Luke's revision of Mark's Gospel. The ethic of Luke-Acts, while it has many subsidiary and mostly conventional elements, including the ideals of civic concord, communitarian economics, freedom, and courage, in its narrative dimension is principally a missionary ethic. The story is the conquest of the world by the word of God that is, itself, the story. How that story subverts and subsumes the history of Israel is a third major and peculiar focus of Luke-Acts, to which we shall return in the final part of this chapter.

The Acts narrative of heroic and miraculous adventures by irresistible proclaimers of Christ's message in near and distant lands set a pattern that was followed by many Christian writers beginning in the second century. Some expanded on the story already told, like the *Acts of Paul*, a large part of which focuses on a new character, the holy virgin Thecla, or the *Acts of Peter*, which climaxes in a new confrontation between the apostle and the magician he had previously overcome in Samaria (Acts 8:14–25). Others provide accounts of apostles neglected in the earlier work: John, Andrew, Thomas, and eventually Philip, Matthew, Bartholomew, Simon and Judas, Thaddaeus, and Barnabas. Some of these are told to reinforce a quite specific vision of Christianity and of the morality Christianity required, such as the encratite message in the *Acts of Thomas* already discussed in an earlier chapter, equally central to the story of Paul and Thecla. For the most part, however, the atmosphere is that of the popular romance: the apostles solve all problems by miracles, the piety of the converts is simple and naïve, and the moral implications are unremarkable.[25]

The Cosmic Story

There was another way of telling the story that began very early, the scene of which was broader still. It begins and ends in heaven, the whole universe is implicated, and in some versions the central characters are not human. In the liturgy of the Christian groups, particularly in their hymns, they sang about Jesus as a cosmic figure even before Paul and his disciples wrote their letters. Jesus, in these poems, was "with God"—like Lady Wisdom in earlier Jewish literature—"in the beginning," and all things were created through his mediation. He was "equal to God," but instead of exploiting that status, he "emptied himself, taking the form of a slave" and "was obedient to the point of death." Therefore God, who in one strand of Jewish tradition always elevates his righteous servants who humble themselves and suffer, "has highly exalted him," giving him his own name, "Lord," so that all the powers and spiritual beings not only on earth, but also in the sky and in the underworld, would make obeisance to him and make the same confession that every human convert to the Christian movement made when baptized: "The Lord is Jesus Christ." Paul shows, in his letter to the Philippian Christians (chap. 2), how this extravagant hymnic picture could be made real and earthy in the dispositions of ordinary Christians: "Base your practical reasoning on what you see in Christ Jesus" (as I would translate the difficult introductory clause in Phil. 2:5).[26] Thinking in humility of the other's concerns rather than one's own was to think after the pattern of Christ's story; that was the way such mundane crises in the church as the feud between the two women apostles, Euodia and Syntyche (4:2), would be solved.

But the cosmic story of Jesus as a divine figure who invaded the world and then returned to heaven was subject to elaboration in more exotic ways. In the Fourth Gospel it becomes the image for portraying the mystery of Jesus' identity and the mystery especially of his rejection by "his own people," the Jews—and thereby it becomes also the key for interpreting to a beleaguered community of Jews expelled from their synagogues the meaning of their own alienation, of their own experience of "not belonging to the world." The moral implications of that communal self-identity, and especially of that way of stigmatizing their enemies, were ambiguous. In the long run this way of talking, in a triumphant church, would bear the bitter fruit of Christian anti-Semitism, but it could also remind a church grown comfortable in the world of its countercultural origins.[27]

In the second century the cosmic story of Jesus took a new form when Valentinus took up these narratives from Paul and John and blended them with speculative readings of the Genesis stories of creation by the obscure sect of Gnostics. From Valentinus and his followers and from other thinkers of speculative bent arose an endlessly elaborated series of myths that describes the origin of this world and of human life in it as the results of cosmic mistakes and accidents, which leave us in a hostile universe, alienated from our own true selves and from the world of light and truth out of which the lost spirits of the true Gnostics fell. In each of these permutations of the cosmic story, the narrative, which we now are accustomed to call a myth, offers its audience a way to understand their place in the world and the appropriate way of behaving in that cosmic context.

The Christian Story and Israel's History

The Gnostic form of the cosmic story becomes an antihistory, and the moral goal of the Gnostic's life is anticosmic: the point is to discount this world and to escape it. It was not only the Gnostics, however, who were tempted to dissolve the worldly history into timeless episodes of moral or theological significance. In one way the apocalyptic yearning for transformation of the political and social world stands opposed to such dissolution of the historical. Yet the apocalyptic mentality itself sees in the events of the past only "types," "models," written down, as Paul says, "to provide admonition for us, who have encountered the ends of the ages" (1 Cor. 10:11; see also Rom. 15:4). While Paul did have a keen sense for the reality and the problematic character of the history of Israel, the same was not always true of other Christian interpreters of Israel's scriptures. The discovery in scripture of moral examples, like the models of faith in Hebrews 11 or the *exempla* of hospitality, of righteousness, of jealousy, and so on, in the letter we call 1 *Clement*, need not carry any *historical* sense at all. In one of the most elaborate and influential compilations of this sort, the *Testaments of the Twelve Patriarchs*, narrative is minimal. The patriarchs are each a type, almost a cipher, for a virtue; what remains of their *stories* is merely moral tales, lacking that movement of encompassing narrative that gives the stories in the Bible itself their weight and connectedness.[28]

It was by no means a foregone conclusion, then, that the early Christians would preserve that sense of rootedness in Israel's history that is an indispensable ingredient in the narrative they would ultimately produce. In the first century Paul had enunciated the dialectic of continuity and discontinuity implicit in his "gospel" with peculiar intensity and a subtlety that could hardly be preserved, or even understood, as the situation of the Christian groups evolved independently of the Jewish communities. Nevertheless his formulations, in two of his surviving letters, did leave for future generations of Christian interpreters a continuing provocation to reflect on the meaning of Israel's history for the church. Other first-century writers as well, as we have already seen in the cases of Matthew, the Fourth Gospel, and Luke-Acts, were preoccupied with the conflict between the Christian groups and other Jewish communities over claims to represent an authentic reading of scripture and legitimate continuity with Israel. There was, moreover, a strong apologetic pressure to discover a past. In the Roman world, antiquity was one of the defining characteristics of a valid religious tradition. The Christians had to prove that they were not the upstart superstition that traditionalist members of the society were bound to see in them. For both internal and external reasons, then, it was essential that they find ways to incorporate Israel's story into their own.

There were several ways of making the connection, and this is not the place to survey the whole variety. The anonymous tract that has come down to us as the *Epistle of Barnabas,* written sometime in the first half of the second century, is probably representative of a broad segment of Christian thought in the period, and its scheme of interpretation was popular enough that the writing was often treated as canonical. The fundamental conviction that drives Barnabas's reading of the Jewish scriptures is that they speak in hidden ways of Jesus. Consequently the biblical narratives are dismantled; only "types" are plucked out. The binding of Isaac is a type fulfilled in Jesus' crucifixion (7:3); the goat driven into the wilderness on the Day of Atonement is a type of Jesus (7:7–10); and so on. Yet the author knows that "some of what is written about him applies to Israel, some to us" (5:2), and he develops his own story to explain the connection and to justify his contrarian readings. According to this new story, Israel has sinned again and again, and God has finally rejected them altogether, choosing instead "a new people" with a "new law" (for example, 5:6; 2:6). That story itself is now read into the ancient texts. For example, the blessing by Jacob of Ephraim and Manasseh (Gen. 48) is explained: "But Jacob saw in the spirit a type of the people of the future" (*Barn.* 13.5, trans. Lake). The biblical narrative's own outcome is directly supplanted, here and elsewhere, by the new plot that Barnabas imposes.

A few decades later, writing in Rome, Justin follows a similar way of reading. The acuteness of the issue for Christians of the mid-second century is apparent in the seriousness with which Justin composes his longest surviving work as a dialogue with a Jewish teacher. Although more elaborate and somewhat less crude than Barnabas's explanations, Justin's readings of the Septuagint text lead to results that are not fundamentally different. Both represent mainstream Christianity's effort to commandeer the scriptures of Israel for their own. Justin's reading is particularly important in that it epitomizes the church's emerging tendency to read the whole text under a single, unifying perspective. In his *First Apology* Justin construes the Septuagint as a prophetic epic, its unity created by a single author, "the divine Logos," and urges a specifically "literary" reading of the whole: "When you hear the words of the prophets spoken as in a particular character, do not think of them as spoken by the inspired men themselves, but by the divine Word that moved them. For sometimes he speaks as in the character of God the Master and Father of all, sometimes as in the character of Christ, sometimes in the character of the people answering the Lord or his Father. You can see the same thing in your own writers, where one man is the author of the whole work but introduces different characters in dialogue" (1 Apol. 36.1–2, trans. Hardy).[29]

The decisive impetus had come from Marcion, active in Rome just a few years earlier than Justin's writing of the *Dialogue,* who threw his powerful mind and organizing ability against all continuity with Israel. The God of love who appeared in Jesus Christ, Marcion taught, had nothing to do with the God of Israel, and his people was the antithesis of the people elected by that other God, who had created such an unpleasant world. The Christian story was an absolutely new story, and Marcion revised and expurgated the Gospel of Luke and the letters of Paul to create a new scripture to replace the superseded writings of the "Old Testament." The battle against Marcion that rallied diverse thinkers in the emerging catholic church was a battle for a single story from creation to final judgment, a story that wedded Israel and the church inextricably, however hostile the connection might sometimes be between Christian groups and living Jews. The battle was for one God who was the author of the one story and its principal character, as both creator and redeemer, both just and loving, both the God of Israel and the God of Jesus Christ.

The opponents of Marcion thus came to see in the traditions and scriptures that they had inherited a world history that constituted a moral drama. It had the classic elements that every narrative needs: a beginning, a middle, and an end. Though the beginning was the beginning of the universe, with the God who, through his Logos/Son created the heavens and the earth, the opponents of Valentinus and the other Gnostics insisted that it was a human story from start to finish. In it God acted with and through human actors, and human accountability to God was its leitmotif, dramatized at each of the turning points: the debacle of Adam and Eve, the primeval stories from Cain to Babel, the repeated sin, exile, and return of Israel, the rebellious lynching of God's Son and Messiah by leaders of his own people and by the government of the ruling empire, and the final judgment when all must stand before the throne of God. By the end of the second century the whole plot had come to be perceived, by the Christians who were calling themselves "catholics," as a thread holding together the diverse writings that constituted Christian scripture. A "canon" was emerging comprising an "Old Testament" and a "New Testament," which together narrated one drama.

Irenaeus, the bishop of Lyons in the last decades of the second century, is the first, in the documents that survive, to make explicit this plot as the guiding theme for reading scripture and for understanding the moral contest in which every person is engaged. Especially in his *Proof of the Apostolic Preaching*, a brief summary of the Christian faith that Irenaeus wrote near the end of his career for a certain Marcianus, he both exhibits the various strategies for a figural reading of the biblical texts that had become common in most non-Marcionite interpretation and then, for the first time, outlines the whole story in some detail.[30] Its beginning point is the creation of the world and the primal innocence and subsequent disobedience of the first human couple, as told in Genesis. Its climax is the incarnation of the Word and Son of God; its dénouement, his coming again to judge all humankind.

Each of these major "acts" of the drama had been part of much Christian belief since the first century. What is new about Irenaeus's exposition is that he systematically fills in the narrative between Creation-and-Fall and the account of Jesus' appearance by following the biblical narrative—especially the narratives of the Pentateuch, but also parts of the subsequent accounts of Israel's history. Thus Israel's history, construed in the prophetic (and Deuteronomistic) perspective of sin and redemption, is subsumed into what has emerged by Irenaeus's time as the universal history of God's plan for human redemption. In this plan, a "new people" replaces Israel (something we saw hinted already in Matthew and made explicit in Barnabas), but Israel continues to have a necessary and instructive part. The "figural" or "typological" reading of the Bible had implied many if not most of the parts of this way of understanding Christianity's antecedents, yet the dramatic plot as a whole had not previously been worked out.

This moral drama was a new thing. The moral narratives within which Greek and Roman writers depicted the development of character are small and fragmentary by comparison. If anything may be said to be unique in Christianity's contribution to Western ethical sensibilities, it is this dramatic history of everything and all peoples, centering on the erratic response of God's elect people to God's speaking and acting, and culminating in the calling to account of every creature for what they have done in God's world.

POSTSCRIPT
History, Pluralism, and Christian Morality

❖　❖　❖　❖　❖　❖　❖　❖　❖　❖

Our ethnographic journey into the foreign world of Christian beginnings is at an end. We return to our present, wondering perhaps whether our own world will now look a bit different from before, as it often does to the eyes of a traveler returning from strange places. The purpose of this inquiry has been resolutely historical and descriptive. It will have succeeded to a large extent if it has done no more than to make the ethos of the early Christians seem even more distant from the ordinary concerns and beliefs of people today than it did before. This is one of the things historians do: it is a large part of our job to try to protect the integrity of the past, and that often has the effect of emphasizing its strangeness. Yet encounter with that strangeness, like living for a time in a strange culture, also may produce an odd distancing from our own culture, not unlike the "alienation effect" of engaging a Brechtian drama. Few of us would inquire seriously about the past if we were not driven by some questions that arise in our own time; we hope to return, if not with "lessons" for the present, at least with an altered perspective on it. With that possibility in mind, I venture here a more personal word, addressed to readers who have some concern for the state of Christian moral discourse today. First, however, it may be useful to review the several facets of the early Christians' ethos that we have examined in the previous chapters.

The Culture of Early Christian Morality

The earliest Christians were *converts*, and their moral and theological language was stamped with the metaphor of turning—away from "the world," "the gentiles," "the idols," the past. They did not invent the metaphor, however; the language was already freighted by common use to express two contrasting relationships to the dominant culture: either a radical turning away from the common norms, rejecting as evil the world's good, or a personal turning from a worse to a better life—"worse" and "better" by standards assumed to be self-evident. A similar ambivalence was built into the very social forms of the early Christian groups in the cities of the Roman Empire. They organized themselves as household cult-associations, like the immigrants who had brought their home culture and home gods with them into their new cities. Like those immigrants, these pseudo-immigrants were part of the society of the city, dependent for their existence upon the urban household, upon the protection of the houseowner, upon the network of friendship and patronage that held urban society together.

The mobility and the common languages that made possible the rapid spread of Christian cells through the cities around the Mediterranean combined with the peculiar sensibilities of their Jewish inheritance to produce a sense, out of the ordinary among real immigrants of the time, of being a single people in whatever place. Not only was the little meeting in Gaius's or Nympha's house "the town meeting of God" for its participants in Corinth or Colossae, it was part of the congregation of God that was potentially in every place. Some of them might say that their real *politeuma*, the immigrant's community with quasi-citizenship, was in heaven, that their true household was God's household, and some would seek to flee, physically or emotionally, from all the ties that bound one to this present social world. Yet for most the tensions between being in the world and not being of the world were inescapable. Was the world a corpse? Or was the world God's good creation? Was the city Babylon, the Great Whore? Or was the city the image of the heavenly Jerusalem? Was the body burden and enemy to the soul? Or was the body the means of the Logos entering human life? Was it the object of God's love and his power of resurrection? Was it the weapon of the martyr's warfare against the powers of evil?

The language of Christian moral discourse, too, was ambivalently of the world yet alien to the world. The Christians' lists of virtues and vices were not much different from those common in popular morality, though they used them to mark boundaries, to insist upon difference. Their leaders borrowed from the topics of philosophical and rhetorical moralizing, though sometimes they twisted them in peculiar ways or set them into unusual contexts. For example, the narrative of crucifixion and resurrection of God's

Son, the myth of Logos incarnate, the pervasive notion of the single will of the one God, the image of a final, universal judgment for all humanity—all these colored and sometimes dramatically transformed the common rhetoric of admonition. Perhaps, however, it was in certain of their social practices that the Christian groups most effectively distinguished themselves from other cult associations, clubs, or philosophical schools—their special rituals of initiation and communion, their practice of communal admonition and discipline, the organization of aid for widows, orphans, prisoners, and other weaker members of the movement.

What is perhaps most striking about the ethos of the early Christians as we have observed it is its multiplicity. Christians responded in different ways to the peculiar niches in the ecology of culture in which each group found itself and to the peculiar pressures and opportunities that each had experienced. Christians disagreed among themselves on such fundamental questions as how one ought to treat one's own body, whether marriage and the raising of children were good or evil, whether the powers of government were instruments of God or of the devil. If there is any word that the ethnographer of the past can bring back to help in our own deliberations, it will surely not be simple. What I offer in this postscript is only a series of theses, growing out of the observations made in this book and observations, considerably less systematic, about the lives of Christians and their neighbors today.

Preliminary Theses on Christian Morality

Thesis 1: Making morals and making community are one, dialectical process.

It follows that rational reflection alone cannot, as Bernard Williams has so bluntly shown, produce that moral confidence which we so much need.[1] None of the forms of rationalism has succeeded in finding a place to stand outside the particularities of a human community and its tradition, nor a first premise purified of interest. This is not to say, obviously, that critical reflection is not essential to ethics. No community is wholly good; the best of them, to be humanly tolerable, are in need of frequent criticism. A fanatical community devoted to a relatively good principle (and *relatively* good principles are the only kind given to humans) can produce great misery. But critical reflection is principally reasoning around within the tradition, even when we try to understand, as we urgently must, traditions not our own.[2] The point to remember is that reformative criticism must attend not only to the ideas, not only to the symbolic expressions, but also to the social practices in which, as Alasdair MacIntyre has taught us, all virtue is embedded.

Thesis 2: A Christian moral community must be grounded in the past.

Within the church's defining past I include both scripture and tradition. The Marcionite experiment sought to sever all ties with the past, and that proved enormously attractive to a great many people. Perhaps the fiction of an absolutely fresh start appeals perennially to all of us who are pretty much stuck in the beds we have made for ourselves. I am sure as the end of our millennium approaches that we shall witness a new outbreak of the flying-saucer cults, this century's rough equivalent to Marcion's faith in the Alien God. From outer space will come the saviors, having no connection with our world or our past, who in a blinding flash that obliterates all previous logic will give to the elect the answers, unprecedented and irrefutable, and will pluck those few fortunate saints out of the stream of causation into a pure and uncontingent future. It is a pathetic fiction, as Justin and Irenaeus and Tertullian had sense enough to see. Less obviously, cutting ourselves off from the past by ignorance and neglect also corrodes our sense of who we are.

The early Christians, for practical as well as principled reasons, had to have a past. Without scripture and tradition they would have had no identity. In time they expanded scripture and began a new tradition, and there are times when both seem to us more a burden than an illumination. Nevertheless, the church has defined itself in these terms, and the Marcionite temptation, which today is more likely to arise from neglect than from choice, must still be resisted. The elementary rule is that Christians must know the church's past in order to be faithful.

Thesis 3: The church's rootage in Israel is a privileged dimension of its past.

This is a corollary of Thesis 2. We have had to be taught in our time by the horror and the guilt of the Holocaust how profoundly evil can be the consequences of denying or distorting this truth, and how deep in Christian traditions and even in Christian scriptures are the roots of the denial and the distortion. But these experiences have taught us something else: Judaism is not only part of Christianity's past, and Christianity for about sixteen centuries a fateful part of Judaism's past; each is also part of the other's present. From that fact it follows—historically and ethically, if not logi-cally—that continuing a dialogue with the Jewish tradition *as interpreted by Jews* is a rich and necessary source of insight and correction for Christian theology and ethics. I particularly stress the qualification "as interpreted by Jews." We have never lacked for Christian interpreters of Judaism, and sometimes they have exercised extraordinary diligence, skill, and fairness. Nevertheless, as we look back with eyes chastened by the history of anti-Semitism, we cannot fail to see that even the best Christian interpreters of Judaism have been infected by one-sidedness, defensiveness, or wishful thinking. This is not to say that Jewish interpretations of Judaism are disinterested. Yet we must not imagine that the adoption by Christians of an aesthetic Jewishness in theology or liturgy will be sufficient to compensate for errors of the past. The point is rather that truth-telling gains where conversation is realistic and honest, and realistic and honest conversation requires that the conversation-partner be a real person, possibly inconve-nient and disagreeable, not a fictional character whom we have made up.

Thesis 4: Faithfulness ought not be confused with nostalgia.

We cannot replicate the past, and we ought not to wish to. To be sure, typology and allegory have a long and hallowed history in Christian reading of scripture, but even when Christians today may want for good reasons to recapture some of the liveliness of those interpretive traditions, they need to recognize that both, in different ways, tend to rob the past of its own integ-rity. Certainly there are places in the life of the church—notably in its liturgy—where we ought to be made to feel as if we were in the presence of the patriarchs, prophets, and apostles, where the language of our interpreta-tion may well seek to function in the way that the screen of icons is supposed to work in the liturgy of the Eastern churches, a window between God's eter-nal realm and our world of time. I would only urge that even in those mo-ments we ought also to preserve what Frank Kermode calls "a clerkly skepti-cism."[3] Pretending that the present is the past may at times be an effective and desirable fiction, but it is a fiction, and we need to be conscious of that. Not least when we try to find warrants for moral rules in scripture and tradi-tion, we need to be acutely aware of the constant danger of anachronism.

Not only can we not replicate the golden age of Christian beginnings, there was no golden age to replicate. Jesus did not arrive in Galilee proclaim-ing a complete, systematic, and novel Christian ethic, nor even a compact set of fundamental principles that had only to be explicated by his apostles. There was not even, I have argued, any such thing as "New Testament ethics." What the ethnographer of early Christianity finds is only a record of experimentation, of trial and error, of tradition creatively misread and innovation wedged craftily into the cracks of custom, of the radically new mixed up with the familiar and old, of disputes and confrontation, of fervent assertions of unity amid distressing signs of schism, of opposite points of view on fundamental matters, of dialectic and change. Because Christian moralizing begins in history, begins in the midst of Israel in the midst of a Hellenized and Romanized world of manifold native cultures, it is not even possible to say precisely where and when it begins to be distinctively Christian, and difficult to know, in the whirl of syncretism, what distinguishes it. There has not ever been a purely Christian morality, unalloyed with the experiences and traditions of others.

In our quest for guidance from the past, do we then wander into the all-devouring fog of deconstruction? Is all meaning not only contingent but indeterminable? I do not believe we have to accept so pessimistic a view. The tradition may be diverse from the beginning, but it is not shapeless. There is no single or unique Christian morality, but there are important family resemblances. It may not be possible to enumerate a finite set of fundamental principles robust enough to survive unchanged when plucked from the soil of history, but there are root-metaphors that have proven to have vast generative power. Faith can find the guidance it needs, so long as it is not blinded by nostalgia.

Thesis 5: Christian ethics must be polyphonic.

One of the unsurprising ironies of early Christian history—of all Christian history—is that the drive to be one (as God is one) leads to conflict and schism. The Christian community ought always to strive and pray for unity—but to admit a considerable measure of diversity. How much unity is achievable? How much diversity is tolerable? These are judgments that each generation must make. Obviously there can be no community and no tradition if everything is permitted ("All things are lawful, but not all things build up"), and therefore there can be no community without some degree of coercion. Yet unity coerced is unstable ("For why is my freedom judged by a conscience not mine?"). I quote Saint Paul not arbitrarily, but because, at his best, he among the earliest leaders of the Christian movement had the clearest knack for polyphony, for bringing into overt expression the conscientious voices of many: of tradition, of scripture, of weak, of strong, of time-honored custom, of the radically new gospel.[4] This is at least one feature of Paul's rhetoric that we could well imitate.

The fact is that the Christian movement has survived despite—or perhaps because of—a large and often raucous diversity. To put the matter in conventional theological terms, the unity that Christians seek, the unity that the one God gives, is an eschatological gift. Like other truly eschatological entities, it exerts its pressure upon our life in the middle, but we do not *have* it. We may at best approach it asymptotically; we cannot wrest it into being in the land of unlikeness where human life is lived. Now, in the middle time, we had best not diminish too greatly our intellectual and spiritual gene pool, our store of metaphors, stories, ideas, and institutions. Common sense is needed; many experiments are silly and some are dangerous, but experimentation we need. Our creative polyphony needs the voices of some sects, some orders, some traditionalists, some experimental communities, some radical prophets. And whence do we get the common sense that judges which are silly and which are dangerous? Common sense, as Clifford Geertz has cleverly and rightly said, is "a cultural system."[5] Common sense is shaped, in the way I have argued in this book moral sensibilities are shaped, by common lore, common tradition, common practices, by our memory and our experience—no other way.

Thesis 6: Moral confidence, not moral certainty, is what we require.

I have had repeated occasion earlier to revert to this maxim inscribed by Bernard Williams, and to his demonstration that reflection alone cannot provide confidence.[6] Confidence emerges only from healthy communities, and the general dearth of moral confidence today (though there are all too many prophets ready to assert an unwarranted certainty) is a sign that all is not well with our communities. Yet there is something self-defeating about a project to build up our communities in order to build up our moral confidence: that is liable to produce a vortex of self-concern—a malady to which churches are only too susceptible. Christian communities are healthy not when they are worrying about their health, but when they are trying to do what they are here for. Some of the central things may only be accomplished, as it were, indirectly: "Lord," say the sheep, "when was it that we saw you hungry and fed you?"

To put the matter theologically, the moral confidence the Christian needs rests upon a certainty that is not our own, as the Reformers said of salvation: it is *extra nos*. That observation leads to my final thesis:

Thesis 7: God tends to surprise.

One of the most remarkable things about the biblical story is that God, who is represented as being faithful to his covenant, is forever surprising and often dismaying his people. That quality of the story was wonderfully convenient to the first Christians, who were able thus to assert that the crucifixion and resurrection of God's Son, the Messiah, might be the greatest surprise of all, but not out of character. Naturally Christians then liked to presume that it was also the final surprise; henceforth God would act just as the Christian understanding of that revelatory event requires. But that presumption, in light of God's previous record, appears unwarranted.

Paul's reflection on the situation of Israel in light of this ultimate surprise, in the Letter to Romans, is a salutary paradigm for a way Christians now would do well to think about God's faithfulness. Paul has told the story (in chapters 9–11) of the "partial hardening of Israel" in their rejection of Jesus as Messiah and their replacement "contrary to nature" by gentiles in the Christian communities. He uses that story, however, as a warning to the gentile Christians. The latter must not imagine that their newly privileged status among God's people is independent of "the root" in Israel, or immune to judgment of the sort that had encountered disbelieving Jews, nor must they think (as Matthew, Barnabas, and most of the succeeding tradition would urge) that God was finished with the Jews and their covenant canceled. On the contrary, Paul imagines an ultimate fulfillment for "all Israel" that, although it violates the expectations nurtured in their scriptures and traditions, yet will prove in retrospect to gather up the great themes of those scriptures and traditions in ways unpredictable.

In some analogous way, perhaps Christians and Jews of the twenty-first century will learn that neither of the different but overlapping stories in their two Bibles—the open-ended, multicentered story of the Jewish Tanak, the powerfully centered and forward-driving story of the Christian Bible[7]—is exclusive of the other or complete in itself. More than that, perhaps they will discover that the flourishing that (to use the traditional theological language) God wills for all earth's creatures is only possible if Christians and Jews can find ways to affirm the narratives and rhythms of yet other peoples and traditions, once again revising and rehearing, but not abandoning, their own. A faithful hermeneutic of the Pauline kind requires confidence in the God who, determined to have mercy on all and to bring into being the things that are not, will astonish those who are loyal to the story of God's past actions, but will not abandon them.[8] In this way the process of inventing Christian—and human—morality will continue.

Notes

❖ ❖ ❖ ❖ ❖ ❖ ❖ ❖ ❖ ❖

Preface

1. Brown 1988, xvi.

Chapter 1. Morals and Community

1. For the negative side, see, e.g., MacMullen 1990, 162–68, and Ste Croix 1975.

2. I claim no competence as a moral philosopher, so I do not intend to enter into this debate, though it will be apparent that I find the historical line of questioning I am pursuing here more congenial with the "Aristotelian" critique than with the "Platonist" and Kantian traditions. For a diverse sample of the "Aristotelians," see MacIntyre 1984, Nussbaum 1986b, Williams 1985, and Stout 1981 and 1988.

3. Lear 1988, 169.

4. Cf. Williams 1985, 94–98, and Rorty 1967.

5. Aelius Aristides, *Apol.* 15.3–7. Translations of ancient and modern sources are all my own unless otherwise indicated. Here I translate the Greek version as printed by Goodspeed 1914 (based on the late romance of *Barlaam and Josaphat*, identified by A. Robinson as adapted from the lost Aristides), correcting it by the fourth-century fragment found at Oxyrhynchus (Brit. Museum inv. 2486), published by Milne 1923. Relevant portions of the Syriac version, which generally seems closer to the original than the *Barlaam and Josaphat* excerpts, are conveniently translated by Womer 1987, 34–39.

6. Grant 1988, 37.

7. The earliest Christian writing to use the motif is the "Preaching of Peter" quoted by Clement of Alexandria: Jews, Greeks, and Christians (*Strom.* 6.5.41); see Malherbe 1970a, 220–21. For the broader development, see Harnack 1972, 240–78.

8. Peacock 1986.

9. Geertz 1973, 5.

10. Ibid., 129.

11. See, e.g., the classic description by Berger and Luckmann 1967, 156–63.

12. Pliny, *Ep.* 10.96.7, trans. Radice 1963, 294.

13. Brown, 1988.

Chapter 2. Turning

1. The pioneer in analyzing the "conversion language" of 1 Thess. is Pax 1971 and 1972. Fullest development of the topic, to date, is by Malherbe 1987, who especially emphasizes parallels in Greco-Roman philosophical schools, following up on points made in the classic work by Nock 1933. In general, my interpretation of 1 Thess. is largely informed by Malherbe's work, both published and unpublished.

2. Of the innumerable studies of Paul's conversion, two are particularly noteworthy: the first chapter of the book by Beverly Roberts Gaventa (Gaventa 1986) and Alan F. Segal's major study (Segal 1990).

3. Cf. 1 Cor. 9:1; 15:8–10. Rom. 7 has often been read as Paul's "confession," but since the publication of Kümmel 1929 (repr. in Kümmel 1974), the consensus has shifted to recognition that the "I" of this chapter is a rhetorical one. Stanley Stowers has recently strengthened and further clarified this conclusion by identifying Paul's strategy here with the standard rhetorical practice of *prosopopoiia*, the adopting of a role for argumentative purposes (Stowers forthcoming a, b).

4. On the literary convention, see Hyldahl 1966, 148–59; Nock (1933, 255–57) nevertheless thinks Justin's report "seems to correspond to the attitude of the time" and compares Lucian's *Hermotimus*. See also Skarsaune 1976.

5. See Fredriksen 1986.

6. Fredriksen 1986; for examples of sociological studies, see Beckford 1978, Richardson 1978, and chap. 2, "Conversion Stories," of Goodman 1972.

7. Wilson 1975.

8. Diogenes Laertius 4.3.16, trans. R. D. Hicks, Loeb Classical Library 2:393.

9. *Double Indictment* 17, trans. A. M. Harmon, Loeb Classical Library 121.

10. *Nigrinus* 1, trans. A. M. Harmon, Loeb Classical Library.

11. E.g., Epictetus, *Diss.* 3.23.37.

12. *Diss.* 3.23.37.

13. See Fitzgerald and White 1983. On comparisons with—and possible influence upon—Bunyan, see pp. 29–30, nn. 7, 8.

14. "Wealth is the viaticum for education"—*ephodion de paideias ho ploutos* (Artemidorus, *Oneiroc.* 4.67; ed. Pack 1963, 289, l. 17). The point is candidly admitted in the anonymous treatise on education that has come down to us among the works of Plutarch (*Mor.* 8E). Answering an imagined objection, the author says that the poor and common folk must not blame him but Luck *(Tychē)*. On the other hand, even among the lower classes the hope is occasionally expressed that children may be educated and thus get ahead in life. Bonner 1977, 101 cites Petronius's account (*Sat.* 46) of the old-clothes dealer Echion, who tells Agamemnon the rhetorician about his little son, who is studying arithmetic, Greek, Latin, and painting, and who he hopes will read law. He says, "Education is a treasure-house, and a special skill never lets you down." Bonner finds a similar sentiment in Juvenal 14.189ff. (102). See also Nussbaum 1986b.

15. Fitzgerald and White 1983, 148, n. 53

16. Trans. Benjamin Fiore, S.J., in Malherbe 1977, 163.

17. The second chapter of book 6 in the collection by Diogenes Laertius contains a sample; some are worked up into the Cynic Epistles.

18. Malherbe 1982; cf. Malherbe 1970b. Both repr. in Malherbe 1989, 11–24, 35–48.

19. See the interesting discussion in Malherbe 1987, 36–40.

20. *Ep.* 6.6, trans. Richard M. Gummere, Loeb Classical Library.

21. For the Epicurean "policy on recruitment and conversion," see Frischer 1982, 67–86—part of an extraordinarily ingenious reconstruction, not altogether convincing. If there were Pythagorean communities in the Roman Empire, and if they resembled the tightly organized cult that Pythagoras had once led at Croton in the sixth century B.C.E., according to the idealized description by Iamblichus written more than eight hundred years later, then we would have an even closer analogy to the Christians' (also ideal) model of conversion. Unfortunately, evidence is lacking; see Meeks 1983, 83, with literature cited there. Loveday Alexander points out that in the second century Galen disparagingly compares medical and philosophical schools of his day with "the schools of Moses and Christ." Alexander argues that the schools, not just the "religious" ones of Epicurus and Pythagoras, were somewhat more like the Christian groups than usually recognized (Alexander forthcoming). On the general question of philosophers' concerns about the anxieties of new disciples, see Malherbe 1987, 36–46.

22. Frischer 1982, esp. 83–84.

23. Nock 1933, 138, 155.

24. I follow the text and translation by Griffiths 1975, which is accompanied by extensive and valuable notes.

25. Cf. Griffiths' commentary, 254f.

26. Griffiths' translation of *sacrorum pleraque initia in Graecia participavi;* see his comments on pp. 3–4.

27. The same is true, I believe, of another text sometimes adduced in support of a conversionist interpretation of the mysteries, an inscription from Philadelphia (Lydia) of the second or first century B.C.E.: see the maximalist interpretation by Barton and Horsley 1981. Nock 1933, 216–17, is more cautious.

28. The classic works in English are Bamberger 1968 (originally published in 1939) and Braude 1940, but they make many questionable assumptions in the use of sources. For a sensible review of the problems and a useful survey of the evidence, see Goodman 1992. Cohen has published a series of incisive articles that clearly are moving in the direction of a new synthesis of the evidence: Cohen 1982–83, 1983, 1986, 1987, 1989.

29. Cohen 1989.

30. Trans. F. H. Colson, Loeb Classical Library 8.225–27.

31. The "political" aspect is emphasized in Philo's curious description of conver-

sion as "passing, as it were, from mob-rule *[ochlokratia]* . . . into democracy *[dēmokratia]*" (*Virt.* 180, trans. Colson). In light of Philo's exaltation elsewhere of what might be called constitutional monarchy, the description, which has parallels in other passages, is a little surprising. An interesting question, unfortunately beyond the scope of the present study; a start on the solution is found in Goodenough 1938, 86–90.

32. Many commentators on 1 Thess. speak of "persecution," but in fact there is hardly anything in the letter to suggest that the *thlipsis* goes beyond the kinds of unpleasantness that relatives and associates commonly apply to someone in their midst who has suddenly joined a peculiar and secretive movement. Malherbe points to identical language in philosophical discussions of conversion as well as in the Jewish novel about a paradigmatic female convert, *Joseph and Asenath*, to suggest that the word in 1 Thess. 1:6 refers to "the distress and anguish of heart experienced by persons who broke with their past as they received the gospel" (Malherbe 1987, 36–52, quotation from 48). Naturally, the pressure was often more than psychological, as 1 Thess. 3:4–5 suggests.

33. This is abundantly illustrated by the several publications of Abraham J. Malherbe on the Thessalonian letters, most compactly in Malherbe 1987. For parallels to the marriage rules, see Yarbrough 1985.

34. For further detail, see Meeks 1983, 84–107.

35. The document did not survive, but in this century scholars have been able to reconstruct it from its reuse in later church handbooks. See Dix 1968 and Botte 1963.

36. See Meeks 1983, 150–57.

37. See Finn 1989.

38. Even the famous inscription of rules of the shrine of Agdistis in Philadelphia seems to me to fall into this category, despite the argument of Barton and Horsley to the contrary. See n. 27 above.

39. See the discussion of Justin's conversion above and n. 4.

40. Trans. C. C. Richardson in Richardson 1953, 249–50.

41. See the discussion by Grant 1988, chap. 8, who says the language Justin uses in telling the story "depicts the normal course of conversion as he describes it" rather than literal history (69). He compares the sexual morality espoused by Justin with that of Musonius Rufus (70–71).

42. *Acts of Peter* (Vercellenses) 17, trans. Schneemelcher and Stead in Hennecke 1965, 300; text in Lipsius and Bonnet 1959, 1:65.19–23.

43. *Acts of Paul and Thecla;* note esp. the accusation against Paul by Hermogenes and Demas in chap. 12 (Lipsius and Bonnet 1959, 1:244.3–4; for trans., see Hennecke 1965, 356) and Paul's defense in chap. 17 (Lipsius and Bonnet 1959, 1:246.12–14; trans. Hennecke 1965, 357).

44. So the Vallicelli MS (U); the major Paris MS has a list of vices: *porneia, moicheia, akatharsia, pleonexia, philargyria, kai pan ho ti kai parablaptein tēn psychēn*

oidate, thus compressing the list of vices that in U follow from adultery (Lipsius and Bonnet 1959, 3:199.29–200,20).

45. Berger and Luckmann 1967, 114–16, 156, 159–60.

Chapter 3. City, Household, People of God

1. Werner Jaeger's exposition (Jaeger 1945) remains the definitive treatment of the polis as the context of all Greek ethical thought. He emphasizes the public character of virtue and conscience in the whole classical tradition.

2. I have outlined some of the principal issues on which polis-oriented ethics impinged on the moral sensibilities of the first Christians in Meeks 1986, 1–39.

3. Compare the story told of Diogenes, chap. 2 above. A fine introduction to the characteristics of the Cynics in the era of Christianity's beginnings can be found in Malherbe 1982.

4. For example, Epictetus, *Diss.* 2.20.6 accuses Epicurus of inconsistency in "wanting to abolish the natural community of humans with one another," while taking such pains and writing "such big books" to persuade others of his views. Perhaps he has in view the proselytizing activities of Roman Epicureans in his own time, on which see De Lacy 1948 and Frischer 1982. Plutarch devotes an entire tract to the topic, "That Epicurus Actually Makes a Pleasant Life Impossible" (*Non posse suav.; Mor.* 1086C–1107C).

5. Martha Nussbaum denies the communal element in Epicureanism. Viewed from Aristotle's standpoint, she says, "Epicurus thinks of the good life as an individual and not a communal matter, to which interpersonal goods of all sorts, even the vaunted good of *philia,* are instrumental, [and therefore] he is free to design a procedure which altogether neglects our political nature and which subordinates *philia* to the ends of individual therapy" (Nussbaum 1986a, 69). The contrast with Aristotle is illuminating, and Nussbaum's reading of Epicurus is a useful corrective to the overenthusiastically communitarian interpretations sometimes offered of Epicureanism (notably by De Witt, e.g., 1936a, 1936b), but she seems to me to go too far in the other direction. A full discussion, however, would lead us far afield from our topic. See Festugiere 1956, Baldry 1965, and Mueller 1972.

6. MacMullen 1988, 69–70.

7. Ibid., 70, 119.

8. Ibid.

9. Varied perceptions of slaves' status, including the slaves' own perceptions, are interestingly discussed by Dale B. Martin in the first chapter of his important book (Martin 1990), 1–49. Flory 1975 and 1978, Weaver 1972, Boulvert 1974, and Chantraine 1967 are among the other significant contributions to this topic.

10. See, for example, Walcot 1970, Campbell 1964, Peristiany, Pitt-Rivers 1963.

11. Geertz 1973; cf. Berger and Luckmann 1967.

12. In the present-day Greek village Vasilika (beloved of anthropologists), a child who misbehaves is admonished, "Aren't you ashamed?" But a young man who is rude in public is chided, "Have you no *philotimo?*" (Walcot 1970, 59–60, with references to field work by Friedl, Sanders, the Blums, and others). Note Walcot's observations (83) on the inevitable progression from "love of honor" to "envy."

13. Alföldy 1980.

14. *Pasin philos outhena lypōn;* Tod 1951. Elias Bickerman calls the Latin equivalent of the quoted sentiment, *neminem laesi,* the "Golden Rule of paganism under the Empire" (Bickerman 1957, 327).

15. Crisis of the poleis: Welskopf 1974; see also the classic surveys by Rostovtzeff 1957, esp. 1:130–50, and A. H. M. Jones 1971. For the role of Roman patronage in linking Rome with the provincial aristocracies—and transforming the latter—Badian 1958 and Bowersock 1965 remain fundamental. An excellent translation of the younger Pliny's correspondence is Radice 1963. Dio's speech to the Tarsians: *Or.* 34.

16. Meeks 1983, 16–23; see also Meeks 1986, 19–39.

17. See esp. MacMullen 1974.

18. Plümacher 1987; see also Fox 1987, 50–53. The whole of Lane Fox's chapter on "Pagans and Their Cities" (27–63) is valuable as background for the present discussion.

19. The best introduction to the political situation of the Jews under the Roman principate is Smallwood 1981. For a broader survey of the internal developments of Judaism, see Cohen 1987a.

20. On Philo, see Meeks 1986, 81–85. The literature on Philo is vast; for the topic at hand Goodenough 1938 remains important, and for Philo's cultural location Heinemann 1962 is fundamental.

21. For the pattern and its implications, see White 1990a. Comparing the philosophical schools, Alexander (forthcoming) makes astute observations on the "political" options presented to the new Christian groups.

22. On inscriptional evidence for the increasing exercise of patronage by women, implying and enabling a greater role in civic life, see MacMullen 1990, 162–68.

23. The point is well made by Fox 1987, 733–34, n. 20, but it hardly follows, as he asserts, that we should therefore not speak of patrons and clients at all when speaking of analogous relations of reciprocity at lower social levels. On Erastus, see Meeks 1983, 58–59, based on Theißen 1982, 79–83.

24. Jeffers 1991, quotation from 134. Some of the steps in Jeffers's cumulative, largely hypothetical argument are shaky, but the divergent potential of the household ethos is well illustrated by what is at least a plausible reading of the texts. Maier 1991, approaching the same texts with different questions, also emphasizes the tensions between the hierarchical order implicit in the patronage system and the countercultural tendencies that are especially prominent in Hermas. He argues that

Hermas treats "ethics as a means of nurturing a common identity which shields the sect from influence by the outside world" (73)—the aim of the work's paraenetic sections. Lane Fox (1987, 381–90) has a number of sage observations about Hermas's visions, in part a useful counterweight to the sociological perspective of Maier, Jeffers, and others, but the last word on this complex and unique work of popular Roman Christianity has not been said. See also Osiek 1983 and Lampe 1987.

25. Elliott 1981.

26. For a fuller explanation of the concept of "reference groups" and "reference individuals" than space permits here, and an analysis of the variety of functions such reference has in the letters of Paul, see Meeks 1990a.

27. For "nihilation" as a strategy of conversion or the maintenance of a conversionist sect, see Berger and Luckmann 1967, 159–60. Lane Fox's assertion that the Christian community "claimed to sidestep status and power altogether" (1987, 321) misstates the case; rather, the Christians redefine both. We may agree, however, that "it could . . . offer an alternative community and range of values to those who were disenchanted by the display of riches, by the harshness of the exercise of power and the progressive hardening of the gradations of rank and degree" (ibid.). The whole of Paul's Corinthian correspondence could be cited in support—though the irony with which Paul peppers his rhetoric in these letters derives from the evident fact that "gradations of rank and degree," defined in old and new ways, are very important and troublesome indeed to the people he is admonishing.

28. Niebuhr 1956.

Chapter 4. Loving and Hating the World

1. *Gospel of Thomas* 56 (42.29–32). For quotations from the *Gospel of Thomas* (henceforth *GTh*), I have used the translation of Layton 1987 throughout. It is customary to refer to passages in *GTh* by the number assigned to each of the sayings of Jesus in an early edition of the text (e.g., here, 56) as well as by the page and line numbers of the Coptic manuscript (here, 42.29–32).

2. Greek fragments had been found at Oxyrhynchus and published around the turn of the century, but their identity was not apparent until the complete work was found among the cache of documents unearthed near Nag Hammadi. There is now a copious literature on the *Gospel of Thomas*, including several editions and translations. The definitive edition, by Bentley Layton, with translation by Thomas O. Lamdin and the Greek fragments edited and translated by Harold W. Attridge, is in vol. 1 of the series *The Coptic Gnostic Library* (Layton 1989).

3. For a survey of the "school of St. Thomas," see Layton 1987, 359–70. We shall consider the Thomas tradition further in chap. 8.

4. See, e.g., MacMullen 1988, 71–84.

5. The last point was helpfully expressed by Elaine Pagels, in comments on a draft of the present work. See also Smith 1965.

6. An English translation of the *Acts of Thomas,* with introduction, is conveniently available in Hennecke 1965, 2:425–31. It is based on the standard Greek text edited by Bonnet (Lipsius and Bonnet 1959, 3:99–288), generally thought to be closer to the original than the extant Syriac version. A. F. J. Klijn has provided an English translation of the latter, with valuable commentary (Klijn 1962).

7. Perkins 1985, 213.

8. Smith 1981.

9. I have adapted this summary of the classic Gnostic myth from Layton 1987, 12–13, where Layton lucidly diagrams the plot of the story recounted in the *Secret Book of John.*

10. For the history of the Gnostic sect and Valentinus's adaptation of its teachings, see McGuire 1983 and the summary in Layton 1987, 5–22, 217–27. Layton also provides the most useful and accessible collection of the relevant primary texts, in English translation. For Valentinus's place in the tradition of textual interpretation at Alexandria, see Dawson 1992.

11. Ambrose, *Letters* 40.16; 41.1.

12. See Meeks 1972; out of the voluminous literature since then, note especially Martyn 1979 and Brown 1979. For a comprehensive assessment of recent Johannine research, see Ashton 1991.

13. Cf. de Jonge 1968, 95: "typerend, exemplarisch."

14. See Marshall 1987 and the discussion in chap. 3 above.

15. My reading of 1 Cor. 1–4 is heavily dependent on Fitzgerald 1988, 117–48.

Chapter 5. The Language of Obligation

1. Robert M. Grant has argued persuasively that Pliny's investigation was shaped by his reading of Livy's account of the Bacchants in Rome (Grant 1967, 55–56; originally published in 1948). He responds to criticisms by A. N. Sherwin-White in Grant 1988, 29–31.

2. Pioneering work on the lists was done by Vögtle 1936, Wibbing 1959, and Kamlah 1964, but all three studies suffer from excessive schematization and preoccupation with the quest for some single antecedent. Potentially more useful to understanding the kinds of things a good person performed on the one hand and avoided on the other would be a thorough analysis of the language of laudatory inscriptions, including epitaphs and the praise or self-praise of benefactors. For illuminating but partial samples, see Lattimore 1942, Tod 1951, Alföldy 1980, Danker 1982.

3. Meeks 1983, 150–57.

4. From Gal. 5:19–21; 1 Cor. 5:9–10,11; 6:9–10; Col. 3:5,8; Eph. 5:3–4,5; 1 Pet. 2:1; 4:3,15; Mark 4:19; 7:21–22; Matt. 15:19; Rom. 1:29–31; Heb. 13:4; Rev. 21:8; 22:15, all as translated by NRSV.

5. Xenophon, *Memorabilia* 2.1.21–34. For a Jewish adaptation of the same fable, see Philo, "The Sacrifices of Abel and Cain," 20–42.

6. Höistad 1948; Malherbe 1988.

7. For a somewhat fuller analysis of the Two Ways in the *Didache*, see Meeks 1986, 148–53; greater detail on the history and uses of the form in Rordorf 1972.

8. Menander, *Sententiae*, ed. Jaekel 1964; convenient access to Epicurus's extant gnomes is provided by Bailey 1970; Iamblichus, *The Pythagorean Life* 80–87, cf. 157, 161–62, 247 (a good English translation in Clark 1989); for the use of Pythagoras's sayings in moral teachings, see also Pseudo-Plutarch, *On the Education of Children* 17 (= *Moralia* 12D–F).

9. Horst 1978, 79.

10. *Sent. Sexti* 73–75,80, trans. Edwards and Wild 1981.

11. Richardson 1953, 250.

12. Wilson 1991. Quotations are from pp. 148, 19, 80–81; he in turn quotes Crenshaw 1974, 231.

13. See Horst 1978, 72–73, 79–80, and the further literature to which he refers, to which should be added Bonner 1977, 172–79, who describes schoolboy exercises and gives examples in photographs.

14. Wilson 1991, 9–23, offers a succinct and useful list of several sapiential forms common in the environment of early Christianity: gnome, proverb, *chreia*, aphorism, epigram, precept, and oracle. He rightly warns that ancient classifications are themselves fluid, and the boundaries between the various forms not strict.

15. See, e.g., the comment by Theon of Alexandria, a sophist flourishing probably in the late first century C.E., "It has the name 'chreia' because of its excellence, for more than the other exercises it is useful in many ways for life" (*Eirētai de chreia kat' exochēn hoti mallon tōn allōn pros polla chreiōdēs esti tō biō*). Text and trans. in Hock and O'Neil 1986, 82f.

16. Diogènes Laertius 6.45.

17. From Theon of Alexandria, trans. Hock and O'Neil 1986, 313. For the use of chreiai in transitional schooling, between the rote literary studies of the grammar school and the more advanced composition of rhetorical training, see the discussion of the *progymnasmata* in Hock's general introduction.

18. See, e.g., the comments by Theon in Hock and O'Neil 1986, 100–103.

19. 49:27–31, trans. Thomas O. Lamdin in Layton 1989, 89.

20. A brief discussion of the chreiai in the traditions of Jesus may be found in Robbins 1988; a more extended discussion in Robbins and Mack 1987 and in Kloppenborg 1987. Of earlier work, Dibelius n.d. (German orig. ed. 1919), 152–64, deserves special mention.

21. In the traditional numbering, Mandates 1–4.

22. Wilson 1991, 20.

23. *Ep. mor.* 95.1, trans. Richard M. Gummere, Loeb Classical Library.

24. Layton 1968; cf. Meeks 1986, 150–51.

25. Brotherly love: for two examples, compare Plutarch's discourse on that theme (*Moralia* 478A–492D), or Hierocles, *On Duties* 4.27.20 (conveniently trans-

lated by Malherbe 1986, 93–95). Friendship in Philippians: White 1990b; Kenneth Berry is presently completing a dissertation at Yale University on the topic of friendship in Philippians; James Ware is at work on a dissertation to show Paul's merging of the friendship conventions with missionary terminology. For a brief general discussion of topoi with examples drawn from Greek and Roman sources, see Malherbe 1986, 144–61.

26. *Ep.* 94.1, trans. Richard M. Gummere, Loeb Classical Library.

27. See also Eph. 5:21–6:9; 1 Peter 2:13–3:7; Ignatius, *Polyc.* 4:3–6:2; *1 Clem.* 1:3,21:6–9 Polycarp, *Phil.* 4:2–6.1.

28. Key works in recent interpretation of the NT examples are Lührmann 1980 and Balch 1981. A useful review of research and an annotated bibliography are found in Balch 1988.

29. Importance of the household: Malherbe 1983, 60–91; Meeks 1983, 75–77; Klauck 1981.

30. On the nature and degree of Christian adaptation of the so-called *Haustafel,* see Balch 1988 and the further literature he surveys. On the larger intellectual context of the Stoic notion of appropriate behavior, see Engberg-Pedersen 1990. On divine impartiality, see Bassler 1979. On the conflicts that emerge in adapting the household pattern, see Fiorenza 1983, 251–84.

31. On protreptic and the style of Romans, see Stowers 1981 and Aune 1991.

32. For examples, see Malherbe 1986, 85–104.

33. Malherbe 1986, 85; Betz 1985, 1–16, but note the criticism by Stanton 1987; Kloppenborg 1987, 289–316, 322–25.

34. Christians as letter writers: Stowers 1986. Paul's influence: Babcock 1990, in particular the essay by Gamble, 265–80, suggesting that even the format of books (codex) may have been made popular by use of the collection of Paul's letters. Further surveys and bibliography: Dahl 1976; Aune 1987, 158–225; White 1988.

35. Malherbe demonstrated the paraenetic character of 1 Thess. in an essay that has been widely influential despite the fact that it did not appear until 1992, after two decades of private circulation. Many of his insights are summarized in Malherbe 1987 and 1989, 46–66; his commentary on the Thessalonian letters is awaited.

36. See especially Fitzgerald 1988, Fiore 1986, Meeks 1988, Stowers 1990, Malherbe 1989, 1992; the last-mentioned surveys older literature as well.

37. See Fiore 1986. For texts and translations of the fictional Cynic letters, see Malherbe 1977.

38. On 1 Peter, see especially Balch 1981. Among the recent commentaries, Best 1971 and Brox 1979 provide useful overviews and introduction to the wider literature. The paraenetic style of James was described by Dibelius 1976 in a way that dominated scholarship on this epistle for many years; recently Luke Timothy Johnson, in a series of important short studies, has altered Dibelius's picture of a random collection of gnomes by uncovering more subtle authorial features of James. Johnson's commentary is eagerly awaited; in the meantime see Johnson 1982, 1983, 1988.

39. The rhetorical figure of comparison (*synkrisis*) as the dominant pattern of Hebrews was first suggested to me by C. F. Evans, in an unpublished paper read to the Columbia University Seminar for Studies in the New Testament, 21 March 1975, though he referred to an earlier comment by Günther Zunz in the letter's Schweich Lectures. For a full discussion of the rhetorical features of the composition, see the superb commentary by Attridge 1989, who also provides a full bibliography of older literature. For the hortatory speech as "pep talk," see Worley 1981, who notes similarities between Hebrews and speeches that Greek and Roman historians put into the mouths of generals addressing their troops on the eve of battle (like the speech accorded by Shakespeare to Henry V [4.3.18–67] on the eve of the Battle of Agincourt).

40. Dio Chrysostom, *Or.* 34.

41. There is a certain irony, perhaps, in *1 Clement*'s ideal of a unified church as polis in light of the fractionated state of Christianity in Rome throughout the first two centuries of its existence; see Lampe 1987. Maier 1991 and Jeffers 1991 have both attempted sociological readings of *1 Clement* in comparison with other early documents from the Roman groups.

42. The rhetorical character of Acts 20:18–35 has been largely neglected, but it is the subject of a Yale dissertation in progress by Kenneth Cukrowski.

43. I take the translated titles from the commentary by Hollander and De Jonge 1985, which is indispensable for any serious study of the Testaments, as is the critical text by De Jonge et al. (Jonge 1978).

44. See further chap. 9 below.

45. See chap. 3 above.

46. Dihle 1957. Rehrl 1961 tries to temper the claim for the uniqueness of the Christian notion, rightly pointing to a long tradition in Greek morality honoring modesty and moderation. But, as Dihle points out, that is not really the same thing as the *tapeinophrosynē* advocated by Christians and classically defined by Augustine.

47. Hengel 1977.

48. See Meeks 1991a.

49. Dahl 1976c.

50. See Meeks 1982a.

51. For a detailed and illuminating study of Josephus's moral historiography, see Attridge 1976.

Chapter 6. The Grammar of Christian Practice

1. MacIntyre 1984, 187.

2. Kamlah 1964 saw the close connection between baptism and many of the stereotyped patterns of moral discourse we examined in chap. 5, though he erred in assuming a *single* pattern, or *Grundparänese*, and a single *Sitz im Leben*. It is Nils Dahl who has seen most clearly the function of "remembering baptism" in the epistolary admonitions of the New Testament: Dahl 1976a.

3. Most elaborately, Cross 1954. For a review and critique of a series of similar proposals, see Best 1971, 20–27; Balch 1981, 10–15; and Brox 1979, 16–24.

4. The two poles are represented in the two sides of the debate between John Elliott and David Balch on whether a "sectarian" or an "assimilationist" model better fits the situation envisioned by the writer of 1 Peter (see their essays in Talbert 1986). Balch has the better of the argument; Elliott's use of Bryan Wilson's sect-typology is too brittle, and he does not adequately distinguish social reality from hortatory imagery. Yet Balch sometimes overemphasizes the assimilationist and apologetic side of the rhetoric of 1 Peter; it is precisely the tension between alienation and belonging that is characteristic of this document and of much early Christian (and other sectarian) literature.

5. I refer to the edition by Botte 1963; his numbering of the sections is different in part from that in the English version by Dix 1968.

6. For an interesting analysis of the way baptism may have functioned in shaping the identity of the Roman churches, see Finn 1989.

7. Pliny, *Ep.* 2.6, trans. Radice 1963, 63.

8. Theißen 1982, 145–74; see also Meeks 1983, 157–62.

9. Hengel 1983, 78–96; nn. 188–90.

10. Further on Philippians: Meeks 1991a; on Colossians, Meeks 1977.

11. See Newsom 1985.

12. Many examples in Sokolowski 1955 and 1962: see indexes s.v. "pureté," "purification(s)."

13. Among the most helpful descriptions of charismatic phenomena and their social setting I know is Goodman 1972. For a surprising picture—wry, funny, but wonderfully sensitive and sympathetic—of the way Pentecostal practice could intersect with a messy, ordinary world, see the play by Romulus Linney, *Holy Ghosts.*

14. Stowers 1986, 15 and passim.

15. Judge 1980; but see my remarks in Meeks 1983, 140.

16. Origen, *Contra Celsum* 6.1–2.

17. Richardson 1953.

18. On *propempein* as a technical term for providing travel expenses, see Malherbe 1983, 68.

19. On the special case of Philippi, see Sampley 1980 and the forthcoming Yale dissertation by James Ware.

20. From the third century Cyprian provides a particularly clear example; see Bobertz 1988. For earlier developments, see Maier 1991 and Countryman 1980.

21. See Malherbe 1983, 92–112.

22. Trans. in Richardson 1953, 287.

23. *Ep.* 22 in the Loeb Classical Library edition, 429D–431B; cf. *Misopogon* 363A,B.

24. See the discussion of the passage by Lampe 1987, 68–69.

25. See Osiek 1983 and Lampe 1987, 71–78. The usual dating of Hermas in the

mid-second century would tend to explain the difference in terms of the passage of time and further acculturation of the Christian groups, but some critics, identifying the Clement of Hermas 8.4 (*Vis.* 2.4.3) with the writer of *1 Clem.*, regard the two writings as contemporary.

26. Lampe 1987, 334–45.

Chapter 7. Knowing Evil

1. *Acts of Peter* 31–32; in Hennecke 1965, 314–36.

2. MacMullen 1984; Smith 1978.

3. Lucian, *The Lover of Lies* 16; trans. A. M. Harmon in the Loeb Classical Library.

4. The most important collection of the Greek material is Preisendanz 1973–74, hereafter referred to as *PGM*. A large selection, mostly from Preisendanz but some from elsewhere, is now conveniently available in English translation in Betz 1986. *PDM* in the following refers to the translations of the Demotic (Egyptian) magic spells that are also included in the Betz collection. I have used the translations from Betz's team throughout in the following discussion.

5. The most complete collection of curse-tablets from the Hellenistic world remains Audollent 1904. For a brief introduction, see Betz 1987. An English translation of a large number of these spells is announced, but not yet available at this writing: Gager 1992.

6. The extant compositions of the *Testament of Solomon* and the *Book of Mysteries* are probably both later than the period of our interest, but the spells and stories of magical action they contain are likely drawn from earlier lore. The *Book of Mysteries (Sefer ha-Razim)* was reconstructed by Mordecai Margalioth from several sources and published in 1966; for an English translation of Margalioth's text, see Morgan 1983. A translation of the *Testament of Solomon*, with notes, is conveniently found in Charlesworth 1983, 1:935–87. For general introductions to Jewish magic, see Alexander 1986 and Schäfer 1990.

7. In addition, there are numerous spells that are more overtly Christian—in the sense that Christian language and, often, liturgical tags predominate over the kinds of god-names and other expressions shared with the other magical material. See the collection of papyri and ostraca numbered separately in Preisendanz 1973, 2.209–35.

8. Thanks to Victor Bers, in an unpublished paper, for the observation about pejorative use of diminutives.

9. See especially Plutarch's *On Isis and Osiris* 25–26 (*Moralia* 360D–361C) and *On the Decline of Oracles* 10 (*Moralia* 415A–B), and the discussions by Soury 1942 and MacMullen 1981, 73–94. On the problem of the common belief in "evil daimons" for Plutarch and the elements of dualism that appear in his system, see Soury 1942, 45–65.

10. Fox 1987, 137.

11. For details, see Garrett 1989.

12. Division of humankind: 1QS 3.13–4.26. King of Righteousness, King of Evil: 11QMelch. War: 1QM. English translations may be found conveniently in Vermes 1987.

13. V. 44 is difficult, probably corrupted in transmission; variant readings in the manuscripts reveal the puzzlement of many copyists in antiquity. See further Dahl 1964.

14. See Dahl 1964.

15. Attridge 1989, 166; see further comments on this passage below.

16. On the tradition of invective and Paul's rhetoric in the Corinthian letters, see Marshall 1987. On the same tradition's effect on anti-Jewish polemic in the Gospels, see Johnson 1989 and, for the fourth century, Wilken 1983, chap. 4.

17. Further on Rom. 14–15, see Meeks 1987; on functions of judgment language both here and in the Corinthian letters, see Kuck 1992.

18. Richardson 1953, 310. See also Rom. 12:20; 2 *Clement* 13.4; Aristides 15.5; Justin, *1 Apol.* 39.3, *Dial.* 85.7.

19. Pagels 1991, 452. In this essay Pagels argues, against the received view, that Valentinian ethics were less dualistic than was common among more "catholic" Christians of the second century.

20. For the Greek conception of defilement, see Parker 1990; for a brief but stimulating introduction to notions of purity in Judaism, Neusner 1973.

21. Trans. Vermes 1987.

22. Cf. Athenagoras, *Supp.* 12.1; Tatian, *Or.* 6.1; 25.2. The relevant passages in Plato are *Gorg.* 523E–524A, *Resp.* 10.615A, *Phaedr.* 249A.

23. Lampe 1987.

24. I owe this observation and much else in my interpretation of Hermas to an unpublished paper by Craig Wansink, dated 2 Nov. 1988.

25. Nussbaum 1986b.

26. See n. 3 above.

27. Mosaics: Levi 1947, 1:32–34, and 2:plate IVa,c; survey of Evil Eye beliefs: Elliott 1988, with literature.

28. Hippolytus, *Ap. Trad.* 41, ed. Botte = 36.11, ed. Dix.

29. Schoedel 1985, 87.

30. See above; other references in Schoedel 1985, 93.

31. Hippolytus, *Ap. Trad.* 20–21, ed. Botte.

32. See pseudo-Phocylides 42–47 (cf. 61, 62) and the parallels cited by van der Horst 1978, 142–46.

33. Moxnes 1988.

34. Countryman 1980.

Chapter 8. The Body as Sign and Problem

1. Brown 1988, 61.

2. Stowers 1988 and 1990. I depend on the latter article for several of the points in the following discussion.

3. See above, chap. 5, and Wilson 1991.

4. The classic statement of the difference remains Bultmann 1951, 1:192–203, despite the excess of existentialist jargon in his formulation.

5. On this passage, see the analysis in Fitzgerald 1988, 166–80, and Garrett 1990.

6. On Paul's use of the body metaphor for political concord, see Moxnes forthcoming, who compares the fable used by Menenius Agrippa speaking to a threatened mutiny of plebs against senators in Rome: Livy 2.32; Dio Chrys., *Or.* 35.16. On Phil. 2, see Meeks 1991a; on 1 Cor. 8–10, Meeks 1988 and Malherbe forthcoming. On Rom. 14–15, Meeks 1987.

7. Layton 1987, 361.

8. Countryman 1988.

9. See, e.g., *On the Migration of Abraham* 1–30, which summarizes many of these themes that recur so often through the corpus of Philo's works; and the treatment in *Questions on Exodus*, bk. 1.

10. In Hennecke 1965, 449.

11. To the foregoing sketch of the Thomas tradition, compare Brown 1988, 97–99. For a more general discussion of second-century Christian radicalism, see Perkins 1985.

12. Valentinus, frag. 3 in Völker 1932, 58 = frag. E in Layton 1987, 238 = Clement Alex., *Stromateis* 3.59.3.

13. Clement Alex., *Excerpta ex Theodoto* 79, trans. Foerster 1972, 230.

14. An excellent brief overview of the medical and philosophical theories may be found in Horst 1990. See also the more extended and anecdotal account in Rousselle 1988, esp. chap. 2.

15. *On the Nature of Things* 4.1208–17, trans. Latham 1951, cited by Horst 1990, 295.

16. Clement Alex., *Excerpta ex Theodoto* 21, trans. Foerster 1972, 224.

17. *Questions on Genesis* 4.15; *On Abraham* 101–02,168; cf. Goodenough 1962, 141–42; on Philo's use of the male/female language more generally, see Baer 1970 and Sly 1990.

18. See, e.g., Cantarella 1987, 135; Sly 1990, 37–39. Boswell 1988, 100–102, is cautious, emphasizing the ambiguity of the evidence.

19. For examples of care for daughters in aristocratic families of Rome, see Hallett 1984.

20. See Laqueur 1990 and Rousselle 1988.

21. Brown 1988, 11.

22. Staden 1992.

23. Herophilus: see Staden 1988a and, for a brief sketch, 1988b; womb in magical gems: Barb 1953; Dura synagogue: Goodenough 1953–68, vol. 11, fig. 56 and plates I, VIII, and IX.

24. See Yarbrough 1985.

25. I follow in part the interpretation of 1 Cor. 7 by Martin 1992, which he kindly showed me.

26. A similar ideology seems to be implied in the Hellenistic Jewish romance *The Testament of Job*, in which at the end the three daughters of Job receive amulets that enable them to speak the language of angels and to escape the realm of the earthly and worldly—i.e., the world of birth, children, household, and death. So Garrett 1993, which she kindly showed me in advance of publication.

27. Saying 114, trans. Thomas O. Lamdin in Layton 1989, 93. More on female-becoming-male in the Thomas tradition: Attridge 1991. For friendships between male and female ascetics: Clark 1979. Athanasius and the virgins: Brakke 1992, 149–73.

28. Texts of the martyr acts are from Musurillo 1972. For a shrewd analysis of the social functions served by the cult of relics in the later, western church, see Brown 1981.

29. See the brilliant evocation of mid-third-century Christian ethos through this story by Lane Fox 1987, 460–92.

30. Gorer 1965.

31. On this symbolism, see Attridge 1991.

32. For a perceptive reading of Perpetua's diary, emphasizing the directness of the woman's language, see Dronke 1984, 1–17. Cf. a similar observation about Christian tracts on virginity in Brown 1988, 25.

33. For literature, see chap. 3, n. 24.

34. Dibelius 1923, 618–19.

35. See also Brown 1988, 69–72.

36. I have used the translation in Edwards and Wild 1981.

Chapter 9. A Life Worthy of God

1. The statement attributed to Socrates in Plato, *Theaetetus* 176B is repeated and commented on endlessly: "We ought to try to escape from earth to the dwelling of the gods as quickly as we can; and to escape is to become like God, so far as this is possible; and to become like God is to become righteous and holy and wise" (trans. Fowler in the Loeb Classical Library). For examples, see Meeks 1990b, 320, n. 14.

2. Lutz 1947.

3. Seneca, *Ep.* 42.1.

4. Other typical examples are Matt. 7:21 and 21:31; Eph. 6:6; Heb. 13:21; 2 *Clem.* 5:1, 8:4, and 14:1; Polycarp, *Philad.* 2:2.

5. For an excellent discussion of the function of this tradition in Mark's narrative, and of discipleship in Mark as "doing the will of God," see Dowd 1988.

6. See Squires 1988, who compares Luke's notion of providence with that of the Stoics and sets Luke-Acts within the context of the debate in the philosophical schools over providence, fatalism, and human freedom, and the application of these notions to the writing of history by other Greco-Roman authors.

7. That 1 Clement's opposition to any form of stasis and its appeal for concord and peace adopts the ideals of the urban elites in the Roman Empire is surely true, and may be contrasted to some extent with the viewpoint of the (contemporary?) Shepherd of Hermas, as Jeffers 1991 argues, though his resulting portrait of the Roman communities is a bit too schematic. See the discussion above in chap. 3.

8. See also the discussion of precepts and commands in chap. 5 above.

9. We must be careful, on the other hand, not to understand this complexity of human and divine intentionality, of which the ancients were well aware, in modern psychological and individualistic categories, which were not yet dreamed of. Augustine is commonly credited with the invention of the notion of the will that predominated in medieval and early modern philosophy and which also shaped the psychological tradition. On its antecedents, see Dihle 1982.

10. In pagan religious language as well, the descriptions of the aretai, the "virtues," or more accurately the performative manifestations of excellence, of the gods closely resemble the language that describes human benefactors or patrons in laudatory inscriptions. An excellent collection of both kinds, with notes on similar language in the New Testament, is to be found in Danker 1982.

11. Carrington 1940; Selwyn 1947, 369–75.

12. Bassler 1979.

13. See Thompson forthcoming.

14. Well observed by Haacker 1990, who perhaps overstates the political implications, however.

15. MacLeish 1958, 11.

16. Richardson 1953, 245, 247.

17. Ibid., 329.

18. In an unpublished paper presented to the Judaic Studies Faculty Seminar at Yale University, 26 Sept. 1990.

19. Brown 1988, 103–05.

20. On the Middle Platonic antecedents of Valentinus's belief, see the article by G. C. Stead and all the papers in part 3 of Layton 1980, vol. 1. For adaptation of the Gnostic myths, see McGuire 1983. For the best outline of the Valentinian myth, see the introductions to individual documents in parts 2 and 3 of Layton 1987. For Valentinian interpretation of biblical texts, see Williams 1988 and Dawson 1991. On interpretation of Paul and John, Pagels 1973 and 1975.

21. See, e.g., Gospel of Truth 16:4–20.

22. Layton 1987, 330.

23. Koschorke 1973; Pagels 1991.

24. This is, I believe, the implication of Peter Brown's view that for the Valentinians "the body was of little value as a declaratory agent" (Brown 1988, 110). See also Pagels 1991.

25. The indispensable basis for any study of Marcion remains the classic by Harnack 1989 (originally published in German in 1921), though one must be somewhat wary of Harnack's tendency to read into Marcion the passions of the young Luther. See also Blackman 1948, May 1987–88, Drijvers 1987–88, Hoffmann 1987–88, and Brown 1988, 83–90.

26. Yoder 1984; Hauerwas 1983.

27. "Tu nos, te autem Deus": *Pass. ss. Perp. et Felic.* 18.8, ed. Musurillo; see also Justin, *1 Apol.* 45.6. We have discussed the notion of final judgment earlier, in chap. 7, and will return to it again in the next chapter.

28. Richardson 1953, 152.

29. Slaves of the gods: Pleket 1981; Fox 1987, 109, 701, n. 20; Martin 1990, xiv–xvi. Servile metaphors in Paul: Marshall 1987, 281–317, and esp. Martin 1990.

30. Roscher 1978, 2.1: cols. 619–20.

31. Besides the standard commentaries on this passage, compare Pseudo-Plutarch, *On the Education of Children,* and see Bonner 1977, 38–46.

Chapter 10. Senses of an Ending

1. Gager 1970.

2. Fox 1987, 265. Justin supports the Christian belief that "consciousness continues for all who have lived, and eternal punishment awaits," by referring to *nekyomanteia,* possession by spirits of the dead, oracles, and the teaching of Empedocles, Pythagoras, Plato, and Socrates, as well as the Nekyia of Homer (*1 Apol.* 1.18, trans. Hardy). Summing up this portion of his argument in §20, he compares Christian belief in creation and providence to that of Plato, "a coming destruction by fire" to Stoicism, and postmortem punishment to teachings of "poets and philosophers." The later apologists adduce the same or similar parallels.

3. Kermode 1968, 6–7.

4. Dieterich 1969. See also Himmelfarb 1983.

5. See MacMullen 1981, 53–57; on divine vengeance and punishments, 58.

6. For a survey of the development of beliefs about postmortem judgment in the centuries before and contemporary with Christianity's beginnings, with extensive bibliography, see Kuck 1992, chaps. 2 (Jewish sources) and 3 (Greco-Roman traditions). See also Nickelsburg 1972.

7. In 11:2 the examples of Sodom and Gomorrah and of Lot's wife show that "the double-souled and the doubters end up in judgment"; since God knows all, we must "leave off evil deeds and dirty passions, that we may be protected by his mercy

from the coming judgments" (28:1). A catena of scriptural texts warns, "Behold the Lord, and his wages before his face, to repay to each according to his work" (34:3). Chaps. 24–26 stress the truth of belief in the resurrection to come, but as a basis for comfort (chap. 27) rather than fear of judgment. Most of the scriptural examples are of punishments in the past of Israel or its foes.

8. For the comparison of *Tab. Cebes* with Hermas and with the *ekphrasis*, see Fitzgerald and White 1983, 7, 16–18. Hellholm 1980 has analyzed in excruciating detail the linguistic characteristics of Hermas that, in his opinion, consign the work clearly to the genre apocalypse. The demonstration, however, is too abstractly formal and the conception of genre too brittle to be finally convincing. Hellholm's promised second volume has not appeared.

9. On 1 Thess. 4 and the rhetoric of consolation, see Malherbe 1987, 57–60; Malherbe 1989, 64–66.

10. The scholarly literature on the topic is boundless; the standard commentaries will provide an entry for the curious reader.

11. The variety and extent of the connections between Paul's language and that of the philosophical and rhetorical schools was sensed by some of the classically trained scholars of the nineteenth century, but largely submerged by the later enthusiasms of the *religionsgeschichtliche Schule*. Only recently have those connections begun to reemerge in new light and greater detail, owing to the work of the *Corpus Hellenisticum ad Novum Testamentum* project and to individual scholars such as E. A. Judge, Hans Dieter Betz, A. J. Malherbe, and their students. The symposium essays in Engberg-Pedersen forthcoming provide a lively and diverse sample of the present state of research.

12. I have written elsewhere at somewhat greater length about Paul's use of apocalyptic language. See Meeks 1982b and 1983, 171–80.

13. On the rhetoric of the Apocalypse as an attack on common sense and habitual conceptions of the world, see Meeks 1986, 143–47.

14. Käsemann 1965, 130.

15. See further Meeks 1987.

16. My discussion of Paul's use of End-time and judgment language is dependent at many points on the full and careful analysis in Kuck 1992, which should be consulted for details, as well as for references to other useful bibliography.

Chapter 11. The Moral Story

1. *On Listening to Poetry (Mor.* 15A), trans. Babbitt, in the Loeb Classical Library.

2. *On the Creation of the World* 3; *Life of Moses* 2.47–51.

3. MacIntyre 1984; Hauerwas 1975 and 1981.

4. MacIntyre 1984, 144, 216.

5. See Nelson 1987, chap. 4.

6. It is well to remember the stories of Judith and Esther in Jewish literature, and in Christianity such stories as the Acts of Thecla and the Martyrdom of SS. Perpetua and Felicitas. Apart from goddesses, heroines as moral examples in pagan literature are equally rare, but some are notable: Sophocles' Antigone, Medea in a richly ambivalent way, the Cynic Hipparchia, some heroines of the romances (in which the melodramatic turns of plot narrowly rescue the virtuous from terrible fates), like Callirhoe and Anthia.

7. C. P. Jones 1971, 103.

8. *Life of Abraham* 4, trans. Colson, in the Loeb Classical Library.

9. For an excellent sketch of the types of ancient historiography and their functions, see Aune 1987, 80–115. The narrative qualities of the Deuteronomistic History as a whole, as well as the complexity of its underlying traditions and component literary parts, have come to be recognized more fully in recent scholarship; see for example Boling 1975 and 1982. Criticism of overblown contrasts between Israel's and other cultures' temporal sense: Barr 1961 and 1962; Momigliano 1966.

10. In the Loeb Classical Library.

11. Josephus's didactic purpose has been examined in some detail and set within the context of contemporary styles of historiography by Attridge 1976.

12. Josipovici 1988, 42; the quotation is from Frye 1983, xiii.

13. The apologetic history of culture is conveniently traced by Droge 1989.

14. Josipovici 1988 has expressed with rare sensitivity this fundamental difference between the open-endedness of the Jewish scriptures' story and the "sense of unity, of an end already implicit in the beginning," that the Christian Bible conveys (48). In contrast, the beginning of the Torah establishes a "rhythm" that reverberates through the varieties of writings that one reads further on, a rhythm that sometimes "falters" and must be renewed, and which imposes no outcome, settles no unified plot. A number of recent interpreters have emphasized the open-ended yet cumulatively interrelated quality of Hebrew biblical narrative: Alter 1981, Kugel (in Kugel and Greer 1986), and Fishbane 1985 may serve, along with Josipovici, as outstanding representatives.

15. See Meeks 1974.

16. For the importance of this underlying narrative in Paul's letters, exemplified in a detailed analysis of the "narrative substructure" of Galatians, see Hays 1983. See also Petersen 1985 and Fowl 1990.

17. Meeks 1988.

18. Neglected through most of Christian history, Mark enjoyed a rediscovery in the nineteenth century under the illusion that here we had a simple folk history, uncontaminated by "dogma." Only recently have the unusual and strangely "modern" qualities of Mark's narrative attracted the concentrated attention of critics. Among the proliferating books that struggle to discover the most appropriate way to

read (or, more in accord with ancient habits, to hear) this Gospel, Farrer 1951 and 1966, Burkill 1963, Best 1983, Robbins 1984, Kermode 1979, Rhoads and Michie 1982, and Tolbert 1989 deserve attention. Yet none of them seems to me to have got it quite right. In many ways the recent Yale dissertation by Whitney Shiner (1992) offers the most persuasive case I have seen both for situating Mark in comparison with ancient biographies and for the way to hear Mark's story on its own terms.

19. What follows is adapted in part from my discussion of Matthew in Meeks 1986, 136–43.

20. Comparisons between Matthew and rabbinic forms: the classic is Davies 1966. See also Smith 1951.

21. See Meier 1979, 45–51.

22. On the use of epitomes, see chap. 5 and the literature given there.

23. See Keck 1984.

24. Garrett 1989.

25. The standard edition of the texts of the apocryphal Acts is by Lipsius and Bonnet 1959 (originally published 1891–1903). English translations are conveniently available in Hennecke 1965. For a review of recent work on the problems of interpreting these works, see Bovon et al. 1981. Bovon and a team of Swiss and French scholars are producing a new series of critical texts in the *Series Apocryphorum* of the *Corpus Christianorum*.

26. Meeks 1991a.

27. Rensberger 1988.

28. This is not to say that there is no narrative in the *Test. XII*. Especially important in the hortatory patterns of most of the *Testaments* are the predictive narratives that project the Deuteronomistic pattern (labeled "Sin-Exile-Return" by De Jonge in his pioneering analysis, Jonge 1975) onto the history of Israel leading up to the advent of Jesus Christ, "future" in the fiction of the last words of the Patriarchs, as well as the eschatological future expected by the Christian author. For an introduction to the complex literary and historical problems of the *Test. XII*, survey of previous research, and extended commentary, see Hollander and Jonge 1985. For an up-to-date critical text, see Jonge et al. 1978.

29. In Richardson 1953, 265.

30. For the following, see Meeks 1986, 159–60.

Postscript

1. Williams 1985.

2. Cf. the stimulating remarks in Stout 1988, 120–23 and chap. 5. On the relation between tradition and reasoning, the remarks on Aristotle's ethics in Lear 1988, chap. 5, are also suggestive.

3. Kermode 1968, passim.

4. Meeks 1988.

5. Geertz 1983, 73–93.

6. Williams 1985.

7. Again I must call attention to the lucid evocation of the different rhythms of the Jewish and Christian scriptures by Josipovici 1988.

8. See Meeks 1991b, 124, from which the last sentence is taken verbatim.

Bibliography of Secondary Works Cited

❖ ❖ ❖ ❖ ❖ ❖ ❖ ❖ ❖ ❖

Alexander, Loveday. Forthcoming. "Paul and the Hellenistic Schools: The Evidence of Galen." In *Paul and His Hellenistic Background*, ed. Troels Engberg-Pedersen. Minneapolis: Fortress.

Alexander, P. S. 1986. "Incantations and Books of Magic." In Emil Schürer, *The History of the Jewish People in the Age of Jesus Christ, 175 B.C.–A.D. 135: A New English Edition*, ed. Geza Vermes et al., 3.1:342–79. Edinburgh: T. & T. Clark.

Alföldy, Géza. 1980. *Die Rolle des Einzelnen in der Gesellschaft des Römischen Kaiserreiches: Erwartungen und Wertmastäbe*. Heidelberg: Carl Winter.

Alter, Robert. 1981. *The Art of Biblical Narrative*. New York: Basic.

Ashton, John. 1991. *Understanding the Fourth Gospel*. Oxford: Oxford University Press.

Attridge, Harold W. 1976. *The Interpretation of Biblical History in the Antiquitates Judaicae of Flavius Josephus*. Missoula, Mont.: Scholars.

———. 1989. *The Epistle to the Hebrews: A Commentary on the Epistle to the Hebrews*. Philadelphia: Fortress.

———. 1991. " 'Masculine Fellowship' in the *Acts of Thomas*." In *The Future of Early Christianity: Essays in Honor of Helmut Koester*, ed. Birger A. Pearson, 406–13. Minneapolis: Fortress.

Audollent, Auguste. 1904. *Defixionum tabellae*. Paris: A. Fontemoing.

Aune, David E. 1987. *The New Testament in Its Literary Environment*. Philadelphia: Westminster.

———. 1991. "Romans as a *logos protreptikos* in the Context of Ancient Religious and Philosophical Propaganda." In *Paulus und das antike Judentum*, ed. Martin Hengel and Ulrich Heckel. Tübingen: J. C. B. Mohr (Paul Siebeck).

Babcock, William S., ed. 1990. *Paul and the Legacies of Paul*. Dallas: Southern Methodist University Press.

Badian, Ernst. 1958. *Foreign Clientelae, 264–70 B.C.*. Oxford: Oxford University Press.

Baer, Richard A., Jr. 1970. *Philo's Use of the Categories Male and Female.* Leiden: Brill.

Bailey, Cyril, ed. and trans. 1970. *Epicurus: The Extant Remains, with Short Critical Apparatus, Translation and Notes.* Hildesheim and New York: Georg Olms.

Balch, David L. 1981. *Let Wives Be Submissive: The Domestic Code in 1 Peter.* Chico, Calif.: Scholars.

————. 1988. "Household Codes," ed. David E. Aune. In *Greco-Roman Literature and the New Testament: Selected Forms and Genres,* 25–50. Atlanta: Scholars.

Baldry, H. C. 1965. *The Unity of Mankind in Greek Thought.* Cambridge: Cambridge University Press.

Bamberger, Bernard J. 1968. *Proselytism in the Talmudic Period.* New York: Ktav.

Barb, Alphonse A. 1953. "Diva matrix: A Faked Gnostic Intaglio in the Possession of P. P. Rubens and the Iconology of a Symbol." *Journal of the Warburg and Courtald Institutes* 16: 193–238.

Barr, James. 1961. *The Semantics of Biblical Language.* Oxford: Oxford University Press.

————. 1962. *Biblical Words for Time.* Studies in Biblical Theology. London: SCM.

Barton, S. C., and G. H. R. Horsley. 1981. "A Hellenistic Cult Group and the New Testament Churches." *Jahrbuch für Antike und Christentum* 24: 7–41.

Bassler, Jouette M. 1979. *Divine Impartiality: Paul and a Theological Axiom.* Chico, Calif.: Scholars.

Beckford, James A. 1978. "Accounting for Conversion." *British Journal of Sociology* 29: 249–62.

Berger, Peter L., and Thomas Luckmann. 1967. *The Social Construction of Reality: A Treatise in the Sociology of Knowledge.* Garden City, N.Y.: Doubleday, Anchor.

Best, Ernest. 1971. *1 Peter.* London: Oliphants.

————. 1983. *Mark: The Gospel as Story.* Edinburgh: T. & T. Clark.

Betz, Hans Dieter. 1985. *Essays on the Sermon on the Mount.* Philadelphia: Fortress.

————. 1987. "Magic in Greco-Roman Antiquity." In *Encyclopedia of Religion,* ed. Mircea Eliade, 9:93–97. New York: Macmillan.

Betz, Hans Dieter, ed. 1986. *The Greek Magical Papyri in Translation, Including the Demotic Spells.* Chicago and London: University of Chicago Press.

Bickerman, Elias. 1957. Review of Ernest Barker, *From Alexander to Constantine. American Journal of Philology* 78: 327.

Blackman, E. C. 1948. *Marcion and His Influence.* London: SPCK.

Bobertz, Charles. 1988. "Cyprian of Carthage as Patron: A Social Historical Study of the Role of Bishop in the Ancient Christian Community of North Africa." Ph.D. diss., Yale University. Microform: UMI 90–09438.

Boling, Robert. 1975. *Judges: Introduction, Translation, and Commentary*. Garden City, N.Y.: Doubleday.

———. 1982. *Joshua: Introduction, Translation, and Commentary*. Garden City, N.Y.: Doubleday.

Bonner, Stanley F. 1977. *Education in Ancient Rome from the Elder Cato to the Younger Pliny*. Berkeley: University of California Press.

Boswell, John. 1988. *The Kindness of Strangers: The Abandonment of Children in Western Europe from Late Antiquity to the Renaissance*. New York: Pantheon.

Botte, Bernard, O.S.B., ed. and trans. 1963. *La Tradition apostolique de saint Hippolyte: Essai de reconstitution*. Münster: Aschendorff.

Boulvert, Gérard. 1974. *Domestique et fonctionnaire sur le haut-empire romain: La Condition de l'affranchi et de l'esclave du prince*. Paris: Belles Lettres.

Bovon, François, et al., eds. 1981. *Les Actes apocryphes des apôtres: Christianisme et monde païne*. Paris: Labor et Fides.

Bowersock, Glen W. 1965. *Augustus and the Greek World*. Oxford: Oxford University Press.

Brakke, David Bernhard. 1992. "St. Athanasius and Ascetic Christians in Egypt." Ph.D. diss., Yale University.

Braude, William G. 1940. *Jewish Proselytizing in the First Five Centuries of the Common Era*. Providence, R.I.: Brown University Press.

Brown, Peter. 1981. *The Cult of the Saints: Its Rise and Function in Latin Christianity*. Chicago: University of Chicago Press and London: SCM.

———. 1988. *The Body and Society: Men, Women and Sexual Renunciation in Early Christianity*. New York: Columbia University Press.

Brown, Raymond E. 1979. *The Community of the Beloved Disciple: The Life, Loves, and Hates of an Individual Church in New Testament Times*. New York, Ramsey, and Toronto: Paulist.

Brox, Norbert. 1979. *Der erste Petrusbrief*. Zurich: Benziger and Neukirchen-Vluyn: Neukirchener Verlag.

Bultmann, Rudolf. 1951. *Theology of the New Testament*, trans. Kendrick Grobel. New York: Scribner's.

Burkill, T. A. 1963. *Mysterious Revelation: An Examination of the Philosophy of St. Mark's Gospel*. Ithaca, N.Y.: Cornell University Press.

Campbell, J. K. 1964. *Honour, Family and Patronage: A Study of Institutions and Moral Values in a Greek Mountain Community*. Oxford: Oxford University Press.

Cantarella, Eva. 1987. *Pandora's Daughters: The Role and Status of Women in Greek and Roman Antiquity*, trans. Maureen B. Fant. Baltimore and London: Johns Hopkins University Press.

Carrington, Philip. 1940. *The Primitive Christian Catechism: A Study in the Epistles*. Cambridge: Cambridge University Press.

Chantraine, Heinrich. 1967. *Freigelassene und Sklaven im Dienst der römischen Kaiser: Studien zu ihrer Nomenklatur.* Wiesbaden: Steiner.

Charlesworth, James H., ed. 1983. *The Old Testament Pseudepigrapha.* Vol. 1. *Apocalyptic Literature and Testaments.* Garden City, N.Y.: Doubleday.

Clark, Elizabeth A. 1979. *Jerome, Chrysostom, and Friends: Essays and Translations.* New York and Toronto: Edwin Mellen.

Clark, Gillian, trans. 1989. *Iamblichus: On the Pythagorean Life.* Liverpool: Liverpool University Press.

Cohen, Shaye J. D. 1982–83. "Alexander the Great and Jaddus the High Priest According to Josephus." *Association of Jewish Studies Review* 7–8: 41–68.

———. 1983. "Conversion to Judaism in Historical Perspective: From Biblical Israel to Postbiblical Judaism." *Conservative Judaism* 36 (Summer): 31–45.

———. 1986. "Was Timothy Jewish (Acts 16:1–3)? Patristic Exegesis, Rabbinic Law, and Matrilineal Descent." *Journal of Biblical Literature* 105: 251–68.

———. 1987a. *From the Maccabees to the Mishnah.* Philadelphia: Westminster.

———. 1987b. "Respect for Judaism by Gentiles According to Josephus." *Harvard Theological Review* 80: 409–30.

———. 1989. "Crossing the Boundary and Becoming a Jew." *Harvard Theological Review* 82: 13–33.

Countryman, L. William. 1980. *The Rich Christian in the Church of the Early Empire: Contradictions and Accommodations.* Toronto: Edwin Mellen.

———. 1988. *Dirt, Greed, and Sex: Sexual Ethics in the New Testament and Their Implications for Today.* Philadelphia: Fortress.

Crenshaw, James L. 1974. "Wisdom." In *Old Testament Form Criticism,* ed. John H. Hayes, 229–36. San Antonio: Trinity University Press.

Cross, F. L. 1954. *I Peter: A Paschal Liturgy.* London: A. R. Mowbray.

Dahl, Nils Alstrup. 1964. "Der Erstgeborene Satans und der Vater des Teufels (Polyk. 7,1 und Joh. 8,44." In *Apophoreta: Festschrift für Ernst Haenchen,* ed. Walther Eltester, 70–84. Berlin: Alfred Töpelmann.

———. 1976a. "Anamnesis: Memory and Commemoration in Early Christianity." In *Jesus in the Memory of the Early Church,* 11–29. Minneapolis: Augsburg.

———. 1976b. "Letter." In *The Interpreter's Dictionary of the Bible, Supplementary Volume,* 538–41. Nashville: Abingdon.

———. 1976c. "Form-critical Observations on Early Christian Preaching." In *Jesus in the Memory of the Early Church,* 30–36. Minneapolis: Augsburg.

Danker, Frederick W. 1982. *Benefactor: Epigraphic Study of a Graeco-Roman and New Testament Semantic Field.* St. Louis: Clayton.

Davies, W. D. 1966. *The Setting of the Sermon on the Mount.* Cambridge: Cambridge University Press.

Dawson, David. 1992. *Allegorical Readers and Cultural Revision in Ancient Alexandria.* Berkeley: University of California Press.

de Lacy, P. H. 1948. "Lucretius and the History of Epicureanism." *Transactions of the American Philological Association* 79: 12–23.

De Witt, Norman W. 1936a. "Epicurean Contubernium." *Transactions of the American Philological Association* 67: 59–60.

———. 1936b. "Organization and Structure of Epicurean Groups." *Classical Philology* 31: 205–11.

Dibelius, Martin. 1923. *Der Hirt des Hermas*. Handbuch zum Neuen Testament, Ergänzungs-Band. Tübingen: J. C. B. Mohr (Paul Siebeck).

———. 1976. *James: A Commentary on the Epistle of James*. Revised by Heinrich Greeven. Philadelphia: Fortress.

———. n.d. *From Tradition to Gospel*, trans. Bertram Lee Woolf and Martin Dibelius. New York: Scribner's.

Dieterich, Albrecht. 1969. *Nekyia: Beiträge zur Erklärung der neuentdeckten Petrusapokalypse*. 3d ed. Stuttgart: B. G. Teubner.

Dihle, Albrecht. 1957. "Demut." In *Realenzyklopädie für Antike und Christentum*, vol. 3, cols. 735–78.

———. 1982. *The Theory of Will in Classical Antiquity*. Berkeley: University of California Press.

Dix, Gregory, O.S.B., ed. and trans. 1968. *The Treatise on the Apostolic Tradition of St Hippolytus of Rome*. Reissued with corrections, preface, and bibliography by Rev. Henry Chadwick. London: SPCK.

Dowd, Sharyn Echols. 1988. *Prayer, Power, and the Problem of Suffering: Mark 11:22–25 in the Context of Markan Theology*. Atlanta: Scholars.

Drijvers, Han J. W. 1987–88. "Marcionism in Syria: Principles, Problems, Polemics." *Second Century* 6: 153–72.

Droge, Arthur J. 1989. *Homer or Moses? Early Christian Interpretations of the History of Culture*. Tübingen: J. C. B. Mohr (Paul Siebeck).

Dronke, Peter. 1984. *Women Writers of the Middle Ages: A Critical Study of Texts from Perpetua (†203) to Marguerite Porete (†1310)*. Cambridge: Cambridge University Press.

Edwards, Richard A., and Robert A. Wild, S.J., eds. and trans. 1981. *The Sentences of Sextus*. Chico, Calif.: Scholars.

Elliott, John H. 1981. *A Home for the Homeless: A Sociological Exegesis of 1 Peter, Its Situation and Strategy*. Philadelphia: Fortress.

———. 1988. "The Fear of the Leer: The Evil Eye from the Bible to Li'l Abner." *Forum* 4 (December): 42–71.

Engberg-Pedersen, Troels. 1990. *The Stoic Theory of Oikeiosis: Moral Development and Social Interaction in Early Stoic Philosophy*. Aarhus: Aarhus University Press.

Engberg-Pedersen, Troels, ed. Forthcoming. *Paul in His Hellenistic Context*. Minneapolis: Fortress.

Farrer, Austin. 1951. *A Study in St. Mark.* Westminster: Dacre and New York: Oxford University Press.

———. 1966. *St. Matthew and St. Mark.* 2d ed. Westminster: Dacre.

Festugiere, A. J. 1956. *Epicurus and His Gods,* trans. C. W. Chilton. Cambridge: Harvard University Press.

Finn, Thomas M. 1989. "Ritual Process and the Survival of Early Christianity: A Study of the Apostolic Tradition of Hippolytus." *Journal of Ritual Studies* 3: 69–89.

Fiore, Benjamin, S.J. 1986. *The Function of Personal Example in the Socratic and Pastoral Epistles.* Rome: Biblical Institute Press.

Fiorenza, Elisabeth Schüssler. 1983. *In Memory of Her: A Feminist Theological Reconstruction of Christian Origins.* New York: Crossroad.

Fishbane, Michael. 1985. *Biblical Interpretation in Ancient Israel.* Oxford: Oxford University Press.

Fitzgerald, John T. 1988. *Cracks in an Earthen Vessel: An Examination of the Catalogues of Hardships in the Corinthian Correspondence.* Atlanta: Scholars.

Fitzgerald, John T., and L. Michael White, trans. and eds. 1983. *The Tabula of Cebes.* Chico, Calif.: Scholars.

Flory, Marlene B. 1975. "Family and 'Familia': A Study of Social Relations in Slavery. Ph.D. diss., Yale University.

———. 1978. "Family in *Familia:* Kinship and Community in Slavery." *American Journal of Ancient History* 3: 78–95.

Foerster, Werner, ed. and trans. 1972. *Gnosis: A Selection of Gnostic Texts.* English trans. ed. R. McL. Wilson. Oxford: Oxford University Press.

Fowl, Stephen E. 1990. *The Story of Christ in the Ethics of Paul: An Analysis of the Function of the Hymnic Material in the Pauline Corpus.* Sheffield: JSOT.

Fox, Robin Lane. 1987. *Pagans and Christians.* New York: Alfred A. Knopf.

Fredriksen, Paula. 1986. "Paul and Augustine: Conversion Narratives, Orthodox Traditions, and the Retrospective Self." *Journal of Theological Studies* n.s. 37: 3–34.

Frischer, Bernard. 1982. *The Sculpted Word: Epicureanism and Philosophical Recruitment in Ancient Greece.* Berkeley: University of California Press.

Frye, Northrop. 1983. *The Great Code: The Bible and Literature.* San Diego: Harcourt Brace Jovanovich.

Gager, John G. 1970. "Functional Diversity in Paul's Use of End-time Language." *Journal of Biblical Literature* 89: 325–37.

Gager, John G., ed. and trans. 1992. *Curse Tablets and Binding Spells from the Ancient World.* New York and Oxford: Oxford University Press.

Garrett, Susan R. 1989. *The Demise of the Devil: Magic and the Demonic in Luke's Writings.* Minneapolis: Fortress.

———. 1990. "The God of This World and the Affliction of Paul: 2 Cor 4:1–12." In *Greeks, Romans, and Christians: Essays in Honor of Abraham J. Malherbe,* ed. David L. Balch, Everett Ferguson, and Wayne A. Meeks, 99–117. Minneapolis: Fortress.

———. 1993. "The 'Weaker Sex' in *Testament of Job*." *Journal of Biblical Literature* 112:55–70.

Gaventa, Beverly Roberts. 1986. *From Darkness to Light: Aspects of Conversion in the New Testament*. Philadelphia: Fortress.

Geertz, Clifford. 1973. *The Interpretation of Cultures: Selected Essays*. New York: Basic.

———. 1983. *Local Knowledge: Further Essays in Interpretive Anthropology*. New York: Basic.

Goodenough, Erwin R. 1938. *The Politics of Philo Judaeus: Practice and Theory*. With a general bibliography of Philo by Howard L. Goodhart and Erwin R. Goodenough. New Haven: Yale University Press.

———. 1953–68. *Jewish Symbols in the Greco-Roman Period*. 13 vols. New York: Pantheon and Princeton: Princeton University Press.

———. 1962. *An Introduction to Philo Judaeus*. Oxford: Blackwell.

Goodman, Felicitas D. 1972. *Speaking in Tongues: A Cross-cultural Study of Glossolalia*. Chicago and London: University of Chicago Press.

Goodman, Martin. 1992. "Jewish Proselytizing in the First Century." In *The Jews among Pagans and Christians in the Roman Empire*, ed. Judith Lieu, John North, and Tessa Rajak, 53–78. London and New York: Routledge.

Goodspeed, Edgar J., ed. 1914. *Die ältesten Apologeten: Texte mit kurzen Einleitungen*. Göttingen: Vandenhoeck & Ruprecht.

Gorer, Geoffrey. 1965. "The Pornography of Death." In *Death, Grief, and Mourning*, Appendix 4, 192–99. Garden City, N.Y.: Doubleday.

Grant, Robert M. 1967. *After the New Testament*. Philadelphia: Fortress.

———. 1988. *Greek Apologists of the Second Century*. Philadelphia: Westminster.

Griffiths, J. Gwyn, ed. and trans. 1975. Apuleius of Madauros, *The Isis-book (Metamorphoses, book XI)*. Leiden: E. J. Brill.

Haacker, Klaus. 1990. "Der Römerbrief als Friedensmemorandum." *New Testament Studies* 36: 25–41.

Hallett, Judith P. 1984. *Fathers and Daughters in Roman Society: Women and the Elite Family*. Princeton: Princeton University Press.

Harnack, Adolf von. 1972 [vol. 1 of 1908 ed.]. *The Mission and Expansion of Christianity in the First Three Centuries*, trans. James Moffatt. Gloucester, Mass.: Peter Smith.

———. 1989. *Marcion: The Gospel of the Alien God*. Durham: Labyrinth.

Hauerwas, Stanley. 1975. *Character and the Christian life: A Study in Theological Ethics*. San Antonio: Trinity University Press.

———. 1981. *A Community of Character*. Notre Dame: University of Notre Dame Press.

————. 1983. *The Peaceable Kingdom: A Primer in Christian Ethics.* Notre Dame: University of Notre Dame Press.

Hays, Richard B. 1983. *The Faith of Jesus Christ: An Investigation of the Narrative Substructure of Galatians 3:1–4:11.* Chico, Calif.: Scholars.

Heinemann, Isaak. 1962. *Philons griechische und jüdische Bildung.* Darmstadt: Wissenschaftliche Buchgesellschaft.

Hellholm, David. 1980. *Das Visionenbuch des Hermas als Apokalypse: Formgeschichtliche und texttheoretische Studien zu einer literarischen Gattung. I. Methodologische Vorüberlegungen und makrostrukturelle Textanalyse.* Lund: C. W. K. Gleerup.

Hengel, Martin. 1977. *Crucifixion in the Ancient World and the Folly of the Message of the Cross.* Philadelphia: Fortress.

————. 1983. *Between Jesus and Paul.* Philadelphia: Fortress.

Hennecke, Edgar. 1965. *New Testament Apocrypha,* ed. Wilhelm Schneemelcher and R. McL. Wilson. Vol. 2. *Writings Related to the Apostles: Apocalypses and Related Subjects.* Philadelphia: Westminster.

Himmelfarb, Martha. 1983. *Tours of Hell: An Apocalyptic Form in Jewish and Christian Literature.* Philadelphia: University of Pennsylvania Press.

Hock, Ronald F., and Edward N. O'Neil, eds. 1986. *The Chreia in Ancient Rhetoric.* Vol. 1. *The Progymnasmata.* Atlanta: Scholars.

Hoffmann, R. Joseph. 1987–88. "How Then Know This Troublous Teacher? Further Reflections on Marcion and His Church." *Second Century* 6: 173–91.

Höistad, Ragnar. 1948. *Cynic Hero and Cynic King.* Uppsala: G. W. K. Gleerup.

Hollander, H. W., and Marinus de Jonge. 1985. *The Testaments of the Twelve Patriarchs: A Commentary.* Leiden: E. J. Brill.

Horst, P. W. van der. 1990. "Sarah's Seminal Emission: Hebrews 11:11 in the Light of Ancient Embryology." In *Greeks, Romans, and Christians: Essays in Honor of Abraham J. Malherbe,* ed. David L. Balch, Everett Ferguson, and Wayne A. Meeks, 287–302. Minneapolis: Fortress.

Horst, P. W. van der, ed. and trans. 1978. *The Sentences of Pseudo-Phocylides, with Introduction and Commentary.* Leiden: E. J. Brill.

Hyldahl, Niels. 1966. *Philosophie und Christentum: Eine Interpretation der Einleitung zum Dialog Justins.* Copenhagen: Munksgaard.

Jaeger, Werner. 1945. *Paideia: The Ideals of Greek Culture,* trans. Gilbert Highet. 2d ed. Oxford and New York: Oxford University Press.

Jaekel, Siegfried, ed. 1964. *Menandri Sententiae.* Leipzig: B. G. Teubner.

Jeffers, James S. 1991. *Conflict at Rome: Social Order and Hierarchy in Early Christianity.* Minneapolis: Fortress.

Johnson, Luke T. 1982. "The Use of Leviticus 19 in the Letter of James." *Journal of Biblical Literature* 101: 391–401.

————. 1983. "James 3:13–4:10 and the *topos Peri phthonou.*" *Novum Testamentum* 25: 327–47.

————. 1988. "James." In *Harper's Bible Commentary*, 1272–78. San Francisco: Harper & Row.

————. 1989. "The New Testament's Anti-Jewish Slander and the Conventions of Ancient Polemic." *Journal of Biblical Literature* 108: 419–41.

Jones, A. H. M. 1971. *The Cities of the Eastern Roman Provinces*. 2d ed., rev. Michael Avi-Yonah et al. Oxford: Oxford University Press.

Jones, C. P. 1971. *Plutarch and Rome*. Oxford: Oxford University Press.

Jonge, M. de. 1968. *De Brieven van Johannes*. Nijkerk: G. F. Callenbach.

————. 1975. *The Testaments of the Twelve Patriarchs: A Study of Their Text, Composition and Origin*. 2d ed. Assen: Van Gorcum.

Jonge, Marinus de, et al., eds. 1978. *The Testaments of the Twelve Patriarchs: A Critical Edition of the Greek Text*. Leiden: E. J. Brill.

Josipovici, Gabriel. 1988. *The Book of God: A Response to the Bible*. New Haven and London: Yale University Press.

Judge, Edwin A. 1980. "The Social Identity of the First Christians: A Question of Method in Religious History." *Journal of Religious History* 11: 201–17.

Kamlah, Ehrhard. 1964. *Die Form der katalogischen Paränese im Neuen Testament*. Tübingen: J. C. B. Mohr (Paul Siebeck).

Käsemann, Ernst. 1965. "Zum Thema der urchristlichen Apokalyptik." In *Exegetische Versuche und Besinnungen*, 2:105–31. Göttingen: Vandenhoeck & Ruprecht.

Keck, Leander E. 1984. "Ethics in the Gospel According to Matthew." *Iliff Review* 40 (Winter): 39–56.

Kermode, Frank. 1968. *The Sense of an Ending: Studies in the Theory of Fiction*. Oxford: Oxford University Press.

————. 1979. *The Genesis of Secrecy: On the Interpretation of Narrative*. Cambridge: Harvard University Press.

Klauck, Hans-Josef. 1981. *Hausgemeinde und Hauskirche im fruhen Christentum*. Stuttgart: Katholisches Bibelwerk.

————. 1982. *Herrenmahl und hellenistischer Kult: Eine religionsgeschichtliche Untersuchung zum ersten Korintherbrief*. Neutestamentliche Abhandlungen. Münster: Aschendorff.

Klijn, A. F. J. 1962. *The Acts of Thomas: Introduction—Text—Commentary*. Leiden: Brill.

Kloppenborg, John S. 1987. *The Formation of Q: Trajectories in Ancient Wisdom Collections*. Philadelphia: Fortress.

Koschorke, Klaus. 1973. "Die 'Namen' in Philippusevangelium: Beobachtungen zur Auseinandersetzung zwischen gnostischem und kirchlichem Christentum." *Zeitschrift für die Neutestmentliche Wissenschaft* 64: 307–22.

Kuck, David W. 1992. *Judgment and Community Conflict: Paul's Use of Apocalyptic Judgment Language in 1 Corinthians 3:5–4:5*. Leiden: E. J. Brill.

Kugel, James L., and Rowan A. Greer. 1986. *Early Biblical Interpretation*. Philadelphia: Westminster.

Kümmel, Werner Georg. 1929. *Römer 7 und die Bekehrung des Paulus*. Leipzig: J. C. Hinrichs.

———. 1974. *Römer 7 und das Bild des Menschen im Neuen Testament: Zwei Studien*. Munich: Ch. Kaiser Verlag.

Lampe, Peter. 1987. *Die stadtrömischen Christen in den ersten beiden Jahrhunderten*. Tübingen: J. C. B. Mohr (Paul Siebeck).

Laqueur, Thomas W. 1990. *Making Sex: Body and Gender from the Greeks to Freud*. Cambridge: Harvard University Press.

Latham, R. E., trans. 1951. Lucretius, *The Nature of the Universe*. Harmondsworth: Penguin.

Lattimore, Richmond. 1942. *Themes in Greek and Latin Epitaphs*. Urbana: University of Illinois Press.

Layton, Bentley. 1968. "The Sources, Date and Transmission of *Didache* 1.3b–2.1." *Harvard Theological Review* 61: 343–83.

Layton, Bentley, ed. 1980. *The Rediscovery of Gnosticism: Proceedings of the International Conference on Gnosticism at Yale, New Haven, Connecticut, March 28–31, 1978*. 2 vols. Leiden: E. J. Brill.

———. 1989. *The Coptic Gnostic Library*. 2 vols. *Nag Hammadi Codex II,2–7 Together with XIII,2*, Brit. Lib. Or.4926(1), and P. Oxy. 1, 654, 655*. Leiden: E. J. Brill.

Layton, Bentley, trans. and ed. 1987. *The Gnostic Scriptures: A New Translation with Annotations and Introductions*. Garden City, N.Y.: Doubleday.

Lear, Jonathan. 1988. *Aristotle: The Desire to Understand*. Cambridge: Cambridge University Press.

Levi, Doro. 1947. *Antioch Mosaic Pavements*. Princeton: Princeton University Press, London: Oxford University Press, and The Hague: Martinus Nijhoff.

Lipsius, Richard Adelbert, and Maximilian Bonnet, eds. 1959 [orig. ed. 1891–1903]. *Acta Apostolorum Apocrypha*. 2 vols. Darmstadt: Wissenschaftliche Buchgesellschaft.

Lührmann, Dieter. 1980. "Neutestamentliche Haustafeln und antike Ökonomie." *New Testament Studies* 27: 83–97.

Lutz, Cora E. 1947. *Musonius Rufus: "The Roman Socrates."* New Haven: Yale University Press.

McGuire, Anne. 1983. "Valentinus and the Gnostike Hairesis: An Investigation of Valentinus's Position in the History of Gnosticism." Ph.D. diss., Yale University.

MacIntyre, Alasdair. 1984. *After Virtue: A Study in Moral Theory*. 2d ed. Notre Dame: University of Notre Dame Press.

MacLeish, Archibald. 1958. *J. B.: A Play in Verse*. Boston: Houghton Mifflin.

MacMullen, Ramsay. 1974. *Roman Social Relations, 50 B.C. to A.D. 284.* New Haven and London: Yale University Press.

———. 1981. *Paganism in the Roman Empire.* New Haven and London: Yale University Press.

———. 1984. *Christianizing the Roman Empire, A.D. 100–400.* New Haven and London: Yale University Press.

———. 1988. *Corruption and the Decline of Rome.* New Haven and London: Yale University Press.

———. 1990. *Changes in the Roman Empire: Essays in the Ordinary.* Princeton: Princeton University Press.

Maier, Harry O. 1991. *The Social Setting of the Ministry as Reflected in the Writings of Hermas, Clement and Ignatius.* Waterloo, Ontario: Wilfrid Laurier University Press.

Malherbe, Abraham J. 1970a. "The Apologetic Theology of the *Preaching of Peter.*" *Restoration Quarterly* 13: 205–23.

———. 1970b. " 'Gentle as a Nurse': The Cynic Background to 1 Thessalonians 2." *Novum Testamentum* 25: 203–17.

———. 1982. "Self-definition among Epicureans and Cynics." In *Jewish and Christian Self-definition,* ed. B. F. Meyer and E. P. Sanders. Vol. 3. *Self-definition in the Greco-Roman World,* 48–59, 193–97. Philadelphia: Fortress.

———. 1983. *Social Aspects of Early Christianity.* Rev. ed. Philadelphia: Fortress.

———. 1986. *Moral Exhortation: A Greco-Roman Sourcebook.* Philadelphia: Fortress.

———. 1987. *Paul and the Thessalonians: The Philosophic Tradition of Pastoral Care.* Philadelphia: Fortress.

———. 1988. "Herakles." In *Realenzyklopädie für Antike und Christentum,* vol. 14, cols. 559–83.

———. 1989. *Paul and the Popular Philosophers.* Minneapolis: Fortress.

———. 1992. "Hellenistic Moralists and the New Testament." In *Aufstieg und Niedergang der römischen Welt,* part 2, 26.1: 267–333. Berlin: Walter de Gruyter.

———. Forthcoming. "Determinism and Free Will in Paul: The Argument of 1 Corinthians 8 and 9." In *Paul in His Hellenistic Context,* ed. Troels Engberg-Pedersen. Minneapolis: Fortress.

Malherbe, Abraham J., ed. and trans. 1977. *The Cynic Epistles: A Study Edition.* Missoula, Mont.: Scholars.

Marshall, Peter. 1987. *Enmity in Corinth: Social Conventions in Paul's Relations with the Corinthians.* Tübingen: J. C. B. Mohr (Paul Siebeck).

Martin, Dale B. 1990. *Slavery as Salvation: The Metaphor of Slavery in Pauline Christianity.* New Haven and London: Yale University Press.

———. 1992. "Female Physiology and the Dangers of Desire in 1 Corinthians

7." Paper presented at Annual Meeting, Society of Biblical Literature, San Francisco, 22 Nov. 1992.

Martyn, J. Louis. 1979. *History and Theology in the Fourth Gospel.* Rev. and enl. ed. Nashville: Abingdon.

May, Gerhard. 1987–88. "Marcion in Contemporary Views: Results and Open Questions." *Second Century* 6: 129–51.

Meeks, Wayne A. 1972. "The Man from Heaven in Johannine Sectarianism." *Journal of Biblical Literature* 91: 44–72.

———. 1974. "The Image of the Androgyne: Some Uses of a Symbol in Earliest Christianity." *History of Religions* 13: 165–208.

———. 1977. "The Unity of Humankind in Colossians and Ephesians." In *God's Christ and His people: Essays Presented to Nils Alstrup Dahl,* ed. Jacob Jervell and Wayne A. Meeks, 209–21. Oslo: Universitetsforlaget.

———. 1982a. " 'And Rose up to Play': Midrash and Paraenesis in 1 Corinthians 10:1–22." *Journal for the Study of the New Testament* 16: 64–78.

———. 1982b. "Social Functions of Apocalyptic Language in Pauline Christianity." In *Apocalypticism in the Mediterranean World and the Near East: Proceedings of the International Colloquium on Apocalypticism, Uppsala, August 12–17, 1979,* 687–705. Tübingen: J. C. B. Mohr (Paul Siebeck).

———. 1983. *The First Urban Christians: The Social World of the Apostle Paul.* New Haven and London: Yale University Press.

———. 1986. *The Moral World of the First Christians.* Library of Early Christianity. Philadelphia: Westminster.

———. 1987. "Judgment and the Brother: Romans 14:1–15:13," ed. Gerald F. Hawthorne. In *Tradition and Interpretation in the New Testament: Essays in Honor of E. Earle Ellis,* 290–300. Grand Rapids: Eerdmans and Tübingen: J. C. B. Mohr (Paul Siebeck).

———. 1988. "The Polyphonic Ethics of the Apostle Paul." *Annual of the Society of Christian Ethics:* 17–29.

———. 1990a. "The Circle of Reference in Pauline Morality." In *Greeks, Romans, and Christians: Essays in Honor of Abraham J. Malherbe,* ed. David L. Balch, Everett Ferguson, and Wayne A. Meeks, 305–17. Minneapolis: Fortress.

———. 1990b. "Equal to God." In *The Conversation Continues: Studies in Paul and John in Honor of J. Louis Martyn,* ed. Robert T. Fortna and Beverly R. Gaventa, 309–21. Nashville: Abingdon.

———. 1991a. "The Man from Heaven in Paul's Letter to the Philippians." In *The Future of Early Christianity: Essays in Honor of Helmut Koester,* ed. Birger A. Pearson, 329–36. Minneapolis: Fortress.

———. 1991b. "On Trusting an Unpredictable God: A Hermeneutical Meditation on Romans 9–11." In *Faith and History: Essays in Honor of Paul W.*

Meyer, ed. John T. Carroll, Charles H. Cosgrove, and E. Elizabeth Johnson, 105–24. Atlanta: Scholars.

Meier, John P. 1979. *The Vision of Matthew: Christ, Church and Morality in the First Gospel.* New York, Ramsey, and Toronto: Paulist.

Milne, H. J. M. 1923–24. "A New Fragment of the *Apology* of Aristides." *Journal of Theological Studies* 25: 73–77.

Momigliano, Arnaldo. 1966. "Time in Ancient Historiography." In *History and the Concept of Time*, 1–23. Middletown, Conn.: Wesleyan University Press.

Morgan, Michael A., trans. 1983. *Sepher ha-Razim: The Book of the Mysteries.* Chico, Calif,: Scholars.

Moxnes, Halvor. 1988. *The Economy of the Kingdom: Social Conflict and Economic Relations in Luke's Gospel.* Philadelphia: Fortress.

————. Forthcoming. "The Quest for Honor and the Unity of the Community in Romans 12 and in the Orations of Dio Chrysostom." In *Paul in His Hellenistic Context*, ed. Troels Engberg-Pedersen. Minneapolis: Fortress.

Mueller, Reimar. 1972. *Die epikureische Gesellschaftstheorie.* Berlin: Akademie Verlag.

Musurillo, Herbert, ed. and trans. 1972. *The Acts of the Christian Martyrs.* Oxford: Oxford University Press.

Nelson, Paul. 1987. *Narrative and Morality: A Theological Inquiry.* University Park: Pennsylvania State University Press.

Neusner, Jacob. 1973. *The Idea of Purity in Ancient Judaism.* Leiden: Brill.

Newsom, Carol. 1985. *Songs of the Sabbath Sacrifice: A Critical Edition.* Atlanta: Scholars.

Nickelsburg, George W. E., Jr. 1972. *Resurrection, Immortality, and Eternal Life in Intertestamental Judaism.* Cambridge: Harvard University Press and London: Oxford University Press.

Niebuhr, H. Richard. 1956. *Christ and Culture.* New York: Harper and Row.

Nock, A[rthur] D[arby]. 1933. *Conversion: The Old and the New in Religion from Alexander the Great to Augustine of Hippo.* London: Oxford University Press.

Nussbaum, Martha C. 1986a. "Therapeutic Arguments: Epicurus and Aristotle." In *The Norms of Nature: Studies in Hellenistic Ethics*, ed. Malcolm Schofield and Gisela Striker, 31–74. Cambridge: Cambridge University Press and Paris: Editions de la Maison des Sciences de l'Homme.

————. 1986b. *The Fragility of Goodness: Luck and Ethics in Greek Tragedy and Philosophy.* Cambridge: Cambridge University Press.

Osiek, Carolyn. 1983. *Rich and Poor in the Shepherd of Hermas: An Exegetical-Social Investigation.* Washington: Catholic Biblical Association of America.

Pack, Roger A., ed. 1963. Artemidorus, *Artemidori Daldiani Oneirocriticon libri v.* Leipzig: B. G. Teubner.

Pagels, Elaine H. 1973. *The Johannine Gospel in Gnostic Exegesis: Heracleon's Commentary on John*. Nashville and New York: Abingdon.

——. 1975. *The Gnostic Paul: Gnostic Exegesis of the Pauline Letters*. Philadelphia: Fortress.

——. 1991. "The 'Mystery of Marriage' in the *Gospel of Philip* Revisited." In *The Future of Early Christianity: Essays in Honor of Helmut Koester*, ed. Birger A. Pearson, 442–54. Minneapolis: Fortress.

Parker, Robert. 1990. *Miasma: Polution and Purification in Early Greek Religion*. Oxford: Oxford University Press.

Pax, Elpidius. 1971. "Beobachtungen zur Konvertitensprache im ersten Thessalonicherbrief." *Studii Biblici Franciscani Analecta* 21: 220–61.

——. 1972. "Konvertitenprobleme im ersten Thessalonicherbrief." *Bibel und Leben* 13: 24–37.

Peacock, James L. 1986. *The Anthropological Lens: Harsh Light, Soft Focus*. Cambridge: Cambridge University Press.

Peristiany, J. G., ed. 1966. *Honour and Shame: The Values of Mediterranean Society*. Chicago: University of Chicago Press.

Perkins, Judith. 1985. "The Apocryphal Acts of the Apostles and Early Christian Martyrdom." *Arethusa* 18: 211–30.

Petersen, Norman R. 1985. *Rediscovering Paul: Philemon and the Sociology of Paul's Narrative World*. Philadelphia: Fortress.

Pleket, H. W. 1981. "Religious History as the History of Mentality: The 'Believer' as Servant of the Deity in the Greek World." In *Faith, Hope and Worship: Aspects of Religious Mentality in the Ancient World*, ed. H. S. Versnel, 152–92. Leiden: E. J. Brill.

Plümacher, Eckhard. 1987. *Identitätsverlust und Identitätsgewinn: Studien zum Verhältnis von kaiserzeitlicher Stadt und frühem Christentum*. Neukirchen-Vluyn: Neukirchener Verlag.

Preisendanz, Karl, ed. and trans. 1973–74. *Papyri Graecae Magicae: Die griechischen Zauberpapyri*. 2d ed., ed. Albert Henrichs. Stuttgart: B. G. Teubner.

Radice, Betty, ed. and trans. 1963. *The Letters of the Younger Pliny*. Harmondsworth: Penguin.

Rehrl, Stefan. 1961. *Das Problem der Demut in der profan-griechischen Literatur im Vergleich zu Septuaginta und Neuem Testament*. Münster: Aschendorff.

Rensberger, David. 1988. *Johannine Faith and Liberating Community*. Philadelphia: Westminster.

Rhoads, David M., and Donald Michie. 1982. *Mark as Story: An Introduction to the Narrative of a Gospel*. Philadelphia: Fortress.

Richardson, Cyril C., ed. and trans. 1953. *Early Christian Fathers*. In collaboration with Eugene R. Fairweather, Edward Rochie Hardy, and Massey Hamilton Shepherd. Philadelphia: Westminster.

Richardson, James T. 1978. *Conversion Careers: In and Out of the New Religions.* Beverly Hills, Calif.: Sage.

Robbins, Vernon K. 1984. *Jesus the Teacher: A Socio-rhetorical Interpretation of Mark.* Philadelphia: Fortress.

———. 1988. "The Chreia." In *Greco-Roman Literature and the New Testament: Selected Forms and Genres,* ed. David E. Aune, 1–24. Atlanta: Scholars.

Robbins, Vernon K., and Burton L. Mack. 1987. *Rhetoric in the Gospels: Argumentation in Narrative Elaboration.* Philadelphia: Fortress.

Rordorf, Willy. 1972. "Un Chapitre d'éthique judéo-chrétienne: Les Deux Voies." *Recherches de Science Religieuse* 60: 109–28.

Rorty, Richard. 1967. "Intuition." *The Encyclopedia of Philosophy,* 4: 204–12. New York: Free Press.

Roscher, W. H., ed. 1978. *Ausführliches Lexikon der griechischen und römischen Mythologie.* Hildesheim: Georg Olms.

Rostovtzeff, Mihail. 1957. *The Social and Economic History of the Roman Empire.* 2d ed., rev. P. M. Fraser. Oxford: Oxford University Press.

Rousselle, Aline. 1988. *Porneia: On Desire and the Body in Antiquity,* trans. Felicia Pheasant. Oxford: Blackwell.

Sampley, J. Paul. 1980. *Pauline Partnership in Christ: Christian Community and Commitment in Light of Roman Law.* Philadelphia: Fortress.

Schäfer, Peter. 1990. "Jewish Magic Literature in Late Antiquity and Early Middle Ages." *Journal of Jewish Studies* 41: 75–91.

Schoedel, William R. 1985. *Ignatius of Antioch: A Commentary on the Letters of Ignatius of Antioch.* Philadelphia: Fortress.

Segal, Alan F. 1990. *Paul the Convert: The Apostolate and Apostasy of Saul the Pharisee.* New Haven and London: Yale University Press.

Selwyn, E. G. 1947. *The First Epistle of St. Peter: The Greek Text, with Introduction, Notes, and Essays.* 2d ed. London: Macmillan.

Shiner, Whitney Taylor. 1992. "'Follow Me!': Narrative and Rhetorical Function of the Disciples in the Gospel of Mark, Greek Philosophical Biographies, and the Wisdom of Ben Sira." Ph.D. dissertation, Yale University.

Skarsaune, Oskar. 1976. "The Conversion of Justin Martyr." *Studia Theologica* 30: 53–73.

Sly, Dorothy. 1990. *Philo's Perception of Women.* Atlanta: Scholars.

Smallwood, E. Mary. 1981. *The Jews under Roman Rule from Pompey to Diocletian.* Leiden: Brill.

Smith, Jonathan Z. 1965. "The Garments of Shame." *History of Religions* 5: 224–30.

Smith, Morton. 1951. *Tannaitic Parallels to the Gospels.* Philadelphia: Society of Biblical Literature.

———. 1978. *Jesus the Magician.* San Francisco: Harper & Row.

————. 1981. "The History of the Term *gnostikos*." In *The Rediscovery of Gnosticism: Proceedings of the International Conference on Gnosticism at Yale, New Haven, Connecticut, March 28–31, 1978,* ed. Bentley Layton, 796–807. Leiden: E. J. Brill.

Sokolowski, Franciszek, ed. 1955. *Lois sacrées de l'Asie Mineure.* Paris: E. de Boccard.

————. ed. 1962. *Lois sacrées des cités grecques: Supplément.* Paris: E. de Boccard.

Soury, Guy. 1942. *La Démonologie de Plutarque: Essai sur les idées religieuses et les mythes d'un platonicien éclectique.* Paris: Belles Lettres.

Squires, John T. 1988. "The Plan of God in Luke-Acts." Ph.D. diss., Yale University.

Staden, Heinrich von. 1988a. *Herophilus: The Art of Medicine in Early Alexandria.* Cambridge: Cambridge University Press.

————. 1988b. "Herophilus." In *Great Lives from History: Ancient and Medieval Series,* 969–74. Pasadena: Salem.

————. 1992. "Women and Dirt." *Helios* 19: 7–30.

Stanton, Graham N. 1987. "The Origin and Purpose of Matthew's Sermon on the Mount." In *Tradition and Interpretation in the New Testament,* ed. G. F. Hawthorne, 181–92. Grand Rapids: Eerdmans and Tübingen: J. C. B. Mohr (Paul Siebeck).

Ste Croix, G. E. M. de. 1975. "Early Christian Attitudes to Property and Slavery." In *Church, Society and Politics,* ed. Derek Baker, 1–38. Oxford: Blackwell, for the Ecclesiastical History Society.

Stout, Jeffrey. 1981. *The Flight from Authority: Religion, Morality, and the Quest for Autonomy.* Notre Dame: University of Notre Dame Press.

————. 1988. *Ethics after Babel: The Languages of Morals and Their Discontents.* Boston: Beacon Press.

Stowers, Stanley K. 1981. *The Diatribe and Paul's Letter to the Romans.* Chico, Calif.: Scholars.

————. 1986. *Letter Writing in Greco-Roman Antiquity.* Philadelphia: Westminster.

————. 1988. "The Diatribe." In *Greco-Roman Literature and the New Testament: Selected Forms and Genres,* ed. David E. Aune, 71–84. Atlanta: Scholars.

————. 1990. "Paul on the Use and Abuse of Reason." In *Greeks, Romans, and Christians: Essays in Honor of Abraham J. Malherbe,* ed. David L. Balch, Everett Ferguson, and Wayne A. Meeks, 253–86. Minneapolis: Fortress.

————. Forthcoming-a. "Construction of *personae (prosōpopoiia)* and Adaptability in Paul's Letters." *Paul in His Hellenistic Context,* ed. Troels Engberg-Pedersen. Philadelphia: Fortress.

———. Forthcoming-b. *Justice, Jews, and Others: A Re-reading of Paul's Letter to the Romans.* New Haven and London: Yale University Press.

Talbert, Charles H., ed. 1986. *Perspectives on 1 Peter.* Macon, Ga.: Mercer University Press.

Theißen, Gerd. 1982. *The Social Setting of Pauline Christianity: Essays on Corinth,* ed. and trans. John H. Schütz. Philadelphia: Fortress.

Thompson, Cynthia L. Forthcoming. "The Earliest Christians and Greco-Roman Gold Rings: Treasures from Pompeii."

Tod, Marcus N. 1951. "Laudatory Epithets in Greek Epitaphs." *Annual of the British School of Athens* 46: 182–90.

Tolbert, Mary Ann. 1989. *Sowing the Gospel: Mark's World in Literary-Historical Perspective.* Minneapolis: Fortress.

Trumpf, Jürgen. 1958. "Fluchtafeln und Rachepuppe." *Mitteilungen des Deutschen Archäologischen Instituts, Athenische Abteilung* 73: 94–102.

Vermes, Geza, ed. and trans. 1987. *The Dead Sea Scrolls in English.* 3d ed. Sheffield: JSOT.

Vögtle, A. 1936. *Die Tugend- und Lasterkataloge exegetisch, religions- und formgeschichtlich untersucht.* Münster: Aschendorff.

Völker, Walther, ed. 1932. *Quellen zur Geschichte der christlichen Gnosis.* Tübingen: J. C. B. Mohr (Paul Siebeck).

Walcot, P[eter]. 1970. *Greek Peasants, Ancient and Modern: A Comparison of Social and Moral Values.* Manchester: Manchester University Press.

Weaver, P. R. C. 1972. *Familia Caesaris: A Social Study of the Emperor's Freedmen and Slaves.* Cambridge: Cambridge University Press.

Welskopf, Elisabeth Charlotte, ed. 1974. *Hellenische Poleis: Krise, Wandlung, Wirkung.* 4 vols. Berlin: Akademie Verlag.

White, John L. 1988. "Ancient Greek Letters." In *Greco-Roman Literature and the New Testament: Selected Forms and Genres,* ed. David E. Aune, 85–106. Atlanta: Scholars.

White, L. Michael. 1990a. *Building God's House in the Roman World: Architectural Adaptation among Pagans, Jews, and Christians.* Baltimore and London: Johns Hopkins University Press.

———. 1990b. "Morality between Two Worlds: A Paradigm of Friendship in Philippians." In *Greeks, Romans, and Christians: Essays in Honor of Abraham J. Malherbe,* ed. David L. Balch, Everett Ferguson, and Wayne A. Meeks, 201–15. Minneapolis: Fortress.

Wibbing, Siegfried. 1959. *Die Tugend- und Lasterkataloge im Neuen Testament und ihre Traditionsgeschichte unter besonderer Berücksichtigung der Qumran-Texte.* Berlin: Verlag Alfred Töpelmann.

Wilken, Robert L. 1983. *John Chrysostom and the Jews: Rhetoric and Reality in the Late Fourth Century.* Berkeley: University of California Press.

Williams, Bernard. 1985. *Ethics and the Limits of Philosophy*. Cambridge: Harvard University Press.

Williams, Jacqueline A. 1988. *Biblical Interpretation in the Gnostic Gospel of Truth from Nag Hammadi*. Atlanta: Scholars.

Wilson, Bryan R. 1975. *Magic and the Millennium*. Frogmore, St Albans, Herts: Paladin.

Wilson, Walter T. 1991. *Love without Pretense: Romans 12.9–21 and Hellenistic-Jewish Wisdom Literature*. Tübingen: J. C. B. Mohr (Paul Siebeck).

Womer, Jan L., ed. and trans. 1987. *Morality and Ethics in Early Christianity*. Philadelphia: Fortress.

Worley, David Ripley. 1981. "God's Faithfulness to Promise: The Hortatory Use of Commissive Language in Hebrews." Ph.D. diss., Yale University.

Yarbrough, O. Larry. 1985. *Not Like the Gentiles: Marriage Rules in the Letters of Paul*. Atlanta: Scholars.

Yoder, John Howard. 1984. *The Priestly Kingdom: Social Ethics as Gospel*. Notre Dame: University of Notre Dame Press.

Index of Early Christian Literature

❖ ❖ ❖ ❖ ❖ ❖ ❖ ❖ ❖ ❖

Subject Index

❖ ❖ ❖ ❖ ❖ ❖ ❖ ❖ ❖ ❖

Stoics: conversion and, 25f.; concern for "the fitting," 78; judgment and, 85; fate and, 126; body and, 130; godlike character and, 150; cardinal virtues and, 69; postmortem judgment and, 177
Suffering, 88

Tablet of Cebes, conversion in, 23f.
Tertullian, 85, 212
Testaments, 82f.
Testaments of the Twelve Patriarchs, 83f., 89, 177
Thanksgiving. *See* Eucharist
Theodicy, 111
Theology, relation between, and ethics, 16. *See also* God
1 Thessalonians: moral advice for recent converts, 18, 80; conversion as social act, 31f., 47, 110; precepts in, 76, 95; *topoi* in, 77; marriage and sex in, 142–43, 151–52; God teaches right behavior, 154, 180
"Third Race." See *Ethnos*
1 Timothy, and the household, 39
Topics *(topoi)* and commonplaces, 77–79
Torah: in Pauline thought, 20; as code of laws, 44; as informing moral discourse, 89f.
Two Ways, 70f., 172

Urban phenomenon, early Christianity as. *See* City

Valentinus: world and, 56–58; scripture and, 90; body and, 137f.; theory of reproduction, 139; morality and, 164f.; God's actions and, 172; endings and, 184–86; cosmic beginning and, 193, 206
Vices, 68; of pagan deities, 161f. *See also* Virtues and vices (human)
Vindication, 179
Virtue: Stoic notion of, 69; embedded in social practices, 91; as contest, 130; God's, 157–63; moral narrative and, 189
Virtues and vices (human), 15, 66–71, 212
Vocabulary. *See* Language
Vows in early Christianity, 67

Walk *(peripatein/halakah)*, 95
Wealth, 53f., 88. *See also* Greed
Will of God, 84–86, 150–57
The Wisdom of Nigrinus, conversion and, 23
Womb, 142
Women: body and, 138–45; as martyrs, 146f.
World *(kosmos)*, Christians' attitudes toward, 13f., 52–65